Cracking the AP
English Literature Exam

Cracking the AP
English Literature Exam

By Douglas McMullen, Jr.

2002–2003 EDITION
RANDOM HOUSE, INC.
NEW YORK

www.PrincetonReview.com

> The Independent Education Consultants Association recognizes The Princeton Review as a valuable resource for high school and college students applying to college and graduate school.

Princeton Review Publishing, L.L.C.
2315 Broadway
New York, NY 10024
E-mail: booksupport@review.com

© 2002 by Princeton Review Publishing, L.L.C.

All rights reserved under International and Pan-American Copyright Conventions. Published in the United States by Random House, Inc., New York, and simultaneously in Canada by Random House of Canada Limited, Toronto.

Excerpt from "Keats' Sylvan Historian: History Without Footnotes" in *The Well Wrought Urn: Studies in the Structure of Poetry*, copyright 1947 and renewed 1975 by Cleanth Brooks, reprinted by permission of Harcourt Brace and Company.
"next to of course god america I," copyright 1926, 1954 © 1991 by the Trustees for the e. e. Cummings Trust. © 1985 by George James Firmage, from COMPLETE POEMS: 1904–1962 by e. e. Cummings, Edited by George J. Firmage. Reprinted by permission of Liveright Publishing Corporation.
Excerpt from "Ultramarine" reprinted by permission of The Peters Frasers and Dunlop Group Limited, on behalf of © as printed in the original volume.
"Woodchucks," © 1972 by Maxine Kumin, from *Selected Poems 1960–1990* by Maxine Kumin. Reprinted by permission of W.W. Norton & Company, Inc.
Every effort has been made to trace and acknowledge copyright material. The author and publisher would welcome any information from the people who believe they own copyright to material in this book.

ISSN: 1092-0099
ISBN: 0-375-76225-6

AP and Advanced Placement are registered trademarks of the College Entrance Examination Board, which was not involved in the production of, and does not endorse, this book.

Editor: Maria Dente
Production Editor: Maria Dente
Production Coordinator: Ryan Tozzi

Manufactured in the United States of America.

9 8 7 6 5 4 3 2

2002–2003 Edition

ACKNOWLEDGMENTS

The author would like to thank Corinna Snyder for more than space allows. Big thanks to Sylvia Sarrett, Maria Dente, Illeny Maaza, and Ryan Tozzi.

CONTENTS

Introduction ix

Author's Foreword xi

PART I: INTRODUCTION 1

1 **A Brief Introduction to the AP English Literature and Composition Test** 3

PART II: CRACKING THE SYSTEM: THE MULTIPLE-CHOICE SECTION 13

2 **Basic Principles of the Multiple-Choice Section** 15

3 **Advanced Principles: Reading the Multiple-Choice Passages** 27

4 **Cracking the System: Multiple-Choice Questions** 37

5 **Answering Prose Passage Questions** 41

6 **The Poetry Passage and Questions** 65

PART III: CRACKING THE SYSTEM: THE ESSAYS 77

7 **Basic Principles of the Essay Section** 79

8 **The Idea Machine: Starting Your Essays with a High Score** 89

9 **Sample Prose and Poetry Essays** 103

10 **The Open Essay** 115

11 **A Tiny Grammar Review with Sample Questions** 123

PART IV: THE PRINCETON REVIEW AP ENGLISH LITERATURE 129
AND COMPOSITION PRACTICE TEST 1

PART V: ANSWERS AND EXPLANATIONS—PRACTICE TEST 1   147

PART VI: THE PRINCETON REVIEW AP ENGLISH LITERATURE 165
AND COMPOSITION PRACTICE TEST 2

PART VII: ANSWERS AND EXPLANATIONS—PRACTICE TEST 2   183

PART VIII: GLOSSARY   195

INTRODUCTION

WHAT IS THE PRINCETON REVIEW?

The Princeton Review is an international test preparation company with branches in all the major U.S. cities and several abroad. In 1981, John Katzman started teaching an SAT prep course in his parents' living room. Within five years The Princeton Review had become the largest SAT coaching program in the country.

The Princeton Review's phenomenal success in improving students' scores on standardized tests was (and is) due to a simple, innovative, and radically effective philosophy. Study the test, not what the test claims to test. This approach has led to the development of techniques for taking standardized tests based on the principles the test writers themselves use to write the tests.

The Princeton Review has found that its methods work not just for cracking the SAT, but for any standardized test. We've already successfully applied our system to the GMAT, LSAT, MCAT, and GRE, to name just a few. Although in some ways the AP English Literature and Composition Test is a very different test from those mentioned above, in the end, a standardized test is a standardized test. This book uses our time-tested principle: Crack the system based on how the test is written.

We also publish books and CD-ROMs on an enormous variety of education and career-related topics. If you're interested check out our website at www.PrincetonReview.com.

Author's Foreword

Throughout this book you'll notice that when I refer to myself, I say, "we." I'm not the Queen of England and that isn't the "royal 'we,'" it's just that The Princeton Review's test-taking techniques are the refined product of hundreds of smart people spending thousands of hours figuring out how best to teach standardized tests. Saying "we" is a matter of giving credit where it's due. Just this once, though, I'd like to step out of the collective shadows and say a few personal things about the book you're reading.

Since you're reading this book chances are good that you're a high school student studying English literature. I was once where you are, and I never thought I'd be here on the other side of the page, writing about English. In high school, I loved reading (that is, the books I wanted to read) and I even sometimes liked writing, but I definitely wasn't sure I liked studying English. It seemed to me that my teachers were bent on ripping literature into tiny little pieces so they could squint at the wreckage. My English teachers seemed like maniacs who spent their time shooting birds out of trees so that they could take a bird's body, pluck its feathers, pry it open, and talk about its intestines. I just wanted to listen to the birds sing. At the time, I was sure I had the better attitude. But now look at me: carving into books and poems as if they were cooked turkeys and serving them up, supposedly for your benefit.

Well, it *is* for your benefit. First and foremost to help you on this test, but there's much more than that. Reading poetry and fiction is an art—not a skill, *an art*. If you'd told me when I was 15 that I didn't really know how to read fiction I would have laughed at you. But, if you'd told me I didn't know how to read music or how to play the violin, well, it would obviously have been true.

When it comes to literature, great authors are great composers, and you, the reader, are the violinist, the pianist, the conductor—the whole orchestra. The difference is that the performance is one only you can hear, and only you can really know how well you've played the piece. It takes years of practice and study to read (or write) truly well, just as it does to master an instrument. There's no shame in being less than perfect. You'll know when you get it right—it will sound right inside. That maniac English teacher is just a stern piano-instructor, making you practice your scales over and over again. Does it get boring? Yes. Does it seem totally pointless at least half the time? Yes! Is it fun? No, not really—except that every now and then you discover that you can play a new, harder piece just right. When that happens it's exciting; you realize, hey, all this practice is starting to pay off! I'll bet you've already come across a piece of literature or two that's made you sit up and say, "Wow, there really *is* something special about this book." I want to remind you that English teachers are not part of a secret conspiracy to drive students crazy, and that there's a method (and a love of literature) behind your English teacher's and my madness. Maybe, when you get bogged down, remind yourself that the point of all this study is the mastery of an art—intelligent reading and writing—an art you'll be able to make use of every day of your life.

That makes this book my small contribution to your career as a concert soloist in literature. Good luck. Who knows? Maybe I'll see you reading in Carnegie Hall some day.

—Douglas McMullen, Jr.

PART 1

INTRODUCTION

1

A Brief Introduction to the AP English Literature and Composition Test

WHY DO YOU NEED THIS BOOK?

The book you hold in your hands has been designed to meet the differing needs of English students around the country. Above all, this book is for the student whose goal is to achieve the best possible score on the AP English Literature and Composition Test. The Princeton Review believes that the best way to achieve this goal is to understand the test, especially how the test is written. By understanding the limitations the test writers (and essay readers) face, you will know how to approach the test for the maximum score—that's what matters most here. If, like many students, you have had excellent English instruction in a course specifically designated as AP English, then you primarily want a book that will help ensure that you ace the test. We provide that.

But this book is also for students who aren't confident about the course they took, or who haven't taken an AP English course at all. For these students, we go into a little extra depth on many topics, especially in the essay-writing portion of the book. Although no book can replace several semesters with a good teacher, motivated students are their own best teachers and can accomplish amazing things. This book offers instruction and points the way to further learning for those kinds of students.

Finally, this book is for the not-so-uncommon student who loves literature and writing and can't get enough of it; we aren't saying this book is fine literature itself, but we think it can help you toward greater understanding, appreciation, and yes, love of literature (all the while helping you ace the test, of course).

AP ENGLISH

Each May, roughly 176,221 students take the AP English Literature and Composition Test. The AP English Literature and Composition Test has a sister test, the English Language and Composition Test, which is also given in May and is taken by about 139,000 students a year. (This book is for students who intend to take the Literature Test. Near the end of this chapter, on page 11, you'll find a brief description of the AP Language Test and how it differs from the Literature Test.)

Almost all of these 304,000 students have at some point taken a class structured, at least partially, with an AP English test in mind. Most often this course is called, naturally enough, AP English. Some schools do not have specifically titled AP courses, but do have accelerated courses which can be adequate preparation for the AP tests. There is no prerequisite for either AP test. Anyone who wants to take the tests can.

AP English courses (in fact all AP courses) are essentially first year college courses. AP English could very easily be called College English. In fact, AP English courses are often better than the corresponding course available at college. Nearly everyone in an AP course is a superior student and wants to be there, as does the teacher. Conversely, at many colleges freshman English is taught by junior faculty members or even graduate students. Typically, this means the teacher is bright, enthusiastic and knowledgeable, but lacks teaching experience. More importantly, untenured faculty and graduate students have all kinds of career distractions and worries outside the classroom that can't help but interfere with teaching. Even worse is the situation sometimes found at larger schools: Freshman English is taught in "Important Name Memorial Hall," which as it turns out is basically a stadium. Class itself is one endless 8:00 A.M. lecture by a world famous but completely senile professor who mumbles obliviously into his microphone with an impenetrable Peruvian-Belgian accent while the frat boys in the back row snore face down into their notebooks and the girl next to you (invariably) eats crackers with her mouth open. You're left thinking, "Isn't college grand?" A learning experience indeed.

So, if AP English is available at your school, and if you're motivated and interested, do take it if you haven't already. AP English credit lets you skip ahead of the pack, saves money, looks great on your transcript, and opens up your college schedule so you can get to the really interesting courses faster.

GETTING CREDIT

The catch is that getting AP English credit is harder than simply passing Freshman English, which takes only a C or higher. To get credit for AP English you need to meet two requirements. You need to attend a college that recognizes the AP program, and you need a good score on one of the two AP

English tests (Literature and Composition or Language and Composition). Your guidance counselor (or AP teacher) might be able to provide information on whether the schools you are applying to award AP credit, how much credit, and just what scores you need. Chances are they won't know exactly, and you'll want to know—exactly. By far the most reliable way to find out what you need to know is to write or e-mail (not call) the admissions department of the schools you're interested in and ask what their AP English policy is. When they write back, *keep the letter, and take it with you when you register for courses.* College registration, especially freshman registration, is a weird kind of hell, and the last thing you want is to be left pleading with some stressed-out clerk: "But they *told* me..."

In general, the AP tests are widely accepted, but which test is preferred, what score is needed to obtain credit, and how much credit is actually awarded varies from school to school. A four or a five will always get you credit when it's available. A three is borderline. Many schools give credit or partial credit for a three, others give none. A score of one or two won't cut it.

About 70 percent of the students who take an AP English course receive a three or lower. Almost 40 percent of the students who take the Literature Test receive a one or two. It isn't an easy test, but it is well worth the effort.

AP ENGLISH CURRICULUM AND ITS TEACHERS

It may come as a surprise to some students but there is no standard AP curriculum. The course you take is undoubtedly different from the one given at the high school across town, and both are different from the one given 10 states away. What you study is up to your teacher and, to a lesser extent, the English department faculty of your school. Despite all this diversity, however, the courses share a common task: *to teach you to read and write about English Literature at a college level.* In college you will be expected to read difficult texts for meaning. You will also be expected to formulate ideas about what you read and to express those ideas in clear grammatically correct writing. AP courses share these same goals. But because so much leeway is given to the teacher, and individual teachers have their own likes and dislikes, the emphases of one course will differ from those of another. Some courses spend half the year on Shakespeare, others focus on personal and creative writing, some deal almost exclusively with nineteenth- and twentieth-century novels, while still others focus on ancient texts. Finally, many of the best teachers do not teach AP English with the test in mind at all. They believe that maintaining and building your enthusiasm for the subject is more important than any test score (and they're probably right). In general, an English teacher's expertise is in English Literature, not the AP English Literature Test.

Well, our expertise is test taking. As we discuss what you can expect on the AP Literature Test, keep a look-out for what you haven't studied—for your weaknesses. A little extra study in those areas could go a long way.

THE FORMAT OF THE AP ENGLISH LITERATURE EXAM

Test Date: Early May
Total Time: 3 hours
Section I: Multiple choice (60 minutes)—45 percent of your grade
Total number of questions: 50–55
Four or five prose and/or poetry passages: 10–15 questions per passage

Section II: Essay (120 minutes)—55 percent of your grade
Three Essays:
1. Analysis of a single poem (40-minute essay on a poem that ETS provides, or comparisons of two poems)
2. Analysis of prose (40-minute essay on a given story, novel excerpt, or essay)
3. Open essay (40-minute essay on a given literary topic supported by the student's own reading)

WHO WRITES THE AP ENGLISH EXAM?

The test is written by the AP English Development Committee—sort of. The committee is assisted by ETS (the Education Testing Service), the folks who write the SATs as well as other tests you'll no doubt take if you head for graduate school. The AP people (there are eight on the committee, all English teachers, either high school or college) pick the passages and write first drafts of the test questions. But then the ETS people step in. They fine tune the test. ETS's primary concern is to ensure that the test, especially the multiple-choice portion, is similar to previous administrations and tests a broad spectrum of student ability. The ETS contribution is what concerns us and you. ETS has predictable ways of shaping questions and creating the wrong answers. On multiple-choice tests, knowing how the wrong answers are written and how to eliminate them is always key. We'll discuss this topic in detail in the Cracking the System: Multiple-Choice section.

SCORING

WHAT YOUR FINAL SCORE MEANS

After taking the test in early May, you will receive your scores sometime around the first week of July, which is right about when you've just started to forget about the whole experience. Your score will be, simply enough, a single number, 1–5. Here is what those numbers mean:

Score—Meaning	Approximate percentage of all test takers receiving this score at participating colleges	Equivalent first-year college course grade	Will a student with this score receive credit?
5—Extremely Qualified	10.6%	A	Yes
4—Well Qualified	22.4%	A–, B+	Yes
3—Qualified	35.8%	B–, C	Maybe
2—Possibly Qualified	25.1%	C, D	Very Rarely
1—Not Qualified	6.2%	D	No

YOUR MULTIPLE-CHOICE SCORE

In the multiple-choice portion of the test, you receive one point for each question you answer correctly. You receive zero points for a question left blank. You receive a deduction of a quarter of a point for a question which you answer incorrectly. This quarter point deduction is the infamous "guessing penalty." (You might be familiar with this scoring method from the SAT.) We'll discuss that so-called penalty in detail in chapter 4.

YOUR ESSAY SCORE

Each AP essay is scored on a scale from zero to nine, with nine being the best score. The scores of each essay are added together and this total, anywhere from 0 to 27, is your essay section score. A Reader (a high school or college level English teacher) goes through your essay and gives you a score based on a holistic evaluation. This is called "holistic" scoring. We will go into the details of essay scoring in the Cracking the Essay Section portion of this book, but here is the general outline of the zero to nine system: A "nine" essay answers all facets of the question completely, making good use of the passage to support its points, and is "well-written," which is a catch-all phrase that means sentences are complete, properly punctuated, clear in meaning, show an educated vocabulary, and are spelled correctly. Lower scoring essays are deficient in these qualities to a greater or lesser degree. At the zero level, the student has written what amounts to gibberish (misspelled gibberish). If you write in perfect medieval Latin, or Esperanto, or perhaps write a funny, publishable, prize-worthy story about your AP teacher, you will receive a "—." This score is the equivalent of a zero.

The essay Readers do not award points according to a standardized predetermined checklist. The essays are scored individually by individual readers. Each Reader scores essays for only one type of question. ETS says (and we have no reason to doubt them) that the reader of your open essay will be familiar with the work about which you write. If, for your open essay on mistaken identity, you chose to write about Sophocles' *Oedipus Rex*, then your essay reader would have read that work. (Of course, you could choose something stunningly obscure and mess with their heads, but we don't recommend it.) If a certain test has an essay on a poem by John Donne, an essay on a prose extract by Jean Toomer, and an open essay on the topic of mistaken identity in a novel or play of your choice, there will be three distinct Readers: a Reader for your Donne essay, a Reader for your Toomer essay, and a Reader for your open essay. Each will give you a score based solely on the essay she/he reads. The other readers will not see your other essays or know how you were scored on them, nor will they know how you performed on the Multiple-Choice Section.

YOUR FINAL SCORE

Your final one to five score is a combination of your section scores. Remember that the multiple-choice section counts for 45 percent of the total and the essays count for 55 percent. While this makes them almost equal, they are not entirely equal. ETS adopts a somewhat annoying mathematical formula to arrive at your score. This formula involves a 150 point scale, but first you multiply your essay score by 3.0556 and your multiple-choice score by slightly less than 1.3 (the exact multiplier is determined by the number of multiple-choice questions on your test; for example, on a 52 question test the multiplier is 1.298).

Did your eyes glaze over? Yeah, we thought so. Who cares what gets multiplied by what? In fact, neither you, nor the colleges you apply to, will ever know what your individual section scores are. ETS doesn't tell. You get a one to five score. That's it.

Does this mean you don't need to think about how your multiple-choice and essay scores combine? No. You should get a feel for how your multiple-choice score affects your final, total score.

Look at the overall test as two separate assessments:
Multiple-Choice = 52 – 55 questions for a total of 45 percent of the score.
Three Essays = 3 questions, each scored on a 0 – 9 scale, for a total of 55 percent of the score.

Your writing can pull up your multiple-choice scores and vice versa. But, a good bottom line goal is on, say a 55-question multiple-choice test, to get at least 29+ questions right and to earn at least 18 points on the essays. These two scores will net you a final passing grade of 3. Increases in either category can increase your final scores. On a 55-question multiple-choice test, it looks something like this:

Number of Questions Right	+	Number of Essay Points	=	Final Score	Approx. Percentage of Scores Awarded
29		18 – 21		3	23 %
29		24 – 26		4	1 %
29		27		5	1 %
30 – 38		18 – 20		3	59 %
30 – 38		21 – 24		4	19%
30 – 38		25 – 27		5	1 %
39 – 45		18 – 20		3	32 %
39 – 45		24 – 26		4	52 %
39 – 45		25 – 27		5	14 %
46 – 55		18 – 20		3	6 %
46 – 55		21 – 24		4	39 %
46 – 55		25 – 27		5	55 %

CONCLUSIONS

1. The goal on the multiple-choice section is roughly one-half plus one (1/2 of 55 = 27.5, rounded up = 28, then plus one = 29). The goal on the essays is the minimum passing score on each essay, 6 (3 x 6 = 18). The percentage of the higher final scores increases in each category.

2. Set makable goals for yourself. Look what happens if you raise your multiple-choice score one point (from a 29 to a 30) and your essays one point each (from a 20 to a 21): you have a 4!

Let's look again at those multiple-choice scores, this time to see how many students received each final score:

Multiple-Choice Range	AP Final Score				
	1	2	3	4	5
	Approximate Number of Students				
0-18	2900	1400	15	0	0
19-29	1250	12700	4400	200	2
30-38	60	3900	11300	3600	140
39-45	5	270	4200	6900	1840
46-55	0	15	250	1600	2200

The odds are long, but it is even possible to get a 5, even if you only scored within the 19 – 29 range—two people did! And, within that range, 200 people got a 4!

Now let's start practicing ways for YOU to get your best possible score!

Pacing Chart for AP English Literature Subject Test				
My Score on Practice	Shooting for Minimum of	Time Spent	Must Get Right	Guess or Leave Out
_____	29 of 55	60 mins	29	15

Two ways to get 29 right:

1. Answer 29 and get every one of them right.

2. Answer more than 29 to adjust for the ones missed and for the 1/4 right-wrong penalty (or 3/4 right-wrong bonus!)
    Roughly: answer 36, miss 6 = penalty of 1.5
    36 – 6 = 30
    30 – 1.5 = 28.5 (rounded up = 29)

    answer 40, miss 6 = penalty of 1.5
    40 – 6 = 34
    34 – 1.5 = 32.5 (rounded up = 33)

CONCLUSION: You do not have to get every answer right to get a good score!
Look at it this way:

	The Numbers Game				
	Number Right	Penalized Answered	Number Guessed	Number Omitted	Number Penalized Right-Wrong
Before:	_____	_____	_____	_____	_____
After:	_____	_____	_____	_____	_____

Use a set of our questions in the practice sets (see chapters 3 and 5) to give yourself Before and After scores. The Before score reflects your just taking the practice set cold, and the After score shows what you can do after you've tried our suggestions.

The AP English Literature and Composition test is unlike other AP tests in one other factor: Time. The multiple-choice test is always one hour long and contains four or five passages with a total of 52 – 55 questions. Obviously, you could evenly divide your time, say 15 minutes each for 4 passages or 12 minutes each for 5 passages.

When you are practicing on getting the feel of the passage and the kinds of questions, take all the time you need. Your purpose, after all, is different at this stage. Then, when you are practicing for the real experience, limit your time to precisely one hour.

Again, use our practice tests for just that—practice!

Remember—you can Guess (with right-wrong bonus!) and you can Omit. Look at it this way:

Time: 1 hour
Practice Test of 55 questions (page 131+)

Passage	Number of Questions	Number To Get Right	Number To Omit or Guess On
1	15	8	26 (from any section)
2	14	7	
3	11	6	
4	15	8	
		29	

The Time Factor				
Time Evenly Divided 15 minutes	Time I Spent	Time Shooting For	Number to Get Right	Number to Omit
____	____	____	____	____

THREE STUDY NOTES FOR THE AP ENGLISH EXAM

You'll see a total of six or seven reading passages on the AP test: four or five multiple-choice passages plus a passage each for the first two essays. ETS is careful to draw these passages from different time periods. Among these six passages (there actually could be seven if one of the essays asks you to compare and contrast two poems or short prose works), there will be at least one passage from each of the following periods: 1558–1659; 1660–1798; 1799–1917; 1918–present. Whether you're on a multiple-choice or essay section, comprehension of these passages, both in detail and overall, is key. Typically, students find prose easier to understand than poetry, and modern writing easier to comprehend than that of earlier periods. Furthermore, students do better on what they've studied than on what they haven't studied. The general rule is this:

Study to eliminate weaknesses, but on the test itself, emphasize your strengths. We will discuss in detail how to do both these things in the chapters that follow.

Second, notice that although two thirds of the test-taking time is devoted to essays, the multiple-choice section is almost its equal in terms of your score. Many students fixate on the essay questions and act as though the multiple-choice section is just extra. It isn't. **Don't blow off the multiple-choice.** It can and should be studied for.

Third, many students don't just fixate on the essays, they get obsessed with the Open Essay. The essays are all weighed equally. The open essay is about 18 percent of your score. **Prepare for the whole test.**

THE ENGLISH LANGUAGE AND COMPOSITION TEST

As we mentioned above, there are two AP English tests: English Literature and Composition and English Language and Composition. The reason for this is the differing emphases of freshman college English courses. The Literature Test, which is the more popular of the two tests, is meant to assess the knowledge and skills that are developed by first year English courses. The Language Test assesses the knowledge and skills developed by courses with titles like Expository Writing or Rhetoric. In such courses, the emphasis is distinctly on nonfiction writing. Students study the means by which an author develops an argument in writing, and produce persuasive writing of their own.

In keeping with these differences, the AP Language and Composition Test uses a format similar to the Literature Test, with multiple-choice questions on four different passages and a second section that calls for three essays (there is no "open essay," however). The difference is that the Language Test's passages are drawn from critical writing and other kinds of nonfiction rather than the fiction and poetry that make up most or all of the Literature Test. The emphases of the multiple-choice questions and the essay topics on the Language Test are also somewhat different from those of the Literature Test. The Language Test focuses on the student's ability to grasp the overall structure of an argument, to identify the rhetorical devices the author has used, and to discern the important elements of logical reasoning that are present in any argument.

In previous years, both tests were administered on the same day and it wasn't possible to take both senior year. (Many students elected to take the Language Test junior year.) The tests are now scheduled on consecutive weekends and it is possible to take both in the same year. Whether this is practical depends on the course work you have done and the schools to which you are applying. Some schools prefer one test, some, the other. If you write well and think logically, but hate (and can not make sense of) poetry, the Language Test is worth investigating.

BUT, WHAT'S IN IT FOR ME?

There's a mysterious little box on the form you'll be given on the AP test you take. It asks your permission to use your writing as a sample for research. If you check that box you have just thirty seconds to leave the building or else . . . actually, checking the box will not affect your score. It simply means that when ETS publishes samples of student writing they make sure they only use student work that has that box checked off.

HOW TO USE THIS BOOK

We strongly recommend that you read the chapters on test-taking techniques before you take the sample tests at the end of this book. You'll have a better idea of what you're doing, and be able to put into practice the techniques we've taught you. After you've taken the sample tests we advise that you read all the explanations, even the explanations to the questions you've answered correctly. You'll often find that your understanding of a question and the best way to have gone about answering it will be much clearer after you've read the explanation. You'll also catch those times when you got the question right, but for all the wrong reasons. Finally, some of the explanations have tidbits of information you won't find elsewhere in the book.

ABOUT THE INFORMATION HERE

We've seen some awful books on the AP test. We've even seen a book that isn't merely useless but is actually damaging: a book that badly misrepresents the format of the test and completely misunderstands the scoring system. If, looking at other test-prep books, you find that material there doesn't match what you see here—don't wonder who's right. *We're right.* Seriously. It seems there are some greedy publishers out there who don't care at all about what happens to you after you leave the bookstore.

STILL HAVE QUESTIONS?

That's the bare bones of the AP English Literature and Composition Test. We hope you still have questions, because we still have lots of answers. What are the passages like? What kinds of questions are on the multiple-choice section? What book(s) should you read to prepare for the open essay? Does handwriting count? When should you guess? How do you ace the essays? We'll answer all these questions and much more in the chapters that follow.

HOW TO GET MORE INFORMATION

Additional information on AP policies and the AP English Literature exam is available on the College Board's web site at www.collegeboard.org or by contacting:

The AP Program
PO Box 6671
Princeton, NJ 08541-6671
609-771-7300 or toll free 888-CALL-4-AP [888-225-5427]
Fax: 609-530-0482
TTY: 609-882-4118
E-mail: apexams@info.collegeboard.org

PART II

Cracking the System: The Multiple-Choice Section

2

BASIC PRINCIPLES OF THE MULTIPLE-CHOICE SECTION

WHAT ARE THE BASIC PRINCIPLES OF CRACKING THE SYSTEM?

As with any multiple-choice test, there will come a time when the studying is over, and you are as prepared as you are ever going to be. You will be sitting at your desk with a sealed exam booklet and an answer sheet in front of you. The proctor, droning on at the front of the room, will finally finish reading all those instructions no one needs to hear and say, "You may break the seal and begin the test."

At that moment, what you know isn't going to change. Your head will be crammed with knowledge, and you might wish you knew even more, but that's it. Now your score depends on getting what you know onto that answer sheet.

Imagine your exact double sitting at the next desk. In terms of English literature, your double knows exactly what you know. Will you and your double's scores be the same? *Not if you know how to take a standardized test and your double doesn't.* You will squeeze every possible drop of what you know onto that answer sheet. Your double will let half her knowledge go unused and wasted. The scores will reflect the difference.

The multiple-choice portion of the AP English Literature and Composition Test is not different from any standardized test in that there are two critical concerns.

> 1. You must manage a limited amount of time well.
> 2. You must guess wisely and aggressively.

If you manage your time poorly you will not get a chance to use your knowledge. Questions you could have easily answered will vanish into oblivion taking their points with them.

Guessing wisely and aggressively calls for the ability (and courage) to use partial knowledge. When you fail to guess, you let whatever partial knowledge you have go to waste. For that question at least, it's as though you didn't know a thing. In both cases you withhold exactly what the test wants from you: your knowledge. The test, in turn, withholds points.

Of course, we're here to make sure that doesn't happen.

HAVE A PLAN

In order to do your best on the AP Literature Test, you need a plan. A plan lets you stop worrying about whether you are going about things the right way and lets you concentrate on what's important—earning points. The plan we suggest isn't complicated, in fact it's simplicity itself, but with it you'll know that you are going about things the right way.

THE PLAN

Here's an outline of what you should do on the multiple-choice section:

1. NOTE THE TIME

When the section begins make a note of the time. Most proctors put the starting time up on the board, but don't count on it. Sometimes there's a clock in the room, sometimes there isn't (or it's not in your line of vision). Take a watch. You have 60 minutes on the multiple-choice section, which has four passages for you to read and answer questions about. That means you've got an average of 15 minutes per passage. Keep track of your pace. If you finish the first passage in over 15 minutes you know that you should speed up slightly if possible. That doesn't mean go crazy, panic, and rush. It means that if you worked at a comfortable pace on that first passage, nudge the mental accelerator and work at the edge of an uncomfortable pace. Push yourself. If after two passages you find yourself significantly over the 30-minute mark, take a second to calm down. You'll begin to freak, and although it's not good to freak, it is perfectly normal. Say to yourself, "Okay, I can still get a great score doing just three passages, and with even just a few minutes left over for the last passage, I can pick up a bunch of points. I'm fine."

2. PICK A PASSAGE TO DO LAST

This is a key safety device for your time and your score. It's your way of assuring yourself that if you get into time trouble on the last passage at least it's the one that would have given you the most trouble anyway. Put a big X at the top of the page to remind yourself which passage is going to be the last passage.

3. PICK A PASSAGE TO DO FIRST

This isn't nearly as important as figuring out which one to do last. Most students get to three passages, and you should definitely shoot for at least three. (If you only get to two passages you still have a realistic shot at a final score of three if you write well.) Don't take a lot of time figuring out which one to do first, just go with your best guess. Ideally, you pick the passage that you find easiest in order to get going on the right foot and build your confidence.

4. READ THE PASSAGE
Get started. *Don't read the questions first*. Some folks advise this and they're dead wrong. It's a huge waste of time. You'll forget all but the last three (and there are between 12 and 15 questions per passage) and you'll have to read them all again carefully when it comes time to pick answers. Not only that, but the passages are difficult enough that if you try to remember the questions and understand the passage at the same time, you'll end up with a total mental garble, a vicious headache, and a low score. Just read the passage with concentration and care. Remember not to blank out when you hit a difficult stretch. How best to read AP passages is covered in detail in the next chapter.

5. ANSWER ALL THE QUESTIONS ON THE PASSAGE, IN THE ORDER THAT YOU CHOOSE, USING THE PRINCETON REVIEW TECHNIQUES YOU'LL LEARN FROM THIS BOOK
There's a lot to learn, and unless you study like crazy, you won't remember all of it. Don't sweat that. We don't expect you to remember every little detail we teach here. Your subconscious will zero in on the things you really need. The really important thing is to answer all the questions using Process Of Elimination (POE) when necessary and to guess aggressively.

GUESS AGGRESSIVELY BY UNDERSTANDING YOUR RAW SCORE
It all comes down to points. More points mean a higher score. It's that simple. But, because of the marking system—one point for a correct answer, zero points for a blank, and a quarter point deduction for an incorrect answer—*there are several ways of arriving at the same score*.

The AP English Literature and Composition Test you take will have between 50 and 55 multiple-choice questions. Our examples here assume a test with 52 questions. What if your test has more questions, or fewer? Don't worry about it at all. Whether the test has 50 questions, 55 questions, or some number in between, your approach to guessing will remain exactly the same.

Okay, suppose there are 52 points available. Here are three ways to score 32 points on the multiple-choice section. Why 32? Because that's a score we think puts you in a solid position to get a final score of four. Thirty-two points is a good, high number of multiple-choice points to shoot for. If you can do even better, great.

1. To get a score of 32, student A might answer all 52 questions and miss 16. That means she got 36 questions right, but lost four points because of the guessing penalty.
2. Student B might score 32 points by answering 32 questions correctly and leaving 20 blank.
3. Student C might mix and match a little a bit, leaving some questions blank but answering most of them. For example, he might answer 34 questions correctly, get eight wrong and leave ten blank. Thirty-four minus two penalty points is 32.

WHICH WAY IS THE RIGHT WAY?
When most students look at the examples above they think, "Well, student A seems to have answered too many questions and might have scored better by leaving more blank. Student B was too chicken and should have answered more. Student C seems to have found a good balance."

It sounds like common sense, but *it is completely wrong*.

Both student B and student C left too many blanks. Both could have done better. Student B obviously knew her stuff, since she got all of the questions she answered correct. Maybe she worked too slowly, or maybe she was too timid; either way, it's certain she could have earned more points. If she'd answered half of the questions she left blank correctly, she'd have picked up seven more points and been in the running for a final score of five. Student C is closer to his best score but still hasn't achieved it. By answering questions he left blank, he could have squeezed another two or three points out of the test and made things much easier for himself when it came time to write the essays. Student A maxed out. She went after every question and took her lumps (small quarter points) in order to get the rewards—big, full points. If student A had approached the test like either of the other two students her score would have been lower.

Yes, all three students got the same score, but that's because students B and C did worse than they could have, while student A did her best.

At this point a lot of students say, "I don't know . . . I'm not convinced. I don't like the sound of that guessing penalty. Why should I just take a dumb guess at a question I don't know the answer to and get penalized? Why not admit I don't know the answer and leave the question blank? At least I'll avoid the penalty." Okay, if this sounds like your thoughts, please read the next section carefully, *and believe it.*

THE GUESSING PENALTY SHOULD BE CALLED THE GUESSING BONUS

Most students are afraid of the guessing penalty. They think it's going to eat up their score. These students don't answer a question unless they're pretty sure they've got it right. If the question is hard they think, "I'll leave it blank and avoid the guessing penalty." What they end up avoiding is their best score. *You can't get points if you don't answer questions.* A blank means you definitely won't get the point that's available. "Yes," you say, "but at least there's no penalty." No penalty!? I guess that means you can just leave the whole test blank and get a perfect score! It doesn't work that way. Leave the whole test blank and you'll score a humiliating zero. Don't think of a blank as a no-penalty, think of it as minus one point. We know ETS says a blank is zero, but that's a zero *when you're supposed to get a* plus one. Each question is worth one point. Leave a question blank and it's essentially an automatic subtraction of one because you're losing an opportunity to earn that point.

The term *guessing penalty* is just a head-game. *Blank* looks so neutral, so harmless. It isn't. *Guessing penalty* seems nasty—*penalty*—and it looks nasty because it's a negative fraction. Who likes negative fractions? But the truth is wrong answers hurt your score because you don't get the point that's available. That dropped quarter of a point is nothing but a pathetic little kick in the shins following the big damage. *The missed point is the big damage.* Don't even think about the guessing penalty. Ignore it. You'll score higher.

Still don't believe us?

Okay, suppose you've got ten questions you aren't sure about. If you leave them all blank you get zero points. If you guess on all of them and get eight questions wrong and two questions right you break even and get zero points. No harm done. Get just three questions right out of ten and you're picking up bonus guessing points—full points, not little fraction-point jobs. How badly do you have to do to actually get hurt by guessing? You'd have to miss at least nine out of ten questions before you'd even get penalized! The *guessing penalty* should be called the *guessing bonus*.

If you've spent any time on a question, if you have the slightest inkling of what the answer might be, guess! That inkling is knowledge; don't waste it. Sure, you'll lose a quarter of a point here and there. So what? You'll harvest enough whole points to more than make up the difference. Guessing is the only way to take advantage of your partial knowledge. You may not know enough to be comfortable with an answer, but that isn't the issue. You don't have to be comfortable. You have to guess! Do you know anything? If so, then guess.

SHOULD YOU LEAVE ANY BLANKS?

Completely blind guessing on questions you haven't even read is not a good idea. Yes, it could help your score, but it could also hurt it. The odds are guessing randomly will do nothing. We say don't chance it. Don't guess blindly.

> The rule is this: If you've read the passage, the question, and the answer choices, then always answer the question.

There are no exceptions to this rule. There are times, however, when some students will want to leave a block of questions unread (and unanswered) for strategic time management reasons. We will go into that case fully in the time management part of this chapter.

GUESSING WISELY WITH POE

POE is an acronym for the process of elimination. You are probably already acquainted with POE in its simplest form: Cross out answers you know are wrong. The Cracking the System approach to POE isn't really different, just more intense.

There are always two ways to correctly answer a multiple-choice question. The first is to have the answer in mind right from the moment you read the question. This happens on easier questions and when you've read a passage you understood very well. In these cases, you'll see the right answer among the choices and pick it. Great. Far more often, however, you'll be slightly (or not-so-slightly) unsure. ETS is pretty good at spotting places in a text where students are likely to have trouble, and they tend to write questions about these spots. ETS is also pretty good at writing appealing wrong answers. As a result, no matter how strong a reader you are, there will be questions where you have doubts about the answer. That's when you use The Princeton Review-style POE. What does that mean? It means: *Stop looking for the right answer. Don't look for the right answer; look for wrong answers and eliminate them.* Let's look at an example. Here's a part of a passage, followed by a typical question:

Keats fell by a criticism. But who ever died of poor poetry? Ignoble souls!—De L'Omelette perished of an ortolan*. The story then, in brief:

Line
(5) That night the Duke was to sup alone. In the privacy of his bureau he reclined languidly on that ottoman for which he sacrificed his loyalty in outbidding his king—the notorious ottoman of Cadet.

He buries his face in the pillow. The clock strikes! Unable to restrain his feelings, his Grace swallows an
(10) olive. At this moment the door gently opens to the sound of soft music, and lo! The most delicate of birds is before the most enamored of men! But what inexpressible dismay now overshadows the countenance of the Duke? *"Horreur! Dog! Protestant! —the bird! Ah*
(15) *Good God! This modest bird you've quite unclothed and served without paper!"* It is superfluous to say more:— the Duke expired in a paroxysm of disgust . . . .

*an ortolan is a small dove-like bird considered a supreme delicacy by nineteenth century gourmets.

1. Lines 1–12 of the passage best describe the author's portrayal of the Duke De L'Omelette as:

(A) a sympathetic portrait of a man with overly delicate sensibilities.
(B) a comically ironic treatment of an effete snob.
(C) a harshly condemnatory portrait of a bon vivant.
(D) an admiring portrait of a great artist.
(E) a farcical treatment of the very rich.

This is a typical AP English Literature and Composition question. It asks for an evaluation of a passage for comprehension. The majority of the questions take this form. In the example above you've been asked, essentially, "what's going on in lines 1–12?" The actual passage would have been longer (usually around 55 lines), and the rest of the passage would certainly help you understand this section by putting it in context, but nevertheless, there is enough here to answer the question.

If you don't immediately spot the right answer, use POE. Go to each choice and say, "Why is this wrong?"

WHY IS THIS WRONG? HALF BAD = ALL BAD

The key is to take each answer a word at a time. Don't fixate on what's right about the answer; if any part of the answer is wrong then eliminate the answer. *Half bad equals all bad*. In fact, one-tenth bad equals all bad. Now let's look at the answer choices:

(A) Yes, it's true that the portrait is of a man with delicate sensibilities, but is it sympathetic? Don't know? Come back to it. No one said you can only read an answer choice once.

Go through and eliminate the ones you're sure are wrong and then look more closely at what's left.

(B) You might say, "Ironic? Effete? I'm really not sure what they're talking about." Okay, so leave it. Don't eliminate answers if you don't understand them.

(C) Whatever "effete" means, "harshly condemnatory" should look wrong. The Duke is harshly condemnatory of the servant who brings in his meal, but the passage itself does not disapprove of either of them. Half bad equals all bad. Eliminate this choice.

(D) John Keats was a great artist, but the Duke? From these 12 lines you sure can't say that; eliminate this choice.

(E) "Farcical?" Perhaps. But is this passage about the "very rich"? No, it's about the Duke De L'Omelette. Half bad equals all bad. Eliminate.

ELIMINATE THE OBVIOUS AND COME BACK

That leaves answers (A) and (B). This is another key to POE. Work through the answers in two, or even three sweeps. First eliminate what seems most wrong. When you are down to two (or three) answers, compare. Ask, which one is more wrong? So ask yourself, is the portrait *sympathetic*? You might find yourself thinking, "no, it isn't sympathetic exactly. It's kind of funny. I mean, this is a guy who dies because his dinner isn't cooked exactly right. I'm not supposed to sympathize with that, am I?" However, if you aren't clear about the meaning of effete or ironic in (B), you're left with an answer you don't understand very well. What do you do? Be fearless.

BE FEARLESS!

Pick (B). You couldn't find anything wrong with (B). It had some tough vocabulary. So what? Don't be afraid to pick answers you aren't sure are right. There will be plenty of times that happens. Just make sure you don't pick answers that you think are probably wrong. We know that sounds obvious, but students do pick crummy answers, and know that they're doing it. Why? Because one answer was well, "kind of but not really right," and the other one was totally unfamiliar. The student thinks that the unfamiliar answer might be right, but then again it might be *horribly grotesquely embarrassingly wrong*. The student picks the "kind-of-not-really-I-actually-knew-it-was-wrong" answer and loses points, but that's okay, that's fine, because at least it wasn't the dreaded el chumpo-supremo answer. Hey! *Relax*. The multiple-choice questions are scored by a machine. There is no el chumpo-supremo answer. No person looks at or cares about what answer you pick, which you probably already knew, so just keep it in mind when you answer questions. What's more—your haircut looks great, your clothes are snazzy, and you have a nice smile, so—be fearless. If POE leaves you with an answer choice you aren't sure about, pick it. If POE leaves you with two or three answers you aren't sure about—*pick one*.

In the example above, choice (B) was correct. If you were solid on the definitions of "ironic" and "effete," then you probably got the answer without much trouble. (In which case, we hope you followed our discussion of POE anyway, because you will need to use it many times during the actual test.) If those words gave you trouble, here's what they mean. *Effete* means overly delicate, or overly-refined (it can also mean decadent, worn out, sterile, and depleted). Clearly the Duke is effete, in fact hyper-effete—a caricature. This is where *ironic* comes in. The passage is ironic. It treats the Duke's ridiculous tastes as understandable, which they simply aren't. No one dies of a poorly served dinner. (Of course the Duke doesn't just die, that would be too crude, he "expires." An example of exactly the type of point about diction you want to make in your essays.) Nevertheless, the narrator presents this event as though it is not especially bizarre. The contrast between the narrator's tone and the events described produces *irony*, which in the most common instance is a kind of subtle humor produced when what is said is different from what is meant. But this is just one example, and irony comes in dozens of colors and flavors. *Irony* is an important term for the test and for the study of literature in general. We give it a full treatment in our Glossary of Literary Terms for the AP English Literature and Composition Test.

POE SUMMARY

So what does it all boil down to?

- When in doubt, look for wrong answers and eliminate.
- Eliminate the obviously wrong, then look more closely at what's left.
- Half bad = all bad.
- Don't leave a question you've worked on blank, ever.

TIME MANAGEMENT

A key factor on standardized tests is time management. The AP English Literature and Composition Test is no exception. You've got to answer roughly 50 questions in just one hour, and that includes reading the passages. There's no time to waste. Most students have difficulty getting to all the questions in the allotted time.

The more questions you answer correctly, the better you'll do. The only way to answer questions is to get to them. At the same time there is such a thing as working too fast. Some students can score better by slowing down and answering fewer questions, but getting the ones they work on right. So what should you do?

We don't know you and your specific strengths and weaknesses as a reader and test taker, so in this section you're going to have to analyze yourself carefully and honestly. We're going to present some general guidelines that every student should follow. Then we're going to lay out the time management options you have available, and offer suggestions that will help you decide which of our methods you should employ. They all work; it's just a matter of getting the best fit for you.

DO IT YOUR WAY

Have you ever heard this conversation following a standardized test?

Student A (bummed): " I didn't even get to the last passage."

Student B (rubbing it in): "NO? That was the *easiest* one, it was a total breeze, it was a piece of cake, a cinch, a given . . . ."

Okay, student B deserves a swift kick . . ., but that isn't the point. You don't want to be student A, and there's no reason you should be.

If you can get to all four passages and answer all the questions with five minutes left over, great, but don't count on it. Plan ahead. There's no law that says you should do the passages in the order given. Don't.

As we've already mentioned, as soon as the multiple-choice section begins the first thing you should do is look over the four passages quickly. This is definitely allowed. Decide which passage to do first, but much more importantly—**decide which passage to do last.**

The object is to find the hardest passage and put off doing it until the end. There are a couple of reasons for doing this. First, if you're going to run out of time, why not run out of time on the passage where you were going to miss a lot of questions anyway? Second, the hardest passage is undoubtedly going to take the most time. You don't want to get into a situation where you have to rush just to finish three out of four passages. This is such a simple technique. All you have to do is remember to use it.

WHICH PASSAGE IS THE HARDEST?

There's no way of knowing which passage really has the hardest questions, so don't try to figure that out. You want to avoid the passage that is written in the form you find most confusing. For most students that means older poetry. If you're good with poetry, or recognize the author, or see a prose passage that has six words you don't know in the first paragraph, then pass over a prose passage. In general, shorter passages are easier than long ones and more recent passages are easier than older ones.

Remember, the point is to save time, not waste it. The decision process should take no more than *one minute*. Look at the first couple lines of each passage. Does it make sense? Do you feel comfortable? Yes? Great. But when you see a passage that makes you go, "huh?" put a big X at the top of the page to remind yourself to do it last, then start on the passage you like best, pronto.

SKIP A PASSAGE

There are four or five passages, and you are given 60 minutes to complete the section. This means you have 15 minutes per passage. If there were only three passages, you would suddenly have 20 minutes per passage.

Yes, we are suggesting that you (many of you) skip a passage and gain five minutes on each of the passages that you do attempt.

Essentially, some students will skip a passage whether they want to or not—they won't get to the last passage. The idea here is to prepare yourself for that case. If you know from previous standardized tests that you've taken, such as the PSAT, that you have trouble finishing the reading comprehension section, then you can be pretty sure that you'll have time trouble with the AP test. There's more time given for multiple-choice reading comprehension on the AP test than on the SATs, but the AP passages are longer and far tougher, and the questions are tougher too. One solution is to skip a passage entirely—don't even think about getting to it. The trade-off is accuracy for questions. You're letting go of those last 15 questions (and remember, they might be the questions for the *first* passage if that's the passage you decided was toughest for you) in order to improve your accuracy on the questions that you do answer.

Suppose you are coming up on the third passage with 20 minutes left in the section. (Remember to bring a watch to the test.) Don't think, "Oh no, 20 minutes left and still two passages to go . . . I've got to fly through this one to get to the next." That isn't reality. If there are 20 minutes left that means that you averaged 20 minutes on *each* of the two passages that came before. You should forget about the last passage (remember, you've already marked that passage out as the hardest one) and take the 20 minutes you need to do a good job on the third passage. You are bound to get more questions correct than if you tried to do both.

YOU CAN DO ONLY THREE PASSAGES AND STILL GET A GOOD SCORE

It's true. It is completely possible to get a final score of five and only do three passages (go back to page 9 to review the evidence.) No, it isn't easy. It calls for excellent essays and accurate answers on the passages you did do. If you'd be satisfied with a final score of four (and you should be; it's an excellent score), and if you know that time is a problem for you on standardized test reading comprehension, then doing just three out of four passages should definitely be considered an option.

A PREVIEW OF COMING ATTRACTIONS

There's one more time management technique that you absolutely have to know. It's called *the Art of the Seven Minute Passage*. We'd like to tell you about it now, but unfortunately the full technique won't make sense until we've outlined the general principles of reading prose passages and poetry passages, and shown you examples of the kinds of questions you'll see on the AP Literature Test. You'll find our full explanation of the Art of the Seven Minute Passage at the end of chapter 5.

But it's such a good technique we think you should get a preview. If, after all is said and done, you forget some of the details of the full Art of the Seven Minute Passage, or just plain like the Art of the Seven Minute Passage (Lite) that you find here better, use it. It's extremely close to the real thing, and a little easier to remember.

THE ART OF THE SEVEN-MINUTE PASSAGE (LITE)

For many, many students there's enough time on the AP test to do three and one-half passages. That is, you get through three passages and start reading the fourth one, maybe answer a question or two and WONK: "Please put down your pencils and close your exam booklet. There will be a five minute break and then we will proceed to the essay portion of . . ."

"Hey, wait a minute, I'm not finished."

Don't let this happen to you. Have a watch. When you get to the fourth passage, *check the time*. If you're running out of time, (seven minutes or less) you've got to take emergency measures. There are points there for the taking, but you don't have time to read the passage and answer the questions. What do you do?

Answer the questions. Don't read the passage. Go directly to the questions. There are *no points given* for reading the passage. The Art of the Seven-Minute Passage is the art of choosing questions. The principle is very simple.

Answer the questions that take no reading, then the questions that take just a little reading, then what's left over until you run out of time.

It's easy. Take the following three questions:

1. What is the main point of the passage?
2. The phrase *cold fire* is an example of:
3. In the context of the passage, the phrase *wang-a-dang-doodle* (line 123) most probably means:

If you had seven minutes to answer these questions, you'd skip question 1 entirely. You'd do question 2 immediately. That question doesn't even need a passage: it just wants to see if you know that *cold fire* is an oxymoron, which is the literary term for a pair of opposites (see the glossary). After doing question 2 (and if you didn't know what an oxymoron was, you still would have done the question using POE and taken your best, most fearless, guess), you'd look around for more questions like it. You might find one or two more, and you'd do them. Then you'd start looking for questions like 3. It sends you back to a specific place in the passage and asks for the meaning of a specific thing. All you'd have to read is a sentence or two. Do it. Then find another and another. (Many of the AP questions are like this.) After you've done all those you'll find you have read enough of the passage to start working on big general questions like number 1 and at least be able to come up with a good guess.

That's the Art of the Seven-Minute Passage (Lite). The full version in chapter 5 is more detailed about what order to do the questions in. If this lite version is the one you remember or like better, great. *Just remember to use it if you need to.*

ONE FINAL TIME TOOL: CONCENTRATION

After you've decided which passage to do last, and have started on the passage you've decided to do first, concentrate. Does that sound foolish and obvious? It really isn't. Reading fast is easy: just blaze your eyes over the page and pronounce yourself finished. Unfortunately, though, you'll have no idea of what you just looked at. The trick is to understand what you read, and the only way to do that is to concentrate. Buckle down and remember that this test is pretty tough. You've got to force yourself to stay with what you're reading. For the purposes of the AP English Test, concentration means just one thing: **Don't blank out.**

What do we mean? We mean that there almost always comes a time in reading a difficult text when you hit a sentence you don't understand. At that point, most students go blank. They're not reading anymore, just running their eyes over the pretty shapes (called *letters*), waiting for the part that makes sense again. About three-quarters of a page later the student snaps out of it thinking, "What's this . . . ? Hey, wait a minute, it looks like some kind of a test! Oh no . . . ." Then the student slogs back to the killer sentence and tries once more, often blanking out yet again.

Blanking out is really easy to do. Everyone does it, especially when tired or stressed or bored. But you can't afford to do it on the AP test. You don't have time. There's only one cure. When a sentence starts to get away from you—stop. Make a conscious effort to totally concentrate on what you're reading. Now try the sentence again, and if it still doesn't make sense, *move on*—not blanking out, not worrying about that tough sentence—but making a conscious, *concentrated* effort to keep reading.

SUMMARY OF THE BASIC PRINCIPLES OF CRACKING THE SYSTEM

HAVE A PLAN

1. Note the time.
2. Pick a passage to do last.
3. Pick a passage to do first.
4. Read the passage, our way.
5. Answer *all* the questions on the passage, using our techniques.

POE

- *Guess Aggressively*. If you work on a question, answer it, always.
- Use POE (process of elimination).
- The best way to use POE is to look closely at the wording of each answer choice for what is *wrong*, and eliminate.
- The *guessing penalty* should be called the *guessing bonus*.

TIME MANAGEMENT

Time trouble on the multiple-choice section is a reality for most AP students.

- Guess aggressively.
- Pick a passage to do last based on what you consider your greatest weakness.
- Complete just three passages and still get a good score.
- Learn the Art of the Seven-Minute Passage (lite or full) and use it.

3

ADVANCED PRINCIPLES: READING THE MULTIPLE-CHOICE PASSAGES

READING THE PASSAGES IN THE MULTIPLE-CHOICE SECTION

Because of the time constraints, you'll want to make sure that you go about reading the passages in the most efficient way possible. You'll want to use a slightly different approach depending on whether the passage is prose or poetry but there are a few things you should keep in mind regarding both types of passage.

- **You are reading in order to answer questions**, not for enjoyment or appreciation. The object is to answer questions. As you read, ask yourself, "Do I understand this well enough to answer a multiple-choice question about what it means?"

- **You can come back to the passage anytime you want**, and you *should* go back to the passage in order to answer the questions.

Both of these points address the same issue. The passages are on a test (yeah, that's pretty obvious) but you don't do most of your reading on tests, not even one percent of it. Reading for a test *is* slightly different. While a few students take test reading too lightly, the worse and far more common mistake is to overcompensate: "OH MY GOD, IT'S A TEST!!!" Out come the quintuple color highlighter pens: "Let's see . . . pink for verbs, blue for nouns, yellow for adjectives. Huge circles for main points. Little stars for little points. Then the arrows to link it all together, let's see . . . yellow arrows for . . . ." That's not reading, it's coloring. Ninety-nine percent of underlining on multiple-choice tests is worse than a waste of time; it actually distracts from real reading. If you just have to underline, go ahead, but don't fool yourself—it's just a way of releasing nervous energy. (By the way, there is good reason to mark up books when you study, especially when done with an intelligent system. We're only talking about the AP test here.)

A mistake related to obsessive underlining is paranoid micro-reading. The student, again overcompensating for the fact that the passage is on a test, thinks: "There could be a question about anything . . . *anything here* . . . I've got to read super carefully . . . I can't miss a thing . . . whatever I miss that's what they'll ask about—I know it, that's just my luck, I've never had any luck . . . I'll show them . . . *I'll memorize the passage . . . they won't get me this time HAHAHAHA*." This form of test-induced insanity (except for the nervous breakdown at the end) is quite common. The student fixates so intently on trying to remember each little detail that the main drift of the passage is lost, or the student takes 10 minutes on the first paragraph, or both. If this sounds like a tendency of yours, ease up. The passage isn't going anywhere. Everyone has to go back to the passage for details and to recheck first impressions.

READING PROSE PASSAGES

The right way to read prose passages in the multiple-choice section is simple. It's the way you should read whenever your purpose is to assimilate information efficiently. (It is not a way to read for pleasure.) On the AP English Literature Test make a point of reading this way:

1. SKIM THE PASSAGE

Skimming the passage should take about 30 seconds and should never take more than a minute. Look at the beginning of the passage and take in the first sentence. Now just drop your eyes over the passage from top to bottom looking at what is going on, barely reading, just getting impressions. Pay closer attention at the end. Read the last sentence of the passage, thinking, "so this is where it ends up." When you're done (about 30 seconds later) you won't have any grand insights, you probably won't understand what the passage is exactly about. You might feel like you've wasted 30 seconds. You didn't.

Your brain does a lot more than it lets you know about, which is a good thing. Imagine if every time you saw an English word your brain sent you the stunning revelation: "Hey! That's English." Or every time you saw someone your brain announced importantly, "She seems to be breathing, she is not holding a small peeled onion . . . ." You would be insane.

As you skim, your mind is taking in thousands of little details that it doesn't bother you with because it would interfere with the larger part of your consciousness, which is taken up with the task of making things make sense. As you look over the passage your brain registers facts like, "There's no dialogue in this one," and "long paragraphs," and "vocabulary looks okay," all of which help you when it comes time to actually read the passage. At the same time, the isolated little bits you skim float into your consciousness like bits of a jigsaw puzzle. However, your brain hasn't taken in enough to make sense of the whole package, so it sends out little help signals like, "Slow down, I don't get it." Don't slow down. Those jigsaw bits are subconscious teasers. Your brain wants to fit them into a coherent pattern, and you'll give it all the information it needs in just a moment. The skim is the wake up call; you'll get to work when you read. Finally, by paying attention to the end of the passage you set up your mind for the flow of it and give yourself an end-point for your slower-reading self to move toward.

Wow. All that in 30 seconds. And you thought skimming was a waste of time.

Most people don't skim because it's uncomfortable, especially in a test situation where every impulse says, "I've got to get this." Let the skimming be slightly uncomfortable; that means you're doing it right. Skimming, also called pre-reading, aids efficient comprehension enormously, which is exactly what you want on the AP test.

2. READ THE PASSAGE

The second step, the step you've been waiting for, is reading—plain old-fashioned reading. Just read, without fixating on details, without getting stuck or going blank. When you hit a sentence you don't understand in a book, you don't panic, do you? You don't assume: "Gosh, I might as well throw this book away . . . without that sentence it's just a useless collection of incomplete alphabets." When you read normally, you read for the main idea. You read to understand what's going on. When you hit a tricky sentence, you figure that you'll be able to make sense of it from what comes later, or that one missing piece of the puzzle isn't going to keep you from getting the outline of the overall picture. This is exactly how you want to read an AP English Test passage.

GET THE MAIN IDEA

Get the main idea of the passage. A clear understanding of the main idea will get you the bulk of the points you need. Yes, ETS will pin you down on a few specific points and insist you come up with an answer. If you have the main idea, however, you'll be able to go back to the passage and get the detail you need. If the detail is still unclear, remember, you don't have to supply the answer yourself, you only need to find it among five answer choices. At worst, using POE (and some other techniques we'll show you shortly), you'll be left with a reasonable guess.

WHAT IS THE MAIN IDEA?

For the AP English Test, *main idea* means the general point. It is the ten-word, or shorter, summary of the passage. The main idea is the gist. For example, suppose there's a passage about all the different ways a man is stingy, how he cheats his best friend out of an inheritance, and scimps on food around the house so badly that his kids go to bed crying with hunger every night. The passage goes on for 50 or 60 lines describing this guy. Okay, the main idea is that this guy is an evil, greedy miser. If the passage gives a reason for the miser's obsession with money, you might include that in your mental picture of the main idea: this guy is an evil, greedy miser because he grew up poor. No doubt the passage tells you exactly how he grew up (in an orphanage, let's say) and where, and exactly what kind of leftover beans he eats (lima) and exactly how many cold leftover lima beans he serves to his starving kids each night (three apiece), but those are details, not essentials. The main idea is what is essential to the passage.

THE MAGIC TOPIC SENTENCE HAS VANISHED

We don't want you to think the main idea can be found in some magic "topic sentence." The writers on the AP test are sophisticated; they often don't use anything like topic sentences. On poetry passages looking for topic sentences is a complete waste of time.

SUMMARY—HOW DO YOU READ AN AP MULTIPLE-CHOICE PROSE PASSAGE?

- Skim (30 seconds)
- Read for the main idea

READING POETRY PASSAGES

Ideally, you read a poem several times, ponder, scratch your head, and read some more. Then again, ideally, you have a hot mug of coffee, leafy shadows that sway in the sunlight falling across your desk, a breeze from the window, your favorite poem by your favorite poet, and all afternoon—not 15 minutes with some seventeenth century freak you couldn't care less about and 15 inane questions staring you in the face.

It's a test, so you've got to read the poem efficiently. (We know, that's a little bit like trying to fall in love efficiently.) Well, the key to the process is keeping your mind open, especially the first time through the poem.

It might help to be clear about the difference between a narrative and the kind of poetry you'll see on the AP test. A narrative unfolds and builds on itself. Although one's understanding of what came earlier in the narrative is deepened and changed by later developments, by and large the work makes sense as it flows; it is meant to be understood "on the run."

Verse is different. Yes, the way it unfolds is important, but one often doesn't even grasp that unfolding until the second or third (or ninetieth) read. A poem is like a sculpture, it is meant to be wandered around, looked at from all sides, and finally, taken in as a whole. You wouldn't try to understand a sculpture until you'd seen the whole thing. In the same way, think of your first reading of a poem as a walk around an interesting sculpture. You aren't trying to interpret. You are just trying to look at the whole thing. Once you've seen it, taken in its dimensions, then you can go back and puzzle it out.

What we've just said applies to poetry in general. The real question is what does this mean for the AP test? Here's the answer: **When you approach a poem on the AP test, always read it at least twice before you go to the questions.**

THE FIRST READ

The first read is to get all the words in your head. Go from top to bottom. *Don't* stop at individual lines to figure them out, not even a little. If everything makes sense, great. If it doesn't, no problem. The main thing you want is a basic sense of what's going on. The main thing to avoid is getting a fixed impression of the poem before you've even finished it.

THE SECOND READ

The second read should be phrase by phrase. Focus on understanding what you read in the simplest way possible. **Get the main idea.**

Don't worry about symbols. Don't worry about deeper meanings. The questions will direct you toward those things. You will need to go back and read parts of the poem, perhaps the entire poem, several more times, but only as is necessary to answer individual questions. To prepare yourself for the questions, all you need is a general sense of what the poem says, and to get that you need only the literal sense of the lines. We can't emphasize this enough: *Keep it simple.* (The very next sub-section gives you instructions on how to do this.)

THE THIRD READ

If you don't have the main idea of the poem after the second read, give it one more read. The third read is just like the second, but chances are needing a third full read for meaning is an indication that the poem is giving you a lot of trouble. Is it just one line, or just a couple of lines that are the problem? If so, forget it. Stop obsessing over a line or two—you're beginning to waste precious time. Move on to the questions. The point is answering the questions. If you've gone through twice, and the whole poem still seems unclear, give it that third read, and pay attention to where it begins to lose you. Often it helps to ignore a difficult line or two. You'll sometimes find that if you do that, the rest of the poem does in fact make sense.

PANIC AND OBSESSION

If, however, you find that after three reads you don't have the poem's main idea, don't panic. Chances are at least half the people in the room with you are completely baffled by the same poem. Don't skip the passage. Move on to the questions. Often the questions will help you understand the poem, or many of the questions are about aspects of the poem which you can answer. But whatever you do, don't obsess over a difficult poem. Don't read and reread and reread as though you could pummel the poem into submission and force it to give up its meaning. This won't work. You'll just use up time and frustrate yourself. If a poem gives you tons of trouble, chances are it's giving everyone trouble. Go to the questions.

THE PROBLEM WITH POETRY

Poetry, especially good poetry, makes conscious use of all language's resources. By pushing at the limits of language, poetry typically creates a heightened awareness of language in the reader. When everything goes according to plan, the poem seems intensely meaningful, suggestive of new ideas and connections, and yet surprisingly exact. But things don't always go according to plan. Much of the time when you read a complex poem, the heightened sense of language sends you down a maze of false alleys, and myriad suggestions lead you so far from the home-base of meaning that you end up feeling just plain lost. Poets use difficult vocabulary, unusual combinations of words in unusual orders, and odd figures of speech; they play with time and stretch the connections we ordinarily expect between ideas. All these things, essential to poetry, can also make things difficult. It's easy to get lost, and it's often a struggle to get *anything* from a poem, let alone find it beautiful or enjoyable. Finally, many poems are deliberately open to a number of interpretations, which are often valid.

NO PROBLEM AT ALL

But here's some really good news. On the AP test you won't see vague unknowable poetry. You won't see poetry that's open to many interpretations, or if you do, the questions will be about aspects of the poem that are certain. The simple reason for this is that it's a test. In other words, the questions must have right answers, not subjective opinions for answers. Otherwise it wouldn't be a fair test.

The kinds of poems you're likely to see on the AP English Literature Test will use complex, challenging language, but underneath it all will be a spine of good old normal straightforward meaning. Find that spine of meaning and you "get" the poem; even if you have a problem here and there with individual lines, you won't be lost. The *spine of a poem* is a fancy way of saying, *the prose meaning of the poem*. The poems on the AP test have prose hidden inside the poetry. Understand that, and you can ace the poetry passages on the AP test.

THE PROS READ POETRY FOR PROSE

The secret to understanding AP poetry passages quickly and well is to simply ignore the "poetry parts." Ignore the rhythm, ignore the music of the language, and above all ignore the form. That means:

- Ignore line breaks.
- Read in sentences, not in lines. Emphasize punctuation.
- Ignore rhyme and rhyme scheme.
- Be prepared for "long" thoughts—ideas that develop over several lines.

When many students approach poetry they tend to do the opposite of what we suggest here: They emphasize lines and line breaks and totally ignore sentence punctuation. If you don't get slammed on the AP test for doing that, you're lucky.

True, sometimes there's no problem: When lines break at natural pauses and when each line has a packet of meaning complete in itself (these are termed *end-stopped* lines) the poem becomes easier to read.

NICE POETRY

Look at these lines from Thomas Gray's *Elegy Written in A Country Churchyard*:

> Now fades the glimmering landscape on the sight,
> And all the air a solemn stillness holds,
> Save where the beetle wheels his droning flight,
> And drowsy tinklings lull the distant folds.

Read that passage aloud and you can't help but stop on the line endings, even without the commas. The lines build, one upon the next, shaping a picture as they combine to form a mildly complex sentence. The ease with which these lines can be read stems from the fact that each line contains only complete thoughts; there are no loose ends trailing from line to line. This is "nice" poetry, that is, it's nice to you. Each line ends on a natural pause that lets you gather your thoughts. Each line holds something like a complete thought with very little run-over into the next line. Although the stanza is written in one sentence, it could have easily been written in four separate sentences:

> The landscape fades.
> The air is still.
> The beetle wheels and drones.
> The tinklings [of bells worn by livestock] lull the folds.*

*Folds are enclosures where sheep graze, or it is the flocks of sheep themselves.

That paraphrase is lousy poetry, but it gets the main idea across. If the poetry you see on the AP test reads like the example above, great. But if you think every poem should be like that stanza, if you try to make every poem read like that one, you're headed for trouble. The poetry on the AP test is much more likely to be not so nice—not so nice at all.

NOT-SO-NICE POETRY

Consider the next selection. It's the first 13 lines of "My Last Duchess" by Robert Browning. This is the kind of poetry you can expect to find on the AP test.

The poem is a monologue, spoken by a nobleman, the Duke of Ferrara, to a representative of the Count of Tyrol. Ferrara seeks to take the wealthy Count's daughter for his bride and is in the midst of discussing the arrangement with the Count's representative. When Ferrara speaks of his "last duchess," he refers to his first wife, who has quite recently died, at the age of 17, under mysterious circumstances. The implication is that Ferrara has had his first wife murdered, an implication the poem brings home with understated menace.

My Last Duchess

Ferrara:

> That's my last duchess painted on the wall,
> Looking as if she were alive. I call
> That piece a wonder, now: Frà Pandolf's hands
> *Line* Worked busily a day, and there she stands.
> (5) Will't please you sit and look at her? I said
> "Frà Pandolf" by design, for never read
> Strangers like you that pictured countenance,
> The depth and passion of its earnest glance,
> But to myself they turned (since none puts by
> (10) The curtain I have drawn for you, but I)
> And seemed as they would ask me, if they durst,
> how such a glance came there; so, not the first
> Are you to turn and ask thus . . . .

Now this isn't particularly difficult poetry, but legions of students have trouble making heads or tails of it. The first few lines present little difficulty: The Duke points to the painting, remarks on its lifelike quality, mentions the artist (Frà Pandolf), and invites his listener to sit and contemplate the portrait for a moment. Although lines 3–4, "Frà Pandolf's hands/ Worked busily a day" are distinctly unmodern speech, and might give some folks a moment's pause, most of us get through the opening without too much difficulty.

Then comes the remainder of the passage, beginning from line 5, "I said/ 'Frà Pandolf' by design, for never read" and the trouble begins. Now, the truth is that what is written there is easy enough that if you can break the habit of placing too much emphasis on line breaks, you can read it as prose. Browning has deliberately written his verse so that the lines break against the flow of the punctuation. If you expect little parcels of complete meaning at every break, you'll end up lost. Let's consider the troubling part written as prose:

"I said 'Frà Pandolf' by design, for never read strangers like you that pictured countenance, the depth and passion of its earnest glance, but to myself they turned (since none puts by the curtain I have drawn for you, but I) and seemed as they would ask me, if they durst, how such a glance came there."

This is just one long sentence, broken by parenthetical asides, in which the Duke says, "I said 'Frà Pandolf'" on purpose because strangers never see that portrait (or its expression of depth and passion) without turning to me (because nobody sees the portrait unless I'm here to pull aside the curtain) and looking at me as though they want to ask, if they dare, 'How did that expression get there?'"

Read the poem as prose and you'll see it isn't so hard. If you have trouble doing this, try putting brackets around each sentence.

Now, if you're really alert, you'll notice that the Duke still hasn't exactly explained why he mentioned Frà Pandolf on purpose. He eventually does (in his sideways fashion), but if you read poetry without being ready for long thoughts that develop over several lines, you're going to read "I said, 'Frà Pandolf' by design, for never . . ." and expect the explanation—pronto. When it doesn't come you think you're lost, and once you think you're lost, you are. How is "that pictured countenance" an explanation of why he said, "Frà Pandolf?" It isn't, and it never will be, but you can spend hours trying to come up with reasons why it is.

Don't get the wrong impression. Browning isn't easy reading. But you'll find that if you follow our suggestions for reading poetry, he, and poets like him, aren't nearly as difficult as they seem to be. **Ignore line breaks and instead pay close attention to punctuation and sentence structure.** Be ready for "long" thoughts that develop over several lines or even stanzas. You'll still find the poems on the AP test challenging for a variety of reasons: because of their vocabulary, because of their compression of a great deal of information into just a few lines, and because of their often complicated and unusual sentence structure. If you read poetry the way we suggest, however, you'll find that you can make sense of those difficulties by using the context of what you do understand.

Taken together, these pieces of advice boil down to one simple concept:

Before you read a poem as poetry, read it as prose.

Here's Browning's "My Last Duchess" in complete form. Read it according to our advice and see what you can get from it. We'll return to the poem later on in this book, and our discussion of it there (page 105) will let you know how you did.

FERRARA

That's my last duchess painted on the wall,
Looking as if she were alive. I call
That piece a wonder, now: Frà Pandolf's hands
Worked busily a day, and there she stands.
Will't please you sit and look at her? I said
"Frà Pandolf" by design, for never read
Strangers like you that pictured countenance,
The depth and passion of its earnest glance,
But to myself they turned (since none puts by
The curtain I have drawn for you, but I)
And seemed as they would ask me, if they durst,
how such a glance came there; so, not the first
Are you to turn and ask thus. Sir, 'twas not
Her husband's presence only, called that spot
Of joy into the Duchess' cheek: perhaps
Frà Pandolf chanced to say, "Her mantle laps
"Over my lady's wrist too much," of "Paint
"Must never hope to reproduce the faint
"Half-flush that dies along her throat": such stuff
Was courtesy, she thought, and cause enough
For calling up that spot of joy. She had
A heart—how shall I say?—too soon made glad,
Too easily impressed; she liked whate'er
She looked on, and her looks went everywhere.

Sir, 'twas all one! My favor at her breast,
The dropping of the daylight in the West,
The bough of cherries some officious fool
Broke in the orchard for her, the white mule
She rode with round the terrace—all and each
Would draw from her alike the approving speech,
Or blush, at least. She thanked men—good! but thanked
Somehow—I know not how—as if she ranked
My gift of a nine-hundred-years-old name
With anybody's gift. Who'd stoop to blame
This sort of trifling? Even had you skill
In speech—which I have not—to make your will
Quite clear to such an one, and say, "Just this
"Or that in you disgusts me; here you miss,
"Or there exceed the mark"—and if she let
Herself be lessoned so, nor plainly set
Her wits to yours, forsooth, and made excuse,
—E'en then would be some stooping; and I choose
Never to stoop. Oh sir, she smiled, no doubt,
Whene'er I passed her; but who passed without
Much the same smile? This grew; I gave commands;
Then all smiles stopped together. There she stands
As if alive. Will't please you rise? We'll meet
The company below, then. I repeat,
The Count your master's known munificence
Is ample warrant that no just pretense
Of mine for dowry will be disallowed;
Though his fair daughter's self, as I avowed
At starting, is my object. Nay, we'll go
Together down, sir. Notice Neptune, though,
Taming a sea-horse, thought a rarity,
Which Claus of Innsbrück cast in bronze for me!

SUMMARY

BASICS OF READING PASSAGES

- You are reading in order to answer the questions—that's the whole point.
- Reading for a test is different than normal reading. You have limited time, and you've got to approach the passages in a way that takes that into account.
- You can reread the passage anytime you want, and you should go back to the passage in order to answer the questions.
- Underlining is a release of nervous energy, not a technique.

READING PROSE PASSAGES

- First, skim the passage.
- Skimming should take about 30 seconds, and should never take more than a minute.
- Skimming is annoying; it's supposed to be. That annoyance is your brain waking up.
- **Read for the main idea.**

READING POETRY PASSAGES

- On the AP test, read a poem at least twice before you go to the questions.
- The first read is to get all the words in your head.
  —The main thing you want is a basic sense of what's going on.
  —The main thing to avoid is getting a fixed impression of the poem before you've even finished it.
- The second read should be phrase by phrase. Focus on understanding what you read in the simplest way possible. Don't worry about symbols. Don't worry about deeper meanings.
- You will need to go back and read parts of the poem, perhaps the entire poem, several more times, but only as necessary for your work on individual questions.

POETRY INTO PROSE

- Find the spine—the prose meaning—of the poem.
  —Ignore line breaks.
  —Emphasize punctuation. Read in sentences, not in lines.
  —Be prepared for "long" thoughts: ideas that develop over several lines.
- **Before you read a poem as poetry, read it as prose.**

4

Cracking the System: Multiple-Choice Questions

THE QUESTIONS

Once you've finished reading a passage, it's time to go after the questions. If you've paid attention thus far, you already know you're going to answer all the questions, taking your best guess when you are less than perfectly sure of yourself. You're fearless, remember? You should also know by now that we think you should approach the test efficiently, making the best possible use of your time in order to get the best possible score.

In order to answer the questions efficiently, you need to be able to recognize three types of questions:

- General comprehension questions
- Detail comprehension questions
- Factual knowledge questions

It should be fairly easy to distinguish among these three broad categories.

GENERAL COMPREHENSION QUESTIONS

General comprehension questions are those that ask about the overall passage. These are the questions that don't send you back to any specific place in the passage.

Here are some examples of general comprehension questions:

> The passage is primarily concerned with . . . ?
>
> Which one of the following choices best describes the tone of the passage?
>
> Which one of the following choices best describes the narrator's relationship to her mother?
>
> To whom does the speaker of the poem address his speech?
>
> It is evident in the passage that the author feels his hometown is . . . ?
>
> Which of the following best describes the author's changing attitude over the course of first, second, and third stanzas, respectively?

DETAIL QUESTIONS

Detail questions almost always send you back to specific places in the passage. They tell you where to look and ask about what is going on at that specific place in the passage.

Here are some examples of detail questions:

> What significant change occurs in the author's attitude toward her mother in lines 5–9?
>
> How do the final words of the third paragraph, "but then, I should have known better than to trust him" alter the remainder of the passage?
>
> What does the author mean by "formalist" (line 19)?
>
> Which of the following is the best paraphrase for the sentence that begins at line 9?

FACTUAL KNOWLEDGE QUESTIONS

Factual knowledge questions ask you about English language and its grammar, and the basic terminology of criticism and poetry. Factual knowledge questions sometimes (but very rarely) ask for a widely known cultural fact related to the passage.

Here are some examples of factual knowledge questions:

> The third line of the first stanza scans most naturally in which of the following meters?
>
> In line 17, the phrase "frozen fire" is an example of . . .?
>
> Which of the following rhetorical devices is used twice in the final stanza?
>
> Which of the following words is used as a gerund in the passage?
>
> When in the third stanza the playwright character says, "I believe my tragedy is worthy of performance at the Globe," he is referring to:

The last question is an example of a question that tests your knowledge of a cultural fact. You can be sure that the right answer mentions that many of Shakespeare's plays were premiered at the Globe Theatre and because of this the Globe Theatre is indelibly associated with Shakespeare's name. This is the sort of cultural fact that ETS expects literate high school students to know. Questions about cultural facts are one type of question that is impossible to study for, and there are very few of this kind of question on the test anyway. One or two at most, and often none.

DO IT YOUR WAY, OR . . . ORDERING THE QUESTIONS

You can do the questions in any order you like, but that doesn't mean you should jump around and do them any old way. After you finish reading a passage, but before you begin answering the questions, ask yourself, "Do I feel confident about this passage? Would I be able to explain this to a friend? Could I explain its main idea?"

The answer to this question determines the order you should do the test questions in:

- If you feel confident about your comprehension of the passage, do the questions in the order ETS gives them to you. Don't worry about the order of the questions; you're in good shape.

- If you don't feel confident about the main idea, do the detail questions first.

The reasoning behind this is simple. The main idea is the crucial thing to get from a reading passage, either prose or poetry. When you've got the main idea nailed down, you aren't likely to miss more than a few questions on the passage. Knowing the main idea will help you answer all the other general questions and many of the specific questions as well.

When you don't feel confident about the main idea (usually that means the passage was pretty tough, you feel confused, and you're sort of, well, bumming—it happens), you want to start with the specific questions because they tell you exactly where to go and give you something to focus on.

As you reread the lines that the specific questions point you toward, you should become more and more familiar with the passage. Often, after doing a specific question or two, the meaning of the passage "clicks" for you, and you get what's going on. Don't answer the general questions until you have a firm sense of the main idea. If, after answering all the specific questions, you still don't really know what the point of the passage was, give the general questions your best shot and move on.

CONSISTENCY OF ANSWERS #1

The main idea is your guiding rule for most of the questions on any passage. We call this principle *Consistency of Answers*. As you work on a passage you will find that the right answer on several of the questions has to do with the main idea. The rule is, **when in doubt, pick an answer that agrees with the main idea.**

CONSISTENCY OF ANSWERS #2

Pick answers that agree with each other. You'll also find that correct answers tend to be consistent. It's a simple idea that comes in very handy. For example, if you're sure the correct answer to question number 9 is choice (B), and choice (B) says that Mr. Buffalo is extremely hairy, you can be sure that question 10's Mr. Buffalo isn't bald. Correct answers agree with each other.

The best way to understand how to use this very effective technique is to see it at work. You'll see plenty of examples in the following chapters; we'll discuss this technique in detail when we work on actual questions.

SUMMARY

- Recognize three basic categories of questions.
  —General
  —Detail
  —Factual

- Do it your way.
  —If you know the main idea, do the questions in order.
  —If you're uncomfortable with the main idea, answer detail and factual questions first.

- Use Consistency of Answers.
  —When in doubt pick an answer that agrees with the main idea.
  —Pick answers that agree with each other.

5

ANSWERING PROSE PASSAGE QUESTIONS

HOW TO USE OUR SAMPLE PASSAGES AND QUESTIONS

There's no limit to the different kinds of questions that ETS can (and does) write for the AP English Test. As a result, we can't show you every type of question that will show up on the test. We can come pretty close, though. ETS has a bunch of questions it uses and reuses on hundreds of tests. The best way to study these questions is by practicing on examples. To understand and use the example questions, you need a passage.

In this chapter and the next, we provide passages with sample questions. Chapter 5 has a prose passage. Chapter 6 has a poetry passage. Read the passages carefully using our reading techniques, and then look over the questions.

There's no need to do the questions immediately since we're going to take you through them one step at time, discussing the best approaches and specific techniques to use in answering them. Of course, if you want to see how you do on them before referring to our instructions, go right ahead.

After you've looked over the passages, read each question, try to answer it, and then follow our explanations. The correct answer to each question is given in the explanation, but don't just skim through the explanation looking for the answer to see if you chose correctly. Read all of each explanation, regardless of whether you got the question right. Our explanations will point out details you overlooked and discuss how you might have approached the question differently.

SAMPLE PROSE PASSAGE AND QUESTIONS: EDGAR ALLAN POE'S "THE DUC DE L'OMELETTE"

Keats fell by a criticism. But who ever died of inept poetry? Ignoble souls!—De L'Omelette perished of an ortolan*. The story then, in brief:

Line
(5)
That night the Duke was to sup alone. In the privacy of his bureau he reclined languidly on that ottoman for which he sacrificed his loyalty in outbidding his king—the notorious ottoman of Cadet.

He buries his face in the pillow. The clock strikes! Unable to restrain his feelings, his Grace swallows an
(10) olive. At this moment the door gently opens to the sound of soft music, and lo! the most delicate of birds is before the most enamored of men! But what inexpressible dismay now overshadows the countenance of the Duke? "*Horreur! Dog! Protestant! —the*
(15) *bird! Ah Good God! This modest bird you've quite unclothed and served without paper!*" It is superfluous to say more:—the Duke expired in a paroxysm of disgust . . . .

"Ha! ha! ha!" said his Grace on the third day after
(20) his decease.

"He! he! he!" replied the Devil faintly, drawing himself up with an air of hauteur.

"Why surely you are not serious," retorted De L'Omelette. "I have sinned—that's true—but, my
(25) good sir, consider!—you have no actual intention of putting such—such—barbarous threats into execution."

"No what?" said his Majesty—"come, sir, strip!"

"Strip, indeed! very pretty i' faith! no, sir, I shall
(30) not strip. Who are you, pray, that I, Duke De L'Omelette, Prince de Foie-Gras, just come of age, author of the 'Mazurkiad,' and member of the Academy, should divest myself at your bidding of the

*an ortolan is a small dove-like bird considered a supreme delicacy by nineteenth century gourmets. (story adapted from Edgar Allan Poe's "The Duc De L'Omelette")

sweetest pantaloons ever made by Bourdon, the
(35) daintiest dressing gown ever put together by
Rombert—take say nothing of undressing my hair—
not to mention the trouble I should have in drawing
off my gloves?"

"Who am I?—ah, true! I am Baal-Zebub, Prince of
(40) the Fly. I took thee, just now, from a rosewood coffin
inlaid with ivory. Thou wast curiously scented, and
labeled as per invoice. Belial sent thee—my Inspector
of Cemeteries. The pantaloons, which thou sayest
were made by Bourdon, are an excellent pair of linen
(45) drawers, and thy dressing gown is a shroud of no
scanty dimensions."

"Sir!" replied the Duke, "I am not to be insulted
with impunity!—Sir! you shall hear from me! In the
meantime au revoir!"—and the Duke was bowing
(50) himself out of the Satanic presence, when he was
interrupted and brought back by a gentleman in
waiting. Hereupon his Grace rubbed his eyes,
yawned, shrugged his shoulders, reflected. Having
become satisfied of his identity, he took a bird's-eye
(55) view of his whereabouts.

The apartment was superb. Even De L'Omelette
pronounced it "quite well done." It was not its length
nor its breadth—but its height—ah, that was appalling!—there was no ceiling—certainly none—but a
(60) dense whirling mass of fiery-colored clouds. His
Grace's brain reeled as he glanced upward. From
above, hung a chain of an unknown blood-red
metal—its upper end lost. From its nether extremity
swung a large cresset. The Duke knew it to be a ruby;
(65) but from it there poured a light so intense, so still, so
terrible. Persia never worshipped such, no great
Sultan ever dreamed of such when, drugged with
opium, he has tottered to a bed of poppies, his back to
the flowers, and his face to the God Apollo. The Duke
(70) muttered a slight oath, decidedly approbatory.

The corners of the room were rounded into niches,
and these were filled statues of gigantic proportions.
But the paintings! The paintings! O luxury! O love!—
who gazing on those forbidden beauties shall have
(75) eyes for others.

The Duke's heart is fainting within him. He is not,
however, as you suppose, dizzy with magnificence,
nor drunk with the ecstatic breath of the innumerable
censers. (It's true that he thinks of these things to no
(80) small degree—but!) The Duke De L'Omelette is
terror-stricken; for, through the lurid vista which a
single uncurtained window is affording, lo! gleams
the most ghastly of all fires!

The poor Duke! He could not help imagining that
(85) the glorious, the voluptuous, the never-dying melo-
dies which pervaded that hall, as they passed filtered

and transmuted through the alchemy of the enchanted window-panes, were the wailings and the howlings of the hopeless and the damned! And there, (90) too!—there!—upon the ottoman!—who could he be?—he, the Deity—who sat as if carved in marble, and who smiled, with his pale countenance, bitterly?

A Frenchman never faints outright. Besides, his Grace hated a scene—De L'Omelette is himself again. (95) Hadn't he read somewhere? wasn't it said "that the devil can't refuse a card game?"

But the chances—the chances! True—desperate; but scarcely more desperate than the Duke. Besides wasn't he the slyest player in the craftiest card-club in (100) Paris?—the legendary "21 club."

"Should I lose," said his Grace "I will lose twice— that is I shall be doubly damned—should I win, I return to my ortolan—let the cards be prepared."

His Grace was all care, all attention, his Majesty all (105) confidence. His Grace thought of the game. His majesty did not think; he shuffled. The Duke cut.

The cards are dealt. The trump is turned—it is—it is—the king! No—it was the queen. His Majesty cursed her masculine habiliments. De L'Omelette (110) placed his hand upon his heart.

They play. The Duke counts. The hand is out. His majesty counts heavily, smiles and is taking wine. The Duke palms a card.

"It's your deal," said his Majesty, cutting. His Grace (115) bowed, dealt, and arose from the table—turning the King.

His Majesty looked chagrined.

Had Alexander not been Alexander, he would have been Diogenes; and the Duke assured his antagonist (120) in taking his leave, "Were one not already the Duke De L'Omelette one could have no objection to being the Devil."

1. The primary purpose of the passage is to portray

   (A) the characteristics of an exaggerated type through the figure of L'Omelette.
   (B) a reassuringly humorous vision of hell through a narrative in which the Devil himself is bested.
   (C) the evil consequences of excessive pride.
   (D) the developing relationship between L'Omelette and the Devil.
   (E) the pivotal change that occurs in L'Omelette through his encounter with the Devil.

2. Which of the following best describes the Duke de L'Omelette?

   (A) He is a typical eighteenth century nobleman.
   (B) He is a caricature of a snob.
   (C) He is a man more wicked than the Devil.
   (D) He is a man with perfect aesthetic judgment.
   (E) He is a man transformed by his encounter with a power greater than his own.

3. In context, lines 29–38 serve to reinforce the reader's impression of the Duke's

   (A) quick temper.
   (B) exquisite taste.
   (C) sense of self-importance.
   (D) accomplishments and social position.
   (E) misunderstanding of his situation.

4. The author's portrayal of the Duke De L'Omelette is best described as:

   (A) A sympathetic portrait of a man with overly delicate sensibilities.
   (B) A comically ironic treatment of an effete snob.
   (C) A harshly condemnatory portrait of a bon vivant.
   (D) An admiring portrait of a great artist.
   (E) A farcical treatment of the very rich.

5. Which of the following descriptions is an example of the narrator's irony?

   (A) "Unable to restrain his feelings, his Grace swallows an olive." (line 9)
   (B) "I took thee, just now, from a rosewood coffin inlaid with ivory." (line 40)
   (C) "The Duke knew it to be a ruby; but from it there poured a light so intense, so still, so terrible." (line 64)
   (D) "And there, too!—there!—upon the ottoman!—who could he be?—he, the Deity—who sat as if carved in marble, and who smiled, with his pale countenance, bitterly?" (line 90)
   (E) "His Grace was all care, all attention, his Majesty all confidence." (line 104)

ANSWERING PROSE PASSAGE QUESTIONS ■ 45

6. Which of the following words is, in context, used in a sense most unlike its customary meaning?

   (A) sacrificed (line 6)
   (B) paroxysm (line 17)
   (C) trouble (line 37)
   (D) appalling (line 58)
   (E) approbatory (line 70)

7. Which of the following best explains the underlying meaning in the phrase "sacrificed his loyalty" within the context of the story?

   (A) The Duke has fallen into disfavor with the King by outbidding him.
   (B) The Duke has betrayed his country.
   (C) The Duke has allowed his desire for the ottoman to override his deference to the King.
   (D) The Duke recognizes no one as more powerful than himself.
   (E) The Duke values the ottoman more greatly than his prestige.

8. In which of the following lines is the narrator most clearly articulating the Duke's thoughts?

   (A) "Ignoble souls!"(line 2)
   (B) "It is superfluous to say more:—" (line 16)
   (C) "Having become satisfied of his identity, he took a bird's-eye view of his whereabouts." (line 53)
   (D) "But the chances—the chances! True—desperate" (line 97)
   (E) "They play." (line 111)

9. Which of the following lines implies a speaker other than the narrator?

   (A) "Who ever died of inept poetry?" (line 1)
   (B) "That night the Duke was to sup alone." (line 4)
   (C) "The apartment was superb." (line 56)
   (D) "His majesty did not think, he shuffled." (line 105)
   (E) "Had Alexander not been Alexander, he would have been Diogenes." (line 118)

10. Which of the following best describes the situation in lines 19–22 and the events that came immediately *before it*?

(A) The Duke has just noticed the Devil and laughs at him. The Devil returns the laugh, but quietly because he feels insulted.
(B) The Duke has just heard the Devil explain the tortures that lie in store for him. He believes the Devil is joking and laughs. The Devil mocks his laughter, implying that it is no joke.
(C) The Duke and the Devil have been talking, but the exact topic has been left purposefully vague.
(D) The Duke has just heard the Devil's plans for him and laughs defiantly at the Devil. The Devil puns on the Duke's use of the word "Ha!" by saying "He!" By doing so, the devil indicates "He," that is the Duke, will be punished for his sins.
(E) The Duke, believing he speaks with a lowly servant, laughs at the threats the Devil has made. The Devil plays along, laughing with the Duke in order to draw out the Duke's eventual humiliation.

11. The style of the passage overall is characterized by a combination of:

(A) light-hearted situations narrated with deep seriousness.
(B) humorous irony at the passage's outset and deadly seriousness at its conclusion.
(C) long, purely descriptive sentences offset by occasional interjections of subjective emotion.
(D) statements of seemingly objective neutrality that only partially conceal an underlying contempt.
(E) first person outbursts of effusive emotion in an otherwise third person narration.

12. The narrator's attitude toward the Duke can be best described as:

(A) complete objectivity.
(B) ambiguous pity.
(C) slight distaste.
(D) bemused confusion.
(E) satiric glee.

13. The passage contains:

    I. abrupt shifts in tense.
    II. an abrupt shift in place.
    III. abrupt shifts in emotional state.

    (A) I only
    (B) I and II only
    (C) I and III only
    (D) II and III only
    (E) I, II, and III

14. The phrase, "as if carved in marble" line 91 is an example of:

    (A) an apostrophe.
    (B) irony.
    (C) lyricism.
    (D) a metaphor.
    (E) a simile.

15. Grammatically, the phrase, "Were one not already the Duke De L'Omelette" line 121 establishes:

    (A) the simple past tense.
    (B) the past imperfect tense.
    (C) the present conditional tense.
    (D) the subjunctive mood.
    (E) the simple present tense.

ABOUT POE'S "THE DUC DE L'OMELETTE"

This passage was adapted from a short story called "The Duc de L'Omelette." You'll sometimes see adapted passages on the AP English Test. All it means is the passage was edited to make it appropriate for all high school students, and to meet the test's length requirements. The actual Poe story uses a great deal of French, but keeping the French parts would give students who had studied French an unfair advantage.

The passage uses the kind of language and stylistic devices you'll see on prose passages on the AP English Literature Test, but all the same it is a difficult one; they aren't all this weird. If it seemed long, don't panic—it is about one-third longer than the usual AP passage. (We wanted to use a long passage in this example to give you plenty to work with and to provide abundant fodder for our sample questions. Keep in mind that with a total of 50 to 55 questions, some passages on the test will have fewer than 15 questions.) If you see a passage of this length on the test, there will then be a shorter passage to compensate.

ANSWERS AND EXPLANATIONS TO THE QUESTIONS

Below, we give detailed explanations to the 15 questions that followed the passage. Fifteen is the number of questions you should expect to see on a passage of this length. The passages and questions on our diagnostic test are designed to imitate a real AP test. Here, we've chosen the questions with an eye toward teaching you our techniques, but even so, the mix of the types of questions is fairly representative of the questions you'll see on a passage. These questions should give you a very good idea of what the questions following an AP passage will be like.

We've broken the questions down into small groups in order to illustrate specific types of questions you're likely to see. Earlier we used the categories of general, detail, and fact. Now we'll break the questions down according to the subject matter. We don't want you to memorize the names of these types or spend a lot of time practicing identifying these types. There are no points for doing that. If you do remember them, great, but all we want is for you to become familiar with the most common types of questions on the test and to see how the same techniques, applied in slightly different ways, work on question after question.

GENERAL QUESTIONS

The first question is a general question. As you no doubt remember from chapter 4, general questions ask about the whole passage, not some detail of the passage.

The question sets will often (but not always) start out with general questions. We've placed the questions on this passage in the order that lets us best explain them to you. Remember that when you actually take the test, you want to do the questions in the order given (if you felt comfortable with your comprehension of the passage). If you felt pretty lost, then you should put any general questions off for last, in the hope that working with the specific questions will give you more confidence about your comprehension of the passage and its main idea.

PRIMARY PURPOSE

The classic general question is the primary purpose question:

1. The primary purpose of the passage is to portray:

    (A) the characteristics of an exaggerated type through the figure of L'Omelette.
    (B) a reassuringly humorous vision of hell through a narrative in which the Devil himself is bested.
    (C) the evil consequences of excessive pride.
    (D) the developing relationship between L'Omelette and the Devil.
    (E) the pivotal change that occurs in L'Omelette through his encounter with the Devil.

HERE'S HOW TO CRACK IT

Understand the question by understanding the answer choices. What does "primary purpose" mean?

When you see primary purpose, it means you must look for an answer that covers the broad outline of the story. This advice goes for all general questions; it is what makes them general. On every general question you are looking for a choice that accurately describes some facet of the entire passage.

Now use the answer choices themselves to focus on exactly what primary purpose the test writers are looking for.

The question itself indicates that the primary purpose of the passage is to portray something. What is it portraying? Use POE. (After all, the passage was written by Edgar Allan **P**rocess **o**f **E**limination.)

Take choice (A). Does the whole passage deal with an exaggerated type? Well, The Duke is an exaggeration of something: this is a guy who takes time to approve of the decor in hell. (A) seems to be a reasonable summation of the whole passage. Leave it. Now take each of the remaining choices in turn.

Now to choice (B). The whole passage is not all about a "reassuringly humorous vision of hell." Each paragraph does not point out how harmless hell is. The humorous part is the Duke's taking it all more or less in stride. Eliminate (B).

Answer choice (C) talks about "the evil consequences of excessive pride." The whole passage is all about the Duke's excessive pride, but what are the consequences? There are none. The end of the story finds the Duke returning to his ill-prepared ortolan, which is right where he started, so you have to wonder if it's going to kill him all over again. Remember, half bad equals all bad. Eliminate (C).

And while you're at it, eliminate (D), unless you think that the whole passage is about the relationship between L'Omelette and the Devil. It isn't. The Devil doesn't have much personality in the story at all. He serves as a foil for the Duke, little else.

Eliminate (E) because the Duke doesn't change at all. When the point of a passage is to show a dramatic change, you'll know it. The whole passage will build to that change.

You're left with (A). The correct answer.

What phrase have we kept repeating? "The whole passage." General questions call for you to consider the whole passage, not one small piece of it.

Another thing we did was focus on key phrases in the answer choices. "What consequences?" we asked when we looked at choice (C). We didn't get taken in by the phrase "excessive pride." Learning how to focus on an answer choice is a skill that comes with practice. As you follow our explanations, your skill will improve. In fact, after that discussion, the next question should be a breeze.

OVERALL CHARACTER

AP passages tend to be focused on one thing. Here the focus is on the Duke. A passage might focus on the description of an event, or a place, but the most common focus is on a character.

2. Which of the following best describes the Duke de L'Omelette?

    (A) He is a typical eighteenth-century nobleman.
    (B) He is a caricature of a snob.
    (C) He is a man more wicked than the Devil.
    (D) He is a man with perfect aesthetic judgment.
    (E) He is a man transformed by his encounter with a power greater than his own.

HERE'S HOW TO CRACK IT

The correct answer is (B), and finding it probably didn't cause you much trouble. About the only problem might have been the term *caricature*, which means "exaggerated portrait." It is a term you should know (it's in our glossary). Do you notice any similarities between the correct answer to question 1 and the correct answer here? You should. One speaks of an exaggerated portrayal of a type, and one speaks of a caricature of a snob. These are almost the same answer. The only difference is that the second question spells out what "type" is being caricatured: the snob. This is an example of Consistency of Answers. Both answers are consistent with the main idea, and naturally when answers are consistent with the main idea, they are consistent with each other. In this case the answers are extremely similar. When in doubt, make your answers agree with each other. If you thought the Duke was an exaggerated portrayal in question 1, why would he suddenly become a "typical eighteenth-century nobleman" in question 2? That would be inconsistent, so eliminate choice (A). The Duke is either exaggerated or he's typical, but he can't be both. Choice (C) is for students who read into things too much. The Duke wins the card game at the end. Does that mean he's more wicked than the Devil? No. Choice (D) is too strong. "Perfect?" De L'Omelette thinks his tastes are perfect, but does the story suggest that his tastes are perfect? No, only that they are extremely, almost comically, particular. Choice (E) isn't supported by the passage. You'd think the Duke would be transformed by his encounter with the Devil, but he isn't. At the end of the story you should have gotten the feeling that De L'Omelette is going to go right back to his old ways.

Consistency of Answers doesn't just apply to general questions. It is just as helpful with detail questions.

DETAIL QUESTIONS

Detail questions (a.k.a. specific questions) make up the majority of questions on the multiple-choice section of the test. These are questions (or answer choices) that direct you to a specific place in the passage and ask about your comprehension of the details.

1. LINE-REFERENCE QUESTIONS

Most of the time (but not always), the detail questions give you a line number or a range of lines with which to work. We call these questions line-reference questions. (Pretty creative, huh?) For line-reference questions there are just two things you need to keep in mind:

- Go back to the passage and reread the lines in question. Also, read at least one full sentence before the line reference and one full sentence after the line reference.

- Keep the main idea in mind, and use Consistency of Answers whenever possible.

TRY THIS ONE

3. In context, lines 29–38 serve to reinforce the reader's impression of the Duke's

   (A) quick temper.
   (B) exquisite taste.
   (C) sense of self-importance.
   (D) accomplishments and social position.
   (E) misunderstanding of his situation.

HERE'S HOW TO CRACK IT

This question calls for you to go back and read a fairly large range of lines—a whole paragraph. Go back and read it. Because the several lines referred to in this question make up a more or less self-contained paragraph, reading a full sentence **before** and **after** the reference doesn't make a big difference in getting the question right, but it doesn't hurt, either, and takes just an extra two or three seconds. Make it a habit to read a little above and below the lines referred to; it'll be worth a couple of points in the long run.

Essentially, the lines in question discuss the Duke's outrage at the Devil's command to disrobe.

If you misunderstand the question, you have a good chance of getting the answer wrong. The passage shows aspects of all the answer choices. The Duke does (A)—show a quick temper, does (B)—mention his tastes (by the way, the Duke's tastes are not so much exquisite as they are ostentatious), does (D)—mention his accomplishments and does (E)—misunderstand his situation. But the correct answer is (C).

Everything seems right, so what gives? The solution lies in understanding the question and how the question relates to the main idea. The question asks: What does the passage serve to reinforce? Nearly everything in this very compact story serves to reinforce the central impression of the story—the Duke's outrageous sense of self-importance. He isn't merely a snob; he's completely besotted with his own fabulous self. The Duke thinks he's the apex of human intellectual and social development. In fact, choices (A), (B), (D), and (E) are all facets of the Duke's vanity. His anger is angered vanity. His tastes are flawless; they must be, thinks the Duke, because they're his. When the Duke mentions his work, the "Mazurkiad", you can almost see him puff up with the greatness of it all. Even his misunderstanding is an aspect of his vanity. The Duke doesn't quite comprehend his surroundings because he can't imagine being in a position to take orders from anyone. All these things revolve like planets around the Duke's sense that he's the center of the universe.

If you had a solid grasp on the central theme of the story, the Duke's self-love, you might have found this question easy. Choices (A), (B), (D), and (E) are details. (C) is the main thing. If you had trouble, all you had to do to get this question correct was muse, "Hmm, they all look possible, but which one is most consistent with the main idea?" Well, a snob thinks he's better than everyone; he thinks he's very important. Choice (C), sense of self-importance, is most in agreement with that.

Question 3 is an example of using the technique we call Consistency of Answers. Here's another:

4. The author's portrayal of the Duke De L'Omelette is best described as:

    (A) A sympathetic portrait of a man with overly delicate sensibilities.
    (B) A comically ironic treatment of an effete snob.
    (C) A harshly condemnatory portrait of a bon vivant.
    (D) An admiring portrait of a great artist.
    (E) A farcical treatment of the very rich.

HERE'S HOW TO CRACK IT

This is the question we used in our discussion of POE back in chapter 2, so you should remember the correct answer, (B). Of course, it probably seems a lot easier after having gone through the explanations to the previous questions. Doesn't this question look similar? It is. Back when we discussed POE we were able to eliminate down to (A) and (B), and then we weaseled our way down to (B). But here's a pop quiz: what technique tells you the answer must be (B)?

If you said Consistency of Answers, you're right.

Now, we aren't saying every single question uses Consistency of Answers. It should be one of the first things you think about when you approach a question, but there are definitely questions that focus on a detail in such a way that Consistency of Answers doesn't come into play. Here's an example:

5. Which of the following descriptions is an example of the narrator's irony?

    (A) "Unable to restrain his feelings, his Grace swallows an olive." (line 9)
    (B) "I took thee, just now, from a rosewood coffin inlaid with ivory." (line 40)
    (C) "The Duke knew it to be a ruby; but from it there poured a light so intense, so still, so terrible." (line 64)
    (D) "And there, too!—there!—upon the ottoman!—who could he be?—he, the Deity—who sat as if carved in marble, and who smiled, with his pale countenance, bitterly?" (line 90)
    (E) "His Grace was all care, all attention, his Majesty all confidence." (line 104)

HERE'S HOW TO CRACK IT
Notice that in this question the line references come in the answer choices. That's not uncommon. Properly speaking, this isn't a specific question or a general question or a literary-term question. The answer choices send you back to the passage to find a specific example of something that occurs throughout the whole passage: irony, which is a literary term. So this question's a mutt. But, you don't get points for putting questions in categories anyway; the important thing is to get the question right, efficiently.

The way to get this question right is to know what irony is. You can count on only a very few specific things showing up on the AP test. One of them is irony. Learn to recognize its many forms. We discuss irony in our glossary of literary terms for the AP English Literature and Composition Test. (Yep, we're going to say that every time we mention irony.)

The correct answer is (A). You should have noticed the entire tone of the piece is somewhat ironic. Most of the passage is written with a deliberate undercurrent of meaning that changes the effect of the literal meaning of the lines. This, above all, is the hallmark of irony; there's more than meets the eye. But let's get back to choice (A). Why is it ironic? Let's take the statement "Unable to restrain his feelings, his grace swallowed an olive." At face value: the Duke's feelings became so strong he had to swallow an olive. Now, in no way can swallowing an olive be the outcome of unrestrained feelings unless one has pretty unusual feelings, which is precisely the point. The Duke's anticipation of dinner having reached a fevered pitch, he buries his face in a pillow. The clock bangs out the long-awaited hour and unable to restrain himself, the Duke swallows an olive. One thing this shows is how fanatically seriously the Duke takes his meals. At the same time, the juxtaposition (to *juxtapose* means to place things side by side) of the Duke's unrestrained feelings and his act of swallowing an olive show something else: the Duke's biggest feelings are actually puny; the Duke's crescendo of passion is capped by swallowing an olive. That's the ironic part. The author in effect says, "In the Duke's opinion this is something big, but we can all see that it's rather small." When the literal meaning of a word or phrase implies its opposite, you're dealing with irony.

Hey, didn't we say that the whole piece was ironic? If that's true, what makes the other choices wrong? Well, okay, the whole piece *is* ironic. In effect, the passage tells us that the Duke thinks he's absolutely first-rate, but we can see that he's really quite laughable. However, for this question you must consider the answer choices in isolation. None of them, by themselves, carry that double meaning which is so crucial to irony. (B) is a description of a coffin. (C) describes the ruby that illuminates the Devil's chamber in Hell. (D) describes the moment the Duke realizes, at last, that the creature he's dealing with is truly the Devil himself. (E) simply describes the Duke's and the Devil's attitude as they begin the card game.

Okay, enough about irony. Here's the next question:

2. **SINGLE PHRASE OR WORD QUESTIONS**
AP questions will often ask you to look at a single word or phrase:

> 6. Which of the following words is, in context, used in a sense most unlike it's customary meaning?
>
>   (A) sacrificed (line 6)
>   (B) paroxysm (line 17)
>   (C) trouble (line 37)
>   (D) appalling (line 58)
>   (E) approbatory (line 70)

HERE'S HOW TO CRACK IT

Yes, on the AP English Literature and Composition Test a strong vocabulary helps a lot (by "helps a lot," we mean "provides copious facilitation"). If you didn't know the meaning of (B), (D), or (E) you'd have to guess. (And after you eliminated (A) and (C)—neither word is used in an unusual way—you would guess.) A *paroxysm* is a convulsion. *Appalling* means shockingly bad. *Approbatory* means expressing approval; it is the opposite of derogatory.

Now, looking at (B), (D), and (E), which one seems out of place? You should see that there's nothing wrong with (B). The Duke died in a convulsion of disgust—that makes sense. But what about (D) and (E)? Both occur in the same paragraph, and are used in sentences that describe the Duke's reaction to the Devil's chamber, yet one means shockingly bad and the other means he swore an oath expressing approval. Which is it? Does he approve, or does he think the chamber's ceiling is shockingly bad? If you read a full sentence before the citation you'd find that prior to "appalling!" the Duke had pronounced the chamber "quite well done." In fact, the Duke thinks the apartment is "superb." From this you should infer that *appalling* is used outside of its conventional meaning. By *appalling* the Duke means just the opposite. The height of the ceiling is both shocking and excessive. He might have said, "*gnarly!*" or "*wicked!*" but he wouldn't be the Duke then, would he? (And yeah, we know our slang's stale.) The correct answer is (D).

Questions 4 and 5 are two questions in a row that don't use Consistency of Answers. The streak's over. Here's a question that asks about a single phrase, but even so you can use Consistency of Answers to assist your POE.

7. Which of the following best explains the underlying meaning in the phrase "sacrificed his loyalty" within the context of the story?

   (A) The Duke has fallen into disfavor with the King by outbidding him.
   (B) The Duke has betrayed his country.
   (C) The Duke has allowed his desire for the ottoman to override his deference to the King.
   (D) The Duke recognizes no one as more powerful than himself.
   (E) The Duke values the ottoman more greatly than his prestige.

HERE'S HOW TO CRACK IT

When approaching this question, you should first go back and read around the citation. Because the citation is a fragment of sentence, you should read at least a full sentence before and after the reference. (If you want to read more, by all means, do. The full sentence before and after is just a guideline. If it takes you a little more reading to get your bearings in the passage, that's fine.)

Now, use POE to get rid of what is obviously wrong. If you stay focused with what the phrase in question means it shouldn't be too hard to eliminate a few answers. Does "sacrificed his loyalty" mean the Duke has betrayed his country? That should sound a little too intense: we're talking about buying a couch here (an ottoman is a kind of couch). Eliminate choice (B). Does the Duke recognize no one as more powerful than himself? That may or may not be true, but how could you get that meaning from "sacrificed his loyalty?" Of course, if you try really hard you can talk yourself into anything. Don't talk yourself into answers. This is process of elimination. Eliminate (D).

Can you eliminate four answers? The best way is to ask yourself which answer choice is most in keeping with the Duke's character. Do you think the Duke cares about his prestige more than his couch? Of course he does. He would never sacrifice his prestige. L'Omelette thinks of appearances above all else. Eliminate choice (E). What about (A)? It is certainly reasonable that the Duke fell into disfavor with the King for outbidding him. But is this what "sacrificed his loyalty" means? No. And if you have any doubts, ask yourself what that interpretation has to do with the rest of the passage. Is the rest of the passage about the Duke's loss of favor with the King? No. That leaves (C), the correct answer. It is perfectly in keeping with the other answers and the rest of the passage: The Duke shows little deference to the Devil; why would he defer to the King?

The next two questions ask for your comprehension of a detail, but the questions center less around the meaning of the words than about what they indicate about the narrator.

3. **QUESTION-COMPREHENSION QUESTIONS**

Some questions are straightforward, some are vague, and a few are downright tricky. You need to pay close attention to the wording of questions, and when you see an unusual phrase, it's a good idea to ask yourself why the phrase is worded that way. On many questions, just understanding what the question is asking is half the battle.

8. In which of the following lines is the narrator most clearly articulating the Duke's thoughts?

   (A) "Ignoble souls!" (line 2)
   (B) "It is superfluous to say more:—" (line 16)
   (C) "Having become satisfied of his identity, he took a bird's-eye view of his whereabouts." (line 53)
   (D) "But the chances—the chances! True—desperate." (line 97)
   (E) "They play." (line 111)

HERE'S HOW TO CRACK IT

This question has little to do with the main idea. Your first task is to understand the question. What is meant by "articulating the Duke's thoughts?" Well, try to put it in your own words. The question could be rewritten as: "When is the narrator speaking for the Duke?" There's nothing wrong with putting a question in your own words so as to understand it better. In fact it's a good idea, as long as you're careful and don't just drop off the parts of a question that confuse you. Reading the questions accurately is just as important as reading the passages. The passage isn't worth any points; the questions are.

Use POE. Eliminate what you can right away. When is the narrator clearly speaking as himself? Choices (B), (C), and (E) all seem like examples of straightforward narration, so eliminate them. That leaves just (A) and (D). In choice (A), the narrator responds to a question. He exclaims in a very Duke-like way, but the Duke hasn't even been introduced yet. How could the reader know it was the Duke speaking? The reader couldn't. All that's left is (D), the correct answer. In (D), the narrator steps into the Duke's mind for a moment to record his thoughts, and then just as quickly steps out with the words, "but no more desperate than the Duke."

Question 9 picks up where question 8 left off; it is a similar, but more difficult variation on the same theme:

> 9. Which of the following lines implies a speaker other than the narrator?
>
>   (A) "Who ever died of inept poetry?" (line 1)
>   (B) "That night the Duke was to sup alone." (line 4)
>   (C) "The apartment was superb." (line 56)
>   (D) "His majesty did not think, he shuffled." (line 105)
>   (E) "Had Alexander not been Alexander, he would have been Diogenes." (line 118)

HERE'S HOW TO CRACK IT

Read questions carefully. The difference between question 8 and question 9 is that question 8 asks which answer choice shows the Duke's speech (or thoughts) whereas question 9 wants to know which *implies* a speaker other than the narrator. Question 9 is tougher. If your approach to question 9 got stuck somewhere back on question 8 and you were still looking for the narrator to speak the Duke's thoughts (or perhaps the Devil's), you might have easily gotten this question wrong.

As always, use POE. Clearly, choices (B), (C), (D), and (E) are spoken by the narrator. What about (A)? Well, (A) is spoken by the narrator as well, but it *implies* another speaker, someone who asks the question, "Who ever died of poor poetry?" The narrator, speaking as himself, responds to that question: "Ignoble souls!" If the structure of this interchange wasn't clear to you, here's an explanation: "Who ever died of poor poetry?" is a rhetorical question (a question to which the answer is obvious—of course, most people would say, no one has ever been killed by a bad poem). That's where the narrator jumps in and says, "Oh ho, you think the answer to that question is so very obvious but that's because your souls have no finer qualities; it may seem unbelievable to you but some very delicate spirits have died of immaterial things like bad poetry. De L'Omelette for example, died of a badly prepared meal." All that (and a little more) is contained in the first paragraph of the passage. This paragraph is a good example of how gifted writers make every word count.

Ready for one more detail question? It's a good example of how weird things can get on the AP test. It's asks about the meaning of a piece of the passage that isn't there.

WEIRDNESS

10. Which of the following best describes the situation in lines 19–22 and the events that came immediately *before* it?

    (A) The Duke has just noticed the Devil and laughs at him. The Devil returns the laugh, but quietly because he feels insulted.
    (B) The Duke has just before heard the Devil explain the tortures that lie in store for him. He believes the Devil is joking and laughs. The Devil mocks his laughter, implying that it is no joke.
    (C) The Duke and the Devil have been talking, but the exact topic has been left purposefully vague.
    (D) The Duke has just heard the Devil's plans for him and laughs defiantly at the Devil. The Devil puns on the Duke's use of the word "Ha!" by saying "He!" By doing so, the devil indicates "He," that is the Duke, will be punished for his sins.
    (E) The Duke, believing he speaks with a lowly servant, laughs at the threats the Devil has made. The Devil laughs in order to play along with the Duke and draw out the Duke's eventual humiliation.

HERE'S HOW TO CRACK IT

Expect the unexpected at least once or twice on the test. Question 10 is not an easy question. Use POE. Remember to read at least one sentence before and one sentence after the citation. **The key to this question is making sense of the line immediately following the line reference:** "'Why surely you're not serious,' retorted De L'Omelette." Which interpretations make that line a non sequitur? (A non sequitur is a statement which doesn't follow from what came before. For example, Q: What time is it? A: Yes.) You see, somehow, the Duke understands that the Devil is serious. It's just that he still can't believe it. That's why he asks this question. If the Devil were merely acting offended (or making some bizarre pun using the word *he*) then the Duke would have no reason to respond as he does. If you apply this thought, you'll see that you can eliminate (A), (C), (D), and (E). And that leaves (B), the correct answer. The Devil's mocking laughter lets the Duke know that yes, the Devil is serious. Notice that this answer is the simplest explanation.

Staying simple doesn't just apply to poetry. Many students get into trouble when reading the answer choices. They think about the wrong answers so much they get led into outer space. This comes from looking at every answer choice as though it could be correct. Four out of the five answer choices are wrong. At least one answer choice is usually wildly wrong. If something looks nuts, don't spend five minutes trying to figure it out. If it looks nuts, it is.

4. **STYLE, STRUCTURE, AND TONE QUESTIONS**

Style, structure, and tone questions are related.

Style questions will test your understanding of the kinds of sentences that the passage contains. Are they simple or complex? Do they contain modifying clauses? Do the sentences interpret or do they describe? Are they loose or periodic (see the glossary)?

Structure questions ask about how the passage is put together. Does it begin with a general statement and then support that statement with examples? Does it describe an isolated incident and make a generalization from it? Does it begin humorously but end seriously? Is there a sudden shift in emphasis in the middle?

Tone questions ask for your understanding of the underlying emotion of the passage, about how the passage *feels*. Is the author angry? Does she care passionately about what she says, or does she seem to describe the scene as a camera would record it, without judgment? By far the most critical aspect of tone is the choice of words the author uses, and what the author says, but unless you are sensitive to structure and style you can easily get the tone wrong. The tone is in part produced by structure and style.

Here's a question which relies on your understanding of all three elements:

> 11. The style of the passage overall is characterized by a combination of:
>
>   (A) light-hearted situations narrated with deep seriousness.
>   (B) humorous irony at the passage's outset and deadly seriousness at its conclusion.
>   (C) long, purely descriptive sentences offset by occasional interjections of subjective emotion.
>   (D) statements of seemingly objective neutrality that only partially conceal an underlying contempt.
>   (E) first person outbursts of effusive emotion in an otherwise third person narration.

HERE'S HOW TO CRACK IT

Again, from the question alone you can't know exactly what the question asks. That's fine. Look over the answer choices. You can see that they refer to the tone, style, and structure of the passage. ETS likes to throw these mixtures at you. The way to work on this kind of question is to break the answer choices into bit-size parts, then check the passage to see if you can find an example of that part. For example, are there light-hearted situations (A)? Well, going to hell isn't exactly light-hearted. (So the choice is already wrong, but let's keep going.) Are the situations narrated with deep seriousness? No, not exactly. Narrated with a straight face perhaps, but not deeply serious. The idea is to break the choices into pieces you can use. **Remember, half bad equals all bad**.

The correct answer is (E). As always, use POE and look at the whole passage. Make your initial eliminations. Choice (A) is wrong because the situations are not so much light-hearted as absurd, and the narrator is not deeply serious, but nearly as bizarre and out of control as the Duke. Choice (B) isn't worth a second look unless you really think cheating the Devil at cards is deadly serious. Choice (D) should be unappealing as well. What "contempt"? What "objective neutrality"? Eliminate it.

This leaves (E) and (C). Take each answer choice and go back to the passage. Do you see any "long, purely descriptive sentences?" Not really; almost every sentence is loaded with one of the Duke's preposterous emotions. Almost everything comes to us through a filter of the Duke's impressions, especially in the longer sentences. It isn't accurate to call the subjective (first person element) "occasional." That is enough to eliminate (C), leaving you with just one remaining choice, (E). For safety's sake you should now examine it. "Outbursts of effusive emotion?" Well, there are all those exclamation points all over the place. As a matter of fact, half the time the author seems to be shouting. The story is told in the third person, yet much of the time the Duke's persona, his voice, or the attitude behind his voice seems to be speaking. (E) is correct.

If any of the terms we've used in this explanation—*first person*, *third person*, *subjectivity*,—gave you trouble, you should refer to their definitions in the glossary of literary terms on page 195.

Attitude questions are just like tone questions; they ask about the underlying emotional content of the passage:

> 12. The narrator's attitude toward the Duke can be best described as:
>
>   (A) complete objectivity.
>   (B) ambiguous pity.
>   (C) slight distaste.
>   (D) bemused confusion.
>   (E) satiric glee.

HERE'S HOW TO CRACK IT

The correct answer is (E). POE, as usual, helps a great deal. On tone questions ETS often has a couple of answers that you can dismiss without a second glance. There's no way you could call the passage an example of (A), complete objectivity; it's much too weird. Doesn't the whole passage feel high-strung, as though old Edgar A. Poe had a few too many cups of coffee on top of what ever else he was drinking that day? That feeling never goes with objectivity. Choice (B), pity, is just off the wall. Choice (C) might have been appealing because it didn't sound too extreme. In general, mild is better than extreme on tone questions, but unfortunately, "slight distaste" is wrong; there's no evidence that the narrator feels a slight distaste for the Duke. Remember, you wanted to pick what the *narrator* feels. You might have felt slight distaste, but the question didn't ask how you felt. Speaking of how you felt, Choice (D) is a type of answer ETS has been known to use occasionally. Students, especially when they're struggling, are drawn to answers that suggest their own mental state. It's amazing, but students really do pick words like *confused*, *depressed*, *anxious*, and *fearful* on tests when it doesn't make sense to. The answer feels right, not because it's correct but because it's how the student feels taking a test. There's no evidence in the story that the narrator is confused or doesn't understand the Duke; in fact, he seems to understand the Duke a little too perfectly.

This brings up (E), the correct answer. "Glee" may seem a bit strong, but it fits. The narrator tells the story with energy, enthusiasm, and a completely unabashed use of exclamation points—that's a tip-off right there. Good writers, and you'll see nothing but very good writers on the AP test, don't overuse exclamation points. (The great Irish novelist James Joyce called them, derisively, "shriek marks.") Poe doesn't overuse them here, but it could easily seem like it. Poe uses exclamation points because, if for the Duke a badly prepared bird is upsetting enough to kill him, the Duke's life must be filled with exclamation points. This is one of the elements (and there are many) which make the passage satiric. *Satire* is an important concept for the AP test. When a passage pokes fun at an exaggeratedly foolish type (in this case, the type of arrogant man who considers himself supreme in all things), you can be sure it's satire (yes, we do cover the concept in the glossary). The gleefulness stems from the evident enjoyment Poe takes in describing the Duke's peculiar foolishness. Of course Poe has the Duke win in the end, which makes sense because Poe himself had a lot of the Duke in him.

5. I, II, III QUESTIONS

Question 13 tests whether you've noticed certain structural and stylistic devices in the passage. The question uses a form you're sure to see on the test; it's one of ETS's favorites.

> 13. The passage contains:
>
>   I. abrupt shifts in tense.
>   II. an abrupt shift in place.
>   III. abrupt shifts in emotional state.
>
>   (A) I only
>   (B) I and II only
>   (C) I and III only
>   (D) II and III only
>   (E) I, II, and III

HERE'S HOW TO CRACK IT

If you've taken an ETS test before, you've seen I, II, III questions. Most students see them and groan. Somehow they look like more work. It's as if three questions are worth one measly point. The truth is you should think of them as questions with just three answer choices. Take each point one at a time, and look to the passage to see if what you want is there. If you know where to look, this question is a snap.

Let's start with point II. (Why point II? It's the easiest of the three to see, and why not? You don't have to examine the I, II, III points in order.) When the Duke dies "in a paroxysm of disgust" (line 17) there is an abrupt change of place—to hell. So eliminate any answer that doesn't contain II—choices (A) and (C).

Now to point I. Did you also notice that there is an abrupt change of tense at that same line about "a paroxysm of disgust"? The change from the Duke's bedroom to hell is so striking that many students overlook the fact that the tense of the story changes. The second paragraph is in the present tense. It changes when the narrator says, "it *is* superfluous to say more—the Duke expir*ed* in a paroxysm of disgust." That's the simple past and the simple present in one sentence; your English teacher would hang you for it! (And the tense changes back to the present for one paragraph at the end when L'Omelette and the Devil play cards. It's easy to overlook.) Okay, so that means you can eliminate anything that doesn't contain item I—choice (D). You're already down to just two answer choices—(B) and (E).

All that's left is item III. Abrupt shifts in emotional state. You probably knew they happened. It felt like they happened, but where exactly? Was it really abrupt? Hey, don't over-think and worry yourself to death. There are abrupt shifts in emotional state. In the middle of the story the Duke goes from admiring the Devil's decor to being stricken with terror when he realizes that he is in fact dealing with Satan, to getting control of himself again and challenging the Devil to cards, all in the space of about 20 lines. That qualifies as abrupt. Points, I, II, and III, are all examples contained in the passage, so they must be in the answer choice. The correct answer is (E).

6. LITERARY TERM QUESTIONS

> 14. The phrase, "as if carved in marble" (line 91) is an example of:
>
>   (A) an apostrophe.
>   (B) irony.
>   (C) lyricism.
>   (D) a metaphor.
>   (E) a simile.

HERE'S HOW TO CRACK IT

This is an absolutely straightforward literary terms question. You are sure to see a few questions like it on the test you take. Of course you should use POE, but the best solution for literary term questions is to know the terms. That's why we've included our glossary of terms (plug). Second, as we mentioned earlier, there are just a few things you can be sure will make an appearance somewhere on the test. Among those things are the terms *simile* and *metaphor*. We define both in our glossary.

The correct answer here is (E). The phrase is a simile. A comparison that uses *like* or *as* is a simile. Even if these terms don't show up on your test as the right answers to a question (and chances are that's exactly how they will show up), at the very least they'll show up as answers you'll be able to eliminate. If you aren't aware that the phrase in question is a simile, eliminate what you can and take your best guess. Believe it or not, all the terms in the question are defined in our glossary.

Okay, one more question.

7. GRAMMAR QUESTIONS

15. Grammatically, the phrase, "Were one not already the Duke De L'Omelette" (line 121) establishes:

    (A) the simple past tense.
    (B) the past imperfect tense.
    (C) the present conditional tense.
    (D) the subjunctive mood.
    (E) the simple present tense.

The correct answer is (D). When a sentence begins with *were*, it's subjunctive, count on it. What's a *mood*? Well, to those who make it their business to know (language scholars, mostly), *mood* is a term that refers to what a verb form indicates besides time. In the sentence *Go away! go* isn't just in the present tense. It expresses command. Thus it is in the imperative mood. In *Jack laughs*, *laughs* indicates a state of being. It is in the indicative mood. Indicative, imperative, and subjunctive are the principle moods of English. The use of the subjunctive and its forms have faded from our language, which is why starting a sentence with the word *were* might sound a little strange. It is grammatically correct English, however.

Unless you intend to teach Latin, or go to graduate school in linguistics, mood isn't a term you'll need to know precisely: for your purposes on the test, and probably for the rest of your life, you can think of a mood as not exactly a verb tense, but close.

There will be a few grammar questions on the AP test you take. Use POE and take your best shot. In general, studying specific points in English grammar for the sake of a few points on the multiple-choice section is not worth the time. Studying grammar for other reasons is by no means a waste of time. A working command of English grammar is essential for effective writing. We'll have more to say about grammar in the next chapter, when we deal with a sample poetry passage and questions.

If you're rusty on your grammatical terms, chapter 11 contains definitions with examples of the basic terms you need to know, such as *direct object*, *indirect object*, *phrase*, and *clause*.

A FEW LAST WORDS (ALMOST)

If you worked through the passage as we instructed, you just learned a great deal about how to take the multiple-choice questions on the AP English Literature and Composition Test. It probably took close to five times longer here than working on a real passage would, but that's to be expected—you're learning. This does bring up an important point though: time. We've taken you through the passage and familiarized you with some typical questions so that when you're on your own you can work efficiently and accurately, answering all the questions in about 15 minutes.

But what if it doesn't work that way? Let's say you had reasoned that this passage was the hardest on the test and decided to do it last. By the time you got to it, you had only seven minutes left. Seven minutes to do that passage! You would use up most of that time just reading it. Should you give up?—No! This is where all the study you've put into the questions can really pay off. Check out the Art of the Seven-Minute Passage. Enjoy!

THE ART OF THE SEVEN-MINUTE PASSAGE

When you hit the last passage on the test, *check your time*. If you have seven minutes or fewer left, you have to change your strategy. You don't have enough time to do the passage the normal way. It's time for emergency measures. What is the worst thing to do in an emergency? Panic. Don't. You'll want to, but don't. The best defense against panic is preparation. Know exactly what you're going to do. Here it is:

- Don't read the passage. Not even a little. Just *don't* do it.
- Go straight to the questions.
- Answer the questions in the following order:
    1. **Answer any literary term or grammar questions.** You barely need the passage at all for these questions. If you know the point at issue you'll just snap up a point. Otherwise apply as much POE as you can and guess.
    2. **Go to any question that asks for the meaning of a single word or phrase.** These questions always include a line reference. Go to the passage and read a sentence before and after the reference. Answer the question.
    3. **Go to any other question that gives you a line reference in the question.** (Not line-reference answer choices, but questions.) Read the reference and answer the question.
    4. **Go to any question on tone or attitude.** By this time, you've read quite a bit of the passage just by answering questions. You've read enough to be able to make a good guess about where the author's coming from.
    5. **Go to any questions that have line references in the answer choices.** Answer them all.
    6. **Do whatever is left over**—character questions, primary purpose questions, weird questions, etc. If you need to, read some of the passage to get them. Go ahead and read. Keep working until the proctor tells you to put down your pencil.
    7. **Put down your pencil.** Take a deep breath. You did great.

That's the Art of the Seven-Minute Passage. It works in six, five, four, three, two, or one minute too; with less time, you don't get as far down the list, that's all.

WHAT IF I HAVE SEVEN-MINUTES AND THREE SECONDS LEFT?

Seven minutes or less is a good rough guideline for when to use the Don't Read the Passage technique. **Your pace on multiple-choice passages should be about 15 minutes a passage.** If you have an awkward amount of time left for the last passage—that is, somewhere between seven and fifteen minutes—you'll have to decide which approach to use. You have two choices. The first is to just read and work faster, to step on the gas big time. The other choice is to go straight to the questions, that is, to use the Art of the Seven-Minute Passage technique. If you're in that rough area between seven and fifteen minutes, it's your call. Seven minutes and three seconds (or 30 seconds etc.), go straight to the questions. With ten minutes left you should probably try to read the passage fast but then do the questions in the seven minute order. At, say, 14 minutes, you should just work normally, but keep in mind that you don't have any time to waste worrying about those psycho things students worry about, like whether you've guessed too many (C)'s, or what the occult meaning of the pattern of dots you've made is.

SUMMARY

- When a question seems unclear, the answer choices can help you make sense of it.
- On every general question you are looking for a choice that accurately describes some facet of the entire passage.
- Learn to focus on key phrases in the answer choices in order to eliminate using the half bad equals all bad technique.
- Use Consistency of Answers.
- On line-reference questions:
    —Keep the main idea in mind, and use Consistency of Answers whenever possible.
    —Go back to the passage and reread the lines in question, as well as one full sentence before and after the line reference.
- Pay close attention to the wording of questions. Put questions in your own words if that makes things easier for you. Be careful not to just ignore confusing parts, though.
- Expect a weird question or two. ETS likes to get creative on the AP English Literature and Composition test. We can't prepare you for everything, just almost everything.
- Don't be bummed out by I, II, III questions. POE works wonderfully on them.
- This is a public service announcement: Our glossary of terms has many valuable definitions and will get you some points. (We know: if you have to hear about irony one more time, you'll scream.)
- Grammar questions aren't worth studying for unless you're really weak on the basic terms. Chapter 11 will help you out there.

THE ART OF THE SEVEN-MINUTE PASSAGE

- When you get to the last passage, check your time.
- If you have seven minutes or fewer left use the Seven Minute Passage technique.
    —Don't read the passage.
    —Answer the questions going from the questions that require no knowledge of the passage to those that require a complete knowledge.
- If you're left with between seven and fifteen minutes for the last passage, it's your call.

6

THE POETRY PASSAGE AND QUESTIONS

INTRODUCTION

Answering multiple-choice questions on poetry passages involves the very same principles as does answering questions on prose. There are some differences, however.

First, the poetry passages tend to contain a few more questions that rely on knowledge than the prose passages do. You will certainly see a question or two on the literary devices (personification, metaphor, etc.) in the poem. You might see a question about the way a line *scans*, or what the rhyme scheme is called, but these are nothing to worry about: recent tests have not included a single question on scansion or the names of classical poetic forms. ETS does, however, like to use poetry for its questions about grammar, since poets use the kind of tangled syntax that makes for challenging grammar questions.

Second, the poetry you'll see on the AP test tends to make for harder reading than the prose passages do. ETS has a style of poetry they like to select for the AP test. In order to write questions properly they find themselves limited in the kind of material they can use. As a result, you won't see poems that stretch language and meaning to its limits or poems that are open to a variety of interpretations. Nor will you see beautiful and elegant but direct and simple poems: ETS wouldn't have anything to write questions about. ETS likes poems of 30 to 70 lines that use difficult language to make a precise point. The poem below, and the questions that follow, should give you a good idea of what to expect on the test. This is an excellent place to practice what you've learned in previous chapters. Use all the techniques we've taught you:

- Read the poem as prose.
- Focus on the main idea.
- When answering the questions, use POE and Consistency of Answers.
- Be sure to read around line references.

ANDREW MARVELL'S "ON A DROP OF DEW" AND QUESTIONS

Read the following poem carefully and choose answers to the questions that follow.

                    See how the orient[1] dew,
                    Shed from the bosom of the morn
                        Into the blowing[2] roses,
        Line   Yet careless of its mansion new,
        (5)   For the clear region where 'twas born
                        Round in itself incloses:
                    And in its little globe's extent,
                Frames as it can its native element.
                        How it the purple flow'r does slight,
        (10)   Scarce touching where it lies,
                    But gazing back upon the skies,
                            Shines with a mournful light,
                                Like its own tear,
                Because so long divided from the sphere.
        (15)   Restless it rolls and unsecure,
                            Trembling lest it grow impure,
                    Till the warm sun pity its pain,
                    And to the skies exhale it back again.
                            So the soul, that drop, that ray
        (20)   Of the clear fountain of eternal day,
                    Could it within the human flow'r be seen,
                            Remembering still its former height,
                            Shuns the sweet leaves and blos-
            soms green,
        (25)   And recollecting its own light,
                    Does, in its pure and circling thoughts, express
                    The greater heaven in an heaven less.

                In how coy[3] a figure wound,
                Every way it turns away:
(30)   So the world excluding round,
                yet receiving in the day,
                Dark beneath, but bright above,
                Here disdaining, there in love.
            How loose and easy hence to go,
(35)   How girt and ready to ascend,
                Moving but on a point below,
                It all about does upwards bend.
        Such did the manna's sacred dew distill,
        White and entire, though congealed and chill,
(40)   Congealed on earth: but does, dissolving, run
        Into the glories of th' almighty sun.

                                —Andrew Marvell

[1] pearly, sparkling
[2] blooming
[3] modest

1. Which one of the following best describes the overall content of the poem?

    (A) The physical aspects of a drop of dew are related to the spiritual aspects of the human soul.
    (B) The life-cycle of a drop of dew is contemplated.
    (C) The human soul is shown to be a drop of dew.
    (D) The spiritual characteristics of a drop of dew are analyzed.
    (E) The poet offers a mystical vision of a drop of dew as a spiritual entity that has all the qualities of the human soul.

2. The poem contains which of the following?

        I. A biblical allusion.
        II. An extended metaphor.
        III. An evocation of spiritual longing.

    (A) I only
    (B) II only
    (C) III only
    (D) I and II only
    (E) I, II, and III

3. In context, "careless of its mansion new" (line 4) most nearly means:

   (A) The dew drop does not understand the value of its beautiful surroundings.
   (B) The dew drop does not assist the flower in any way.
   (C) The dew drop is unconcerned with it's beautiful surroundings.
   (D) The human soul does not value the body.
   (E) The human soul does not take part in the care of the body.

4. Which one of the following does the poem use as a metaphor for the human body?

   (A) "the orient dew" (line 1)
   (B) "the sphere" (line 14)
   (C) "the clear fountain" (line 20)
   (D) "the sweet leaves and blossoms green" (line 23)
   (E) "th' almighty sun" (line 40)

5. Which of the following is the antecedent of "its" in "Does, in its pure and circling thoughts, express" (line 25)?

   (A) soul (line 19)
   (B) day (line 20)
   (C) flow'r (line 21)
   (D) height (line 22)
   (E) leaves (line 23)

6. All of the following aspects of the dew drop are emphasized in the poem EXCEPT:

   (A) its disregard for the physical world.
   (B) its desire to regain the heavens.
   (C) its purity.
   (D) its will to live.
   (E) its roundness.

7. Lines 9–14 suggest the drop of dew is:

   (A) frightened of death.
   (B) full of unhappy longing.
   (C) envious of the rose's vitality.
   (D) part of a larger body of water in the sky.
   (E) uncertain of the future.

8. Lines 19–26 make explicit

   (A) the analogy between the drop of dew and the soul.
   (B) the actual differences between the drop of dew and the soul.
   (C) the true nature of the drop of dew.
   (D) the soul's need for the body.
   (E) the soul's thoughts.

9. Each of the following pairs of phrases refers to the same action, object, or concept EXCEPT:

   (A) "mansion new" (line 4) . . . "purple flow'r" (line 9)
   (B) "globe's extent" (line 8) . . . "the sphere" (line 14)
   (C) "that drop" (line 19) . . . "that ray" (line 19)
   (D) "exhale" (line 18) . . . "dissolving" (line 39)
   (E) "Every way it turns away" (line 28) . . . "It all about does upward bend" (line 36)

10. Which of the following best paraphrases the meaning in context of "So the world excluding round, yet receiving in the day" (lines 29–30)?

    (A) Although the dew drop shuts out the world, it arrives each day.
    (B) The world evaporates the drop of dew when it receives the light of the sun.
    (C) The dew drop is impervious to everything but time.
    (D) Although the dew-drop and the soul shut out the material world, they let in the light of heaven.
    (E) The only thing which matters to the drop of dew is light.

11. In line 40 the sun is symbolic of

    (A) fire
    (B) rebirth
    (C) the soul
    (D) God
    (E) time

12. Which of the following sets of adjectives is best suited to describing the poem's tone and use of symbolism?

    (A) mysterious . . . moody . . . spiritual
    (B) pious . . . proper . . . academic
    (C) intricate . . . delicate . . . worshipful
    (D) witty . . . clever . . . ironic
    (E) straightforward . . . impassioned . . . sincere

13. In the final four lines of the poem the poet suggests that:

    (A) the dew drop will ultimately be destroyed by the sun.
    (B) the cycle of life and death is continual.
    (C) the dew drop will return to earth in the form of 'manna.'
    (D) souls as pure as a drop of dew will ascend to heaven.
    (E) death brings spiritual unity with God.

14. Which of the following adjectives is least important to the poem's theme?

(A) blowing (line 3)
(B) clear (line 20)
(C) pure (line 25)
(D) bright (line 31)
(E) loose (line 33)

ABOUT ANDREW MARVELL'S "ON A DROP OF DEW"

This poem is a challenging one, but absolutely typical of what you will find on the AP test. Marvell (1621–1678) was one of the *metaphysical poets*, and the poem above is an excellent example of this school of poetry's verse. The metaphysical poets were a loosely connected group of seventeenth century poets who rejected what they felt were the overly-sweet, mushy-headed Italian models for poetry that were prevalent in England at that time, and, in reaction, fashioned a type of elaborately clever, often witty verse that has a decidedly intellectual twist to it. The metaphysical poets are noted for taking a comparison—for example, "a drop of dew is like the soul"—and developing it over dozens of lines. Lots of metaphysical poetry appears on the multiple-choice section; this is not because metaphysical poetry is necessarily great, but because unlike most poetry, it lends itself well to multiple-choice questions. So, reading any of the metaphysicals' poetry is great practice for the AP test. Others of the metaphysical school include John Donne, George Herbert, Thomas Carew, Abraham Cowley, and Richard Crashaw.

ANSWERS AND EXPLANATIONS TO THE QUESTIONS

1. Which one of the following best describes the overall content of the poem?

(A) The characteristics of a drop of dew are related to those of the human soul.
(B) The life-cycle of a drop of dew is contemplated.
(C) The human soul is shown to be a drop of dew.
(D) The physical characteristics of a drop of dew are analyzed.
(E) The poet offers a mystical vision of a drop of dew as a spiritual entity that has all the qualities of the human soul.

HERE'S HOW TO CRACK IT

The correct answer is (A). This is a main idea question. Remember, you could have left it alone and come back to it if you hadn't found the main idea yet. Chances are you didn't have too much trouble. If you had any trouble eliminating choices, it was probably with choice (C). Does the poet really show that the human soul is a drop of dew? No. Marvell uses a drop of dew to speak about the human soul, but he isn't suggesting that a person's inner spirit is actually composed of condensed water. In fact, in the poem the drop of dew isn't so much a water droplet as it is a receptacle for light. This point becomes important in later questions. If choice (D) threw you then you weren't paying attention to the word *physical*. You should have asked yourself, "Wait a minute, this dew drop trembles with fear at the thought of becoming impure: can I call that a physical analysis?" Marvell's drop of dew is a being with a personality and desires; all of these things are studied, not just its physical characteristics.

2. The poem contains which of the following?

   I. A biblical allusion.
   II. An extended metaphor.
   III. An evocation of spiritual longing.

   (A) I only
   (B) II only
   (C) III only
   (D) I and II only
   (E) I, II, and III

HERE'S HOW TO CRACK IT

The correct answer is (E). Question 2 is one of the notorious I, II, III questions. Remember to use POE and work from the easiest point to the hardest. You should see that item II is found in the passage: The dew drop is an extended metaphor for the human soul. This is also known as *conceit*. You can eliminate choices (A) and (C); they don't include item II.

Item III might send you back to the poem, where lines 11–13, ("But gazing back upon the skies,/ Shines with a mournful light,/ Like its own tear") should convince you that item III is a keeper. Eliminate choices (B) and (D). You're finished.

Only (E) is left. If you're curious about item I, the biblical allusion is the word *manna*, which refers to a kind of bread that came to the starving Israelites from out of heaven. If you had any doubts about item I (or item III) you might have reasoned that both points are consistent with the main idea and should be kept.

3. In context, "careless of its mansion new" (line 4) most nearly means:

   (A) The dew drop does not understand the value of its beautiful surroundings.
   (B) The dew drop does not assist the flower in any way.
   (C) The dew drop is unconcerned with its beautiful surroundings.
   (D) The human soul does not value the body.
   (E) The human soul does not take part in the care of the body.

HERE'S HOW TO CRACK IT

The correct answer is (C). Question 3 is a straightforward line-reference question. After reading around the line reference, you can easily eliminate choices (D) and (E). The line in question discusses only the dew drop upon a rose petal. It does not refer to the human soul. Of the remaining choices, (A) and (B) both imply that in context, "careless" means that the dew drop does not take care of the rose. This is simply a misreading. Chances are you didn't have much trouble on this question.

4. Which one of the following does the poem use as a metaphor for the human body?

   (A) "the orient dew" (line 1)
   (B) "the sphere" (line 14)
   (C) "the clear fountain" (line 20)
   (D) "the sweet leaves and blossoms green" (line 23)
   (E) "th' almighty sun" (line 40)

HERE'S HOW TO CRACK IT

The correct answer is (D). To answer this question you must either trace Marvell's involved metaphor, noting that in lines 19–21 he describes the soul as being housed within the "human flow'r," or, use POE. All four correct answers refer to either a spiritual entity (the dew) or its source (the sphere, fountain, and sun) and so can be eliminated.

5. Which of the following is the antecedent of "its" in "Does, in its pure and circling thoughts, express" (line 25)?

    (A) soul (line 19)
    (B) day (line 20)
    (C) flow'r (line 21)
    (D) height (line 22)
    (E) leaves (line 23)

HERE'S HOW TO CRACK IT

The correct answer is (A). Question 5 is a typical grammar question. It hinges on your knowing the term *antecedent*. That term, and other grammatical terms you need for the test, are defined in chapter 11. By asking for the antecedent, the question is simply asking what the word *its* stands for in the given phrase. Analyzed grammatically, the only correct usage (and ETS will only ask about correct usage) is the soul. You might also have reasoned, "For which of the choices would it make sense to have 'pure and circling thoughts'?" Again, only choice (A) makes sense.

6. All of the following aspects of the dew drop are emphasized in the poem EXCEPT:

    (A) its disregard for the physical world.
    (B) its desire to regain the heavens.
    (C) its purity.
    (D) its will to live.
    (E) its roundness.

HERE'S HOW TO CRACK IT

The correct answer is (D). Question 6 is an EXCEPT question. An excellent way to proceed is to disregard the EXCEPT; cross EXCEPT out.

Eliminate any choice that fits the remaining question: All of the following aspects of the drop of dew are emphasized in the poem.

To do this you *must* refer back to the passage. **Remember: Never work from memory!** "Careless of its mansion new," lets you eliminate (A). "Like its own tear/Because so long divided from the sphere" takes care of (B). "Trembling lest it grows impure," lets you eliminate (C). The dew drop's roundness is emphasized in several places; choice (E) was easy to eliminate. This leaves only choice (D). This works on NOT and LEAST questions as well.

7. Lines 9–14 suggest the drop of dew is:

    (A) frightened of death.
    (B) full of unhappy longing.
    (C) envious of the rose's vitality.
    (D) part of a larger body of water in the sky.
    (E) uncertain of the future.

HERE'S HOW TO CRACK IT

The correct answer is (B). Question 7 is a line reference question that tests your comprehension of a set of lines. It shouldn't have posed too many difficulties; if you had trouble with this question you should practice on reading poetry for comprehension. You can eliminate choices (C) and (E) easily: they have nothing to do with the poem. The other choices can almost be justified from the poem, but *almost* means *wrong*. Choice (A) could be eliminated because of the word *frightened*. The drop of dew is perhaps frightened of earthly life (remember, it "trembles" at the thought of becoming "impure"), but as a metaphor for the soul, it is not afraid of death. Certainly no such statement can be found in the poem. Choice (D) is incorrect because Marvell treats the dew drop not only as water, but as a container of light and as a metaphor for the soul. For Marvell the drop comes from the sky, not a body of water in the sky.

8. Lines 19–26 make explicit

   (A) the analogy between the drop of dew and the soul.
   (B) the actual differences between the drop of dew and the soul.
   (C) the true nature of the drop of dew.
   (D) the soul's need for the body.
   (E) the soul's thoughts.

HERE'S HOW TO CRACK IT

The correct answer is (A). The key here is to understand the question. When something is made explicit, it is stated or spelled out. *Explicit* is the opposite of *implicit*. Your task is to see what lines 19–26 show clearly. Using POE, you should eliminate choice (C) immediately; it only talks about the drop of dew; the lines in question refer primarily to the human soul. Choice (E) is a trap answer. The lines in question do refer to the soul's thoughts, but they do not spell them out; the thoughts are not made explicit. Choice (D) is similarly wrong: the drop of dew's "true nature" is not the subject of these lines, only the likeness of the drop of dew and the soul. Choice (B) talks about differences between the soul and the drop of dew. This is the exact opposite of the lines' intent. They discuss the similarities of the drop and the soul. In fact, they make the analogy between the drop of dew and the soul explicit—hence (A), the correct answer.

9. Each of the following pairs of phrases refers to the same action, object, or concept EXCEPT:

   (A) "mansion new" (line 4) . . . "purple flow'r" (line 9)
   (B) "globe's extent" (line 8) . . . "the sphere" (line 14)
   (C) "that drop" (line 19) . . . "that ray" (line 19)
   (D) "exhale" (line 18) . . . "dissolving" (line 39)
   (E) "Every way it turns away" (line 28) . . . "It all about does upward bend" (line 36)

HERE'S HOW TO CRACK IT

The correct answer is (B). This is another EXCEPT question. They're common on the AP English Literature Test. Cross out EXCEPT and eliminate answers that satisfy the remaining statement: each of the following pairs of phrases refers to the same action, object, or concept. Use POE. In (A), "mansion new" and " purple flow'r" both refer to the rose the drop of dew perches on. Eliminate it. In (C), "that drop" and "that ray" seem to refer to different things, but both in fact refer to the soul—so eliminate (C). In (D), "exhale" and "dissolving" both refer to the process by which the drop of dew vanishes (evaporation, if you want to be non-mystical about it). In (B), "globe's extent" and "sphere" seem to both refer to the dew drop, but in fact, the sphere refers to the skies above—the "heavenly sphere." Thus, (B) is the correct answer.

Nit-picking? Maybe, but this question provides an excellent example of the kind of careful reading (and nit-picking) you'll be called upon to do on the actual test.

10. Which of the following best paraphrases the meaning in context of "So the world excluding round,/ yet receiving in the day" (lines 29–30)?

    (A) Although the dew drop evaporates in the sun, it arrives anew each day.
    (B) The world evaporates the drop of dew when it receives the light of the sun.
    (C) The dew drop is impervious to everything but time.
    (D) Although the dew drop and the soul shut out the material world, they let in the light of heaven.
    (E) The only thing which matters to the dew drop is light.

HERE'S HOW TO CRACK IT

The correct answer is (D). This is probably the most common type of question on the AP test. ETS gives you a line and asks, "So, what does it mean?" As always, read around the line and then use POE. Paraphrase "the world excluding round" as "the drop that turns away from the world" and you can eliminate (A), (B), and (E). None of those choices include that idea. Choice (C) mentions that the drop of dew is impervious. That isn't a good paraphrase of "world excluding round," and you can eliminate it with confidence by reasoning that *time* is not mentioned in the lines in question at all. That leaves only the correct answer, (D).

11. In line 40, the sun is symbolic of

    (A) fire
    (B) rebirth
    (C) the soul
    (D) God
    (E) time

HERE'S HOW TO CRACK IT

The correct answer is (D). Get used to the range of difficulty on the AP test. Some of the questions are really quite subtle, and challenge even the most experienced readers, others—like question 11—are a piece of cake. Don't freak and think you must have missed something when a question seems easy: just collect the point. Don't miss the easy questions by over-thinking. And don't worry about missing the hardest questions: if those are all you miss, you're on your way to a score of five.

On this question, we hope you saw that the sun symbolized God. The word *almighty* should have been a big clue.

12. Which of the following sets of adjectives are best suited to describe the poem's tone and use of symbolism?

   (A) mysterious . . . moody . . . spiritual
   (B) pious . . . proper . . . academic
   (C) intricate . . . delicate . . . worshipful
   (D) witty . . . clever . . . ironic
   (E) straightforward . . . impassioned . . . sincere

HERE'S HOW TO CRACK IT

The correct answer is (C). This is a tone question. On tone questions, always use POE. On this question, **remember half bad equals all bad**. Every answer choice has something right in it, but only the correct answer choice has *nothing* wrong in it. In (A), yes, the poem's tone is spiritual, but is it mysterious and moody? Not really. Eliminate it. *Pious, proper,* and *academic* sound school-marmish (Choice (B)). That isn't right. Eliminate it. In (D), well, it's true the poem is witty and clever, but is it ironic? Metaphysical poets typically *are* ironic—that is, hidden messages and contradictions often lurk below the surface of a metaphysical poem's text, but "On a Drop of Dew" is an exception. Marvell says what he means, cleverly, but not ironically. Choice (E) should just sound wrong. "On a Drop of Dew" is an intensely crafted work, but it is not impassioned nor straightforward. That leaves (C), which sums things up fairly well: intricate, delicate, and worshipful.

13. In the final four lines of the poem, the poet suggests that:

   (A) the dew drop will ultimately be destroyed by the sun.
   (B) the cycle of life and death is continual.
   (C) the drop of dew will return to earth in the form of 'manna.'
   (D) souls as pure as a drop of dew will ascend to heaven.
   (E) death brings spiritual unity with God.

HERE'S HOW TO CRACK IT

The correct answer is (E). If you answered question 11 correctly, this one shouldn't be much tougher. If you understand that the sun symbolizes God, then you should also understand that the dew's dissolving into the sun is a metaphor for the soul's ascent to heaven. The incorrect answer choices all add extraneous points, or misconstrue the emphasis of this essentially simple idea. Choice (A) suggests that the dew would be destroyed. That misses the point. The dew's evaporation is not a destruction but a reunion with the divine. Choice (B) is extraneous: the cycle of life is not a thematic point of the poem. Choice (C) tries to trap you by confusing the manna with the dew drop. The poem suggests that the dew drop is like manna in that both are distilled from the spiritual realm. The poem does not suggest that the dew will somehow become manna. Choice (D) should have been easy to eliminate: nowhere does the poem talk about whether souls are or are not as pure as a drop of dew.

14. Which of the following adjectives is LEAST important to the poem's theme?

   (A) blowing (line 3)
   (B) clear (line 20)
   (C) pure (line 25)
   (D) bright (line 31)
   (E) loose (line 33)

HERE'S HOW TO CRACK IT

The correct answer is (A). ETS is fond of asking questions about theme, despite the fact that pinning down the theme of many poems is problematic. When ETS asks about the theme, don't try to come up with an exact definition of the theme, just think about the main point, the important stuff. Again, POE is the way to work. Cross out LEAST and work with the remaining question, eliminating choices that are important to the theme. An important aspect of the poem is the metaphor of the dew drop and the soul. A good way to start would be to eliminate those choices which describe any aspect of that relationship. In this way you could eliminate (B), (C), and (D), since all are qualities of the dew drop that relate to qualities of the soul. A moment of study should tell you that (E) is also important. The dew drop is "loose," or ready to ascend; it grips this world only lightly. That is a thematic point. And (A)? Well, *blowing* means blooming. Is it important that the rose is in bloom? Does Marvell return to the fact of the rose being in bloom later in the poem? Does blooming somehow relate to the soul? No. (A) is least thematically important, and thus, (A) is the correct answer.

SUMMARY

- Don't worry about scansion (you know: iambic pentameter, dactyls, spondees, etc.). You probably won't see even one question on it.

- Remember to:
  —Read the poem as prose.
  —Focus on the main idea.
  —When answering the questions, use POE and Consistency of Answers.
  —Be sure to read around line references.

- Metaphysical poetry is excellent practice for the kind of poetry you'll see on the AP test. John Donne, Andrew Marvell, George Herbert, Thomas Carew, Abraham Cowley, and Richard Crashaw are all poets whose work provides excellent AP practice.

- On EXCEPT, NOT, and LEAST questions, cross out the negative word and eliminate any choice that fits the remaining question.

PART III

CRACKING THE SYSTEM: THE ESSAYS

7

BASIC PRINCIPLES OF THE ESSAY SECTION

FORMAT AND CONTENT OF THE ESSAY SECTION

The format of the essay section on the AP English Test has been consistent for the past 17 years. They could conceivably change the format, of course. A meteor could also fall on your head the next time you go outside. Don't worry about it. Here's what to expect:

- You will be asked to write essays on three subjects:
  1. A passage of prose.
  2. A passage of poetry.
  3. An open essay: an essay on a given topic, supported by your own reading.

- You'll be given all the paper you need (including scratch paper), and you'll be instructed to write in pen. Bring a blue or black pen.

- You'll have two hours to complete this section.

WHAT WILL YOU BE WRITING ABOUT?

When ETS considers the mix of literary periods and styles on the test, they include the essay section. If you saw two passages on eighteenth-century poetry in the multiple-choice section, you won't see any eighteenth-century poetry in the essay section. ETS also tries to give male and female authors equal representation (roughly), and takes pains to include at least one person of color among the writers included on the test, so there's a strong chance your essay section will contain a passage by an author who identifies him or herself as African-American, Latino, or Asian.

PACING

On each individual essay, you can take as much or as little time as you like, so long as you don't go over the two hour limit for all three essays. Each essay is worth the same number of points, so it's a good idea to pace yourself and allot 40 minutes for each, give or take a few minutes. If you spend an hour and a half on your first essay, you're not going to finish the other two.

THE IMPORTANCE OF THE ESSAY SECTION TO YOUR SCORE

The essay section of the AP English Literature and Composition Test counts for 55 percent of your total score. It is only slightly more important than the multiple-choice portion of the test. It's obvious, but let's say it anyway: Both sections are important to your score.

Which section feels more important is another issue. For most students, the essay section feels like the whole test. The multiple-choice section seems like a bunch of hoops you have to jump through before getting to the part that matters—the essays. Students tend to look at the essay section with a combination of awe, fear, and excitement, thinking, "They're going to grade my writing!—gulp." Well, yes, some total stranger is going to pore over your words and give you a score from one to nine. It is scary. However, we're going to take the anxiety out of this process and replace it with knowledge and confidence.

Here's the interesting part: The essays are more important. Huh? Didn't we just say the two sections are essentially equal? It's true that the multiple-choice and essay sections are nearly equal in respect to determining your score. In respect to your score *improvement*, however, there is a world of difference between the two sections.

WHEN IT COMES TO IMPROVING YOUR SCORE, THE ESSAYS ARE KING

If you're the kind of student who gets As in class and then bombs on standardized tests, using our multiple-choice techniques will make a huge difference. If you are already a natural test taker, great—our techniques won't help that much because you're doing 90 percent of what we say without even knowing it. You probably actually fall somewhere in between (the vast majority of students do) and so using our techniques for the multiple-choice section squeezes out a half-dozen or so points and ensures that you get your best possible score—why settle for anything less? But when it comes to score improvement (and to your skills as well) the essays are different.

THESE ESSAYS ARE DIFFERENT

Essay points add up fast. If we can show you a way to improve your essays by just one point—*bam*—that means three extra essay points just like that, one for each essay. And there are only 27 total essay points available. One more point on each essay works out to better than a ten percent improvement on your essay score. If you can improve your essays just two notches, from, say, a five to a seven, you're in a whole new scoring bracket. Study this section and you will improve at least one point and probably more.

THESE ESSAYS ARE DIFFERENT (DIDN'T WE JUST SAY THAT?)

Think about this: Unlike familiar old multiple-choice, the essays are completely new. You've never done anything like them before, so you may as well learn to do them in a way that will get you the most points. "What !?" you're thinking, "It's the multiple-choice that's weird; I write essays *all the time* in school."

Sorry, but you're mistaken. You write essays, true—but *not AP essays*.

YOUR TEACHER KNOWS YOU

You write essays for teachers who know you and (we hope) care about you. They know what your writing looked like at the beginning of the semester, they know whether you do your homework, they know whether you spend most of class day-dreaming, they know you occasionally make brilliant comments in class, they know your real passion is for track or violin or painting or science or maybe writing. They even know that there's a kid a few rows over with a hopeless crush on you and they wonder why you haven't noticed yet (why *haven't* you noticed?).

When your teachers see your name at the top of the page they already know a thousand things about you, and they all go into their reading of your writing, and into the grades you get. The AP Reader doesn't know you at all.

YOU KNOW YOUR TEACHER

Secondly, and just as importantly, you don't know anything about the reader of your AP essays. Who is she? He? It? In school, you know your teacher. You know what she wants to hear. You may know that she detests misspellings, or that she loves it when you use humor, or that she gives extra-credit for artistic originality. Or, you may know that she's utterly mad, wears the same neon-purple scarfy shawl thing every day (it's covered in cat fur too), and that she channels Geoffrey Chaucer in her spare time. The AP essays are written to a featureless face: Is it a kind face? Mean? Crazy? You'll never know. When was the last time you wrote an essay to a total stranger for a grade?

READ IT—WRITE IT—GO!

Finally, AP essays are written under intense time-pressure, without a lesson: "Hey kid, here's a passage—read it—write about it—go!" That's totally unnatural. Your teachers have undoubtedly spent a lot time telling you that "good writing is rewriting." Perhaps they've insisted that for assignments you turn in a first draft and then revise that draft. Good. Your teachers are 100 percent correct in doing so. Writing well takes patience and care. One of the joys of writing is getting into its slowed down, reflective pace. (If you're the impatient type, you probably hate writing.) In short, the "ready, set, write" attitude of the ETS is the opposite of the right way to approach writing and is, we hope, diametrically opposed to the way you've been trained to write.

The closest thing to writing for the AP test you might have experienced is an in-class essay test, but even in that case the differences are significant. For example, in-class essay tests come after you've spent at least several classes on the subject at hand and know what your teacher expects you to have learned. Second, on in-class essay tests, the teacher wants to see what you know, not how well you write. On the AP test you'll be writing cold, on a passage you read for the first time just two minutes ago with no time to revise and rework the way good writers always do, and you'll be graded on your writing as well as on what you say. It's ironic (there's that word again), but the very best practice for the AP test comes from the panicked-slacker method of homework preparation. What's that? Oh you know (we know you know): writing a paper—fast—on a book you haven't really read, in the study hall before class. The AP essays call for a kind of speed-writing in which you have to come up with an idea and get it down right, all on the first try.

HORRIBLE? YES, BUT MAKE THE MOST OF IT

It's an awful way to have to write, but at least everyone else is working under the same conditions. In fact, if you know how to make the most out of these bizarre conditions, if you understand that you're doing something you haven't done before and work in the best way possible given the demands of the test, your essay will shine in comparison to the others. This chapter is about giving you the tools to do just that. In order to use those tools, you need to understand how the essays are scored, because really, a high score is all you're after. We aren't going to try to teach you how to write well. We are going to teach you how to write a high-scoring AP essay.

ALL ABOUT AP ESSAY SCORING

THE ZERO TO NINE SCALE

Each of your essays will be given a score between zero and nine. Zero is the worst score you can get, and nine is the best. Students' scores are *not* spread out evenly over that range; the number of nines does not equal the number of fives. In fact the numbers aren't even close. Here's how the scores break down:

Score	Approximate Percentage of Students Receiving Score
9	1%
8	5%
7	10%
6	20%
5	23%
4	22%
3	15%
2	3%
1	1%
0	less than 1%
–	less than 1%

As you can see, about 65 percent of all essays are scored in the middle range: four, five, and six. The extreme scores taper away quickly. ETS doesn't tell its essay Readers to bunch up the scores this way, and they don't fudge the scores around later in order to make them produce this tidy bell-curve. It works out this way because of the nature of student writing and the nature of essay scoring in general.

"HOLISTIC" SCORING

The essays are scored "holistically." What this means is that the reader goes through your essay and gets an overall impression. That impression is translated into a single number, zero to nine, which is your essay's score. There is no checklist of points, such as two points for style, two points for grammar, one point for vocabulary, and one point for writing about, say, the metaphor in paragraph one. Nothing like that.

About a week before the actual grading session, ETS goes through several essays to get a feel for how students did. Next, the ETS staff combs through the student writing looking for the perfect representative nine essay, the perfect five, the perfect three, etc. These representative essays are the "sample essays." The Readers are given the samples and are trained for a day, during which they read student essays, compare them with the samples and discuss the grades they would assign. The next day, the Readers start giving out the real grades. An ETS consultant checks graded essays at random to make sure the scoring is consistent. ETS tries hard to keep things standard and fair. Each Reader only grades one type of essay. But there's no way around the facts: the Readers are individual people making subjective judgments.

THE READERS

Readers aren't there because they love grading essays. It's a part-time job. That doesn't mean they don't care at all, but it does mean they don't care a lot. The Readers mostly just want to pick up their pay check. They want to pick it up without feeling irresponsible or stupid. They want to avoid getting yelled at by the ETS foreman for doing a bad job. They *really* want to avoid being told to go back and re-grade that stack of papers. That's what the Readers want, which means we know what the Reader wants from you.

THE READER WANTS AN ESSAY THAT'S EASY TO SCORE

Your job is to write an essay that's *obviously* better than average. You have to let the Reader feel confident about giving you at least a seven. Ask anyone who's read student essays and he or she will tell you: after a short while their brains get as soggy as yesterday's half-eaten bowl of cornflakes. Everything's bland mush, and it's starting to go sour. Four out of five essays are average or worse. Slogging through these mediocre essays, the Reader gives a score and turns to the next one thinking, "Ugh, here comes another . . . ." The Reader expects it to be medium, lukewarm, and blah, and it usually is. Generic blah gets a five. Blah with lots of spelling and grammar errors gets a four. Blah with a nice turn of phrase here and there gets a six. Those are easy ones (just not the kind of easy grade you want!). But what about the essay that answers the question with extraordinary depth but is built from horribly grammatically flawed sentences? What about the essay that beautifully answers half the question? What about the essay that starts out dull and poorly written but makes one completely original point right at the very end? Those essays are the Reader's nightmares. They want to reward the good qualities, but they aren't going to go out on a limb. They'll think about the score for a while, scratch their heads, and then give it a five or a six. The Reader doesn't want to have to think about things too hard. *When in doubt, the Reader will scrunch your score toward the middle*. You want to make it as easy as possible for the scorer to think your essay is just plain good. Before we get to the basic tips for making it easy for the Reader to give you a high score, let's look at a scoring guide AP Readers use.

A TYPICAL SCORING GUIDE

Every Reader gets a scoring guide for the essay he is grading. The scoring guides for AP essays are always very similar. We've taken a few scoring guides and combined them, taking out the details that are particular to a passage or a poem, such as the author's name and the names of characters and places in the story or poem. Notice as you look over the scoring guide how little specific guidance ETS actually provides; the Readers are given a lot of leeway.

EIGHT TO NINE
These are well organized and well-written essays that clearly analyze the work and how the author dramatizes the situation. These essays use apt, specific references to the passage in order to discuss the author's use of elements such as diction, imagery, pace, and point of view. While not flawless, these papers demonstrate an understanding of the text and of the techniques of composition. These writers express their ideas skillfully and clearly.

SIX TO SEVEN
The content of these papers resembles that of higher scoring essays, but is less precise and less aptly supported. These essays deal with literary elements such as diction, imagery, and pace, but are less effective than the upper range essays. Essays scored at seven will generally exhibit fewer mechanical errors and draw from the passage more incisively than those scored at six.

FIVE
These essays are superficial. Although not seriously in error about the content and literary technique of the passage, they miss the complexity of the piece and offer only a perfunctory analysis of how the subject has been dramatized. The treatment of elements such as diction and imagery is overly generalized or mechanical. The writing adequately conveys the writer's thoughts, but the essays themselves are commonplace, poorly conceived, poorly organized, and simplistic.

THREE TO FOUR
These essays reflect an incomplete understanding of the passage and do not completely respond to the question. The discussion is unclear or simply misses the point. The treatment of literary elements is scanty or unconvincing with little support drawn from the passage. Typically, these essays reveal marked weaknesses in the writer's ability to handle the mechanics of written English.

ONE TO TWO
These essays contain the errors found in three and four scoring essays to an even more pronounced degree. One to two scoring essays either completely misunderstand the passage or fail to address the question. Typically, these essays are incoherent, too short, or both. The writing demonstrates no control of written English, either grammatically or organizationally.

ZERO
This is a response that completely fails to address the question. This is no response, an essay written in a foreign language, an essay written on an unrelated topic, or an essay that is completely illegible.

ANALYSIS OF THE SCORING GUIDE
Look this guide over carefully. What do you see? There are two major points we want blazed into your mind.

First, the high-scoring essays are clear. They aren't perfect, they aren't moving and profound, they're just clear. Practically every point made in the eight to nine description is just another way of saying *clear*. Well-organized means *clearly organized*. *Apt examples drawn from the passages* is another way of saying the writer has used *clear* examples. Clarity is the goal.

Second, notice the jump that happens at the five score. Notice how the whole tone of the guide changes. Suddenly the guide isn't talking about the fine points of answering the question; it's talking about the life-choking drabness of it all. You can almost hear the guide's author muttering under her breath, "I wish we could score these lower but they're just too *common*." Five essays are just a trap. A trap that is easy to fall into if you aren't ready for the AP essays. Many five essays are written by good students, many of them A students, and half of those students *think they wrote a pretty good essay*. But they didn't, they just wrote an essay, a generic essay. Here are the kinds of adjectives that show up in the five category of AP scoring guides: *mechanical, perfunctory, pedestrian, commonplace, adequate*. In other words, the same dull essay most students write (or try to write until they get totally lost, leading to an even lower score). After grading her fifty-fifth essay, the Reader writes down the score and turns to the next essay, praying, "Please, not another one."

If you understand what you read and can write in grammatical English, a five is your absolute low-end score. You will almost certainly do better than that with our help.

HOW TO MAKE IT EASY FOR THE READER TO GIVE YOU A HIGH SCORE

The most important part of your essay is the content. The entire advanced principles part of this section is about writing meaty content-filled essays that just blow the reader away. But the Reader has to get to that content. There are just a few vital things you must do to let your excellence come shining through with full impact. Ignore these simple basic tips at your peril. These basics have to do with the surface of your writing. That might seem cheap, but it's not. If the surface of your essay is clean and clear, the Reader can see through to the depths.

1. **NEATNESS COUNTS, SO PRINT**

Do everything in your power to make your essays readable! Everything! Write twice as slowly as you normally do. Write large. Write dark. Your writing doesn't have to be pretty, but it must be legible.

Print. Don't write in script unless all you've ever heard since fourth grade is, "what beautiful handwriting you have." *If that doesn't sound familiar, don't write in script*. We don't care if you haven't printed since third grade. Print. Put the words down slowly and carefully in block letters. You've got to trust us here. We know you think that this is ridiculous and that your handwriting doesn't, or at least shouldn't, matter. We know you're going to show your script handwriting to a friend and say, "Does this seem decently legible?" And we know your friend is going to say, "Yeah, totally." But unlike your essay Reader, your friend hasn't spent the past six straight hours reading handwritten student essays. As persecuted as you feel writing those essays, the Reader feels twice as persecuted reading them. Script is harder to read than print; it just is. If your normal handwriting looks like a wedding invitation, well, OK, *maybe* you can get away with it. Otherwise print. If that means you have to practice a little—practice a little.

Be as neat as you possibly can. Take pains to be neat. When a neatly written essay shows up, the wave of relief, of *love*, that floods the reader is difficult to describe. A clear, printed essay makes the Reader think, "Ahh, now I can do my job!" A messy essay makes the reader think, "Yeah? You wanna make my life difficult? Well then why should I cut you any slack?" Messy essay writing is like showing up for a job interview with your shoes untied, your fly unzipped, your belt skipping a few loops, ketchup all over your shirt, and gum in your hair. You might be a genius, but you look like an idiot. The Readers will try hard not to let goofy looking handwriting affect the score, but if it's messy and hard to read, they'll lose patience fast.

2. **INDENT**

Your reader's first impressions are crucial. Think about that character at the job interview with gum in his hair. If his battle isn't already lost, it's definitely an uphill fight the rest of the way. The overall look of your essay is a first impression. It's the smile on your face as you walk in the door. Your essay should look neat, organized, and clear. Make your paragraphs obvious. Indent twice as far as you normally would. When in doubt, make a paragraph. Ever look at a book, flip it open, and see nothing but one long paragraph? Your next thought is usually, "Oh please, don't make me have to read this!" That's exactly what the Reader thinks when she sees an essay without paragraphs. Make sure the Reader can see the paragraphs right away. Neat presentation, clear handwriting, paragraphs just screaming out, "I'm so organized it's scary!" and the Reader is already thinking, "Now here's a high-scoring student"—and she hasn't even read a word yet.

3. **WRITE PERFECTLY... FOR THE FIRST TWO SENTENCES**

   Your second first impression (that's an *oxymoron*... see the glossary) comes the first time you open your mouth in the interview, that is, with your first two sentences of the essay. Take triple care with your first two sentences. If you're unsure about the spelling of a word, don't use it. If you're unsure how to punctuate the sentence, rewrite it in a way that makes you feel confident. Don't make any mistakes in the first two sentences. Don't worry about the rest of the passage. The Readers expect mistakes. If you try to write the whole essay perfectly you'll write so slowly, or choke up your brain with so much worry, that you'll either run out of time or write such stilted, dull prose your Reader will wish you had made a mistake just for some relief. All it takes is two good first sentences to convince the Reader that you can write a good sentence when you want to. The glow of a good beginning carries over the whole essay. Mistakes later on look like little oopsy-doodles not even worth bothering with; after all, the Reader's already seen that you can write. Mistakes at the very beginning look like just the opposite—they look like telling signs of inability and a weak grasp of fundamental English mechanics. Take extra care at the beginning of your essay, then relax and just write (*neatly*).

4. **USE SNAPPY VERBS AND TASTY NOUNS**

   Juice up your writing. Try to write with some pizzazz. Try. That's all there is to it. Don't let the test environment, the tension, or worry over writing for a stranger take over your brain. Take risks: you may fall flat every so often, but the Reader will appreciate your effort and reward it. When you've gotten our essay techniques down, you'll understand that 90 percent of dull student writing on AP essays comes from confusion about what to write, which leads to inhibition. Don't be inhibited. Jazz it up a little.

   For example, a student might write, "When Judy first sees Roger going down the street, she thinks he seems interesting." That's probably true, but what a bore. There are a thousand ways to liven up that sentence. It all depends on your personality and what is really happening in the story. How about, "When Judy first glimpses Roger dashing through the shadows of Sullivan Street her heart flutters; she's already in love, she just doesn't know it yet." Or, "When Judy spots Roger flying down the sidewalk with the Sullivan Street gang nipping at his heels, she's dumbstruck by the scrambling wild vitality of his whirling limbs and blazing eyes." Cheesy? Over the top? Who cares? Nobody expects you to write like Marcel Proust. Actually, the Readers expect you to write like someone who's suffering through a tedious nerve-wracking exercise, because that's exactly how most of the essays are written. If you write like someone who enjoys writing, the Readers will be impressed.

   We aren't saying you have to write tangled complex sentences; in fact, you should try to avoid them. Great, long, looping sentences usually just wander off into error and confusion. All you need to do is pay attention to your word choice. When you find yourself using a generic verb like, *look*, *see*, *says*, *walk*, *go*, *take*, or *give*, or a generic noun like *street*, *house*, *car*, or *man*, ask yourself if there isn't a more precise, more colorful word you can use. Why write *house* when you're referring to a *mansion*, or *car* when you're really writing about a *jalopy*? Just a little bit of this goes a long way. It shows you're not scared, and it might even look like you're having fun, which is very good.

   Obviously there's such a thing as too much, and if the Reader gets the impression you're just being silly it won't help your score. But a dash of glitter is much better than none at all. By the way, big important sounding phrases are not glitter and pizzazz, they're an obvious sign that you're full of it. Please don't try to write this kind of gibberish, either: "When Judy initially perceived Roger's rapid ambulatory movement along the pedestrian walkway bordering the automotive thoroughfare, she experienced tachycardia."

5. THE QUESTIONS

Each passage will be preceded by instructions to "Read the passage below carefully and then write a well-organized essay about . . . ." These instructions may also contain some additional material orienting you to the passage, telling you things like who wrote it, the novel it was drawn from, and any other special information ETS feels you need to know in order to understand the passage.

ANSWER THE QUESTION

If you write a great essay that the Reader doesn't think addresses the question, you'll get a lousy score. All three essays will be directed essays; ETS will tell you what they want (that's the theory, anyway). In reality, the questions can be infuriatingly vague. At the same time, not answering the question is the ultimate sin. Understanding and answering the question is crucial to writing a high-scoring essay. In the advanced principles section we'll look at the classic essay question, show you what it means, how ETS modifies this one classic question, and finally how to answer it—in any of its many disguises—for a high score.

ORDERING THE SECTION

Just as with the reading passages in the multiple-choice section of the test, you should put the essays in the order you want to do them. Which one looks easiest? Do it first. Get your writing juices flowing. You definitely want to write all three essays, so don't get lost in your writing and run out of time. If you do happen to run out of time, however, you want it to be on the hardest essay; think of ordering the essays as a safety measure.

But, still, *don't run out of time*. You have 40 minutes per essay.

SUMMARY

GENERAL ESSAY INFORMATION

- There are three essays. One on a prose passage, one on a poetry passage, and one on a work that you select (the open essay).
- You have two hours to complete all three essays.
- The essays are the place to improve your score.

ESSAY SCORING

- Each essay is scored by a Reader who grades only that particular type of essay.
- Each essay is given a score from zero to nine.
- The essays are scored "holistically." There is no checklist of available points.
- The Reader wants to read an essay that's easy to score.
- When in doubt, the Reader will scrunch your score toward the middle range of scores.
- High-scoring essays are clear essays. Middle-scoring essays are generic and boring. Low-scoring essays are plain old bad.

PRESENTATION

- Do everything in your power to make your essays readable.
- Write carefully, in large, dark handwritting. Your writing doesn't have to be pretty, but it must be clear.
- Print!
- Make your paragraph indentations easy to spot.
- When in doubt, create a new paragraph.
- Your first two sentences should be grammatically correct. Your Reader will make a judgment about your ability to write very quickly. Once the reader has decided you can write a sentence, he'll cut you some slack later on (as long as you write neatly).
- Use snappy verbs and tasty nouns. It will impress the Reader and make her think you're comfortable, confident, and smart. Don't worry about overdoing it, but don't go bananas.
- Don't confuse snappy verbs and tasty nouns with ten-dollar vocabulary words. Use the best word you can think of, not the longest.
- Understand the question. (Don't worry, there's much more on this subject in the next chapter.)
- If you write a great essay that doesn't address the question, you'll get a lousy score.
- Order the section. Do the essay you like best first, and save the worst one for last.
- Keep track of time—try to complete each essay in about 40 minutes.

8

The Idea Machine: Starting Your Essays with a High Score

FROM IDEA TO EXECUTION

We're going to take you through our AP English writing process. *The Process has been specifically designed for AP essays.* The hardest part of writing essays under time pressure is coming up with something to say quickly. In this chapter we'll show you how to get the ideas that let you have something to write about in the first place. We aren't going to teach you how to write; you've already spent years learning to write. However, AP essays are unlike anything you've had to write before. You probably haven't spent years learning how to write AP essays.

About 90 percent of this chapter is about how to get an overall conception of your essay and create a great first paragraph. If you can get off to a good start, you're more than halfway to a great score.

THE APPROACH

Just as with the multiple-choice section, you want to have a common sense, step-by-step approach to the essay section (and know how to use it). Here it is:

- Note the time. Remember, 40 minutes per essay.
- Start with either the poetry or the prose passage. Pick whichever one looks easiest (that almost always means the prose).
- Skim the passage (remember, you aren't reading for enjoyment here, this *is* a test).
- Read the passage carefully, keeping in mind that you want to understand what the passage says literally and what emotions the author seeks to arouse. This process should take about five minutes.
- Use the Idea Machine to create your first paragraph. (And remember—neatness counts.) This process should take between five and ten minutes.
- After you've written your first paragraph, do an essay check (thinking about the points you need to make in your essay).
- Support and develop the points you made in your first paragraph. You should have roughly 25 minutes left to complete your essay, but at this point the essay should be flowing, and you should have plenty to say.

DON'T WRITE AN OUTLINE

You don't have time to write an outline. Outlines are for organizing longer, more complex pieces of writing, like research papers—pieces of writing that you have the time to revise and plan. We know you've probably had outlining drummed into you by your teachers. Other books on the AP test recommend making an outline. These people don't understand test taking! Short essays, like the ones you'll write for the AP test, don't call for an outline. You don't even have time to rewrite. Our method shows you how to come up with a solid beginning from which you can build so that you can just write the rest of the essay without an outline.

THE IDEA MACHINE

We've developed a method of approaching AP essays that we call the Idea Machine. Hey, don't get us wrong, the *real* Idea machine is in your skull. The point here is to give you a way of focusing your brain, your imagination, and your analytical skills in a way that's productive for the AP test. This approach won't let you down. Use it and your essays will shine.

The Idea Machine is a series of questions that direct your reading to the material needed to write an essay. Take these questions, apply their answers to the essay question, and in the end you'll find you've written the kind of essay the Readers want to see.

THE IDEA MACHINE

1. What is the meaning of the work?
    a. What is the literal, face-value meaning of the work?
    b. What feeling (or feelings) does the work evoke?
2. How does the author get that meaning across?
    a. What are the important images in the work and what do those images suggest?
    b. What specific words or short phrases produce the strongest feelings?
    c. What elements are in opposition?

That may not look like much, but when we put all the pieces together in this chapter and the next you'll see just how powerful a tool you've been given.

BRILLIANT STUDENTS — DULL ESSAYS

The reason we think we can improve your essay score so much is that chances are you already have what it takes. If you can write an English sentence, if you can write a mediocre, dull, I-hate-writing-this-but-I've-got-to-do-it-anyway kind of essay, then you can write a high-scoring essay, because *you don't actually need any new writing skills at all*. You just need a new approach. Believe us when we say: **Any student who can write an essay that scores a five can write an essay that scores a seven or better.** And remember, any student who can understand what she reads and can write grammatically can get a five. In the scoring guide ETS comes right out and says that there's nothing terribly wrong with the essays that receive scores of five, they're just vague, generalized, mechanical, and dull. Essays like that come out of an incredibly common approach, which is why scores of five are so common.

Let's look at the way *not* to write an AP essay.

THE FIVE-SCORING ESSAY FORMULA

Almost every five-scoring essay is written by a student who doesn't know how to get a real essay idea out of the question and thinks that the "essay formula" can somehow save him. Here's the thought process that invariably leads to a middle score:

"Let's see... they want me to write about the language... well, what *else* would I write about? The whole *thing* is language. This is crazy. And 'how the author dramatized the story'—well, with *language* of course—great, that's about one sentence worth of essay. What am I going to say? I don't know what they want! Oh God. I can't sit here forever; *I've got to write something*. I know! I'll restate the question as a statement and then come up with three examples: one for diction, one for imagery, and one for point of view. Then I'll summarize it all for a conclusion. *That's the essay formula, right*? Okay, here goes."

PANIC + NO IDEA OF WHAT IS WANTED = THE FIVE-SCORING ESSAY FORMULA

This student is perfectly intelligent. The "formula" isn't crazy; in fact, it's taught all over the place:

Restate the question as a statement. Support the statement with three examples from the passage. Summarize it for a conclusion.

It sounds good, but when a student tries to use it he'll realize he still doesn't have one interesting thing to say. From beginning to end he'll feel lost, and writing the essay will feel like one big, meaningless exercise. He'll struggle and pick out bits of the passage that catch his eye and try to discuss them. He won't be exactly sure why they catch his eye, but he'll make something up. The discussion will be vague, over-generalized, and mechanical (that's the description of five-scoring essays in the AP scoring guide, remember). The five-scoring essay has to be vague, because if it were precise the student would be forced to show that he has no precise understanding of what he's supposed to be writing about. The formula turns the essay into garbage.

The formula, however, is actually a heroic effort on the student's part because writing this way is painful and hard. It takes a huge amount of brain power to come up with new and vague ways to say general things about something or other—just what, you aren't quite sure—without looking like a loser. When you're writing this way, a five is a success.

SAY SOMETHING — HAVE AN IDEA

How do you break out of this? How do you make sure you don't get trapped in the soul-sucking bog of formula essay hell? You need to say something. You need an idea, and not just any idea. You need an idea that you can write about. The way to do all this comes from understanding the question. Once you understand the question, you can turn the question into an *essay idea*.

THE ONE CLASSIC ESSAY QUESTION

Whether you're working on a prose or poetry passage, *there is a single classic essay question that ETS uses time after time.* Chances are all the essays you will be asked to write will use this question in some form.

> Read the following work carefully. Then write a well-organized essay in which you discuss the ways by which the author conveys his meaning. Be sure to consider such literary elements as diction, imagery, structure, and point of view.

THE HIDDEN QUESTION IS THE FIRST QUESTION

Okay, so what does ETS want from you on that classic essay question? At first glance, it looks as if you're supposed to write an essay about the "literary elements" in the work, or about how the author "conveys his meaning." That's partly true. But the answers to those questions come later. If you start from there you'll find yourself confused and lost.

How can you start discussing *how* the author conveys his meaning without discussing the author's meaning in the first place? *You can't, and you shouldn't try.* The first question hiding out in every AP question: **"Hey, what does this poem or passage mean?"**

The AP essays never directly ask: "What does this poem or passage mean?" *But they all want you to answer that question.* Your first task is to get the author's meaning and say what that meaning is.

> **The classic essay question breaks down into two questions:**
> 1. What does the poem or passage mean?
> 2. How did the author get you to see that?

The first question is hidden, but totally important. It's the foundation on which you build the rest of your essay. Your (high-scoring!) essay answers those two questions in that order. The question ETS poses will only ask question 2 directly. (They feel question 1 is implied.)

If the first question is "What does the passage or poem mean?" Well . . . what does that mean? What is *meaning*?

THE MEANING OF *MEANING*

For the AP essays, the meaning of a work of prose or poetry is the most basic, flat, literal sense of what is said plus the *emotions and passions* behind that sense.

The passages and poems they ask you to write about on the AP English Literature and Composition Test will present some event or situation in the same way a newspaper article presents an event or a situation. But AP essay passages will, of course, do more than that. They will make the event or situation "come alive" by bringing in human emotions and passions in such a way that those emotions and passions are as important as the facts.

Let's consider a well-known story:

> **ATHENS DAILY NEWS**
> ## Scandal in Thebes!
> The Athens Daily News reports: Murder solved! Popular King Oedipus of Thebes has been revealed as both the son and murderer of the late King Laius. Photos and full coverage of this bizarre incident begin on page 3.

Think of how much will be lost by the newspaper version. Will they really let us know the degree of Oedipus's suffering, his sense of terrible, yet undeserved guilt? Of course not, but those emotions are parts of what the story means, and *the most important part of your essay.*

> **When we say the first question is, "What does the poem or passage mean?" We want you to answer two simple things:**
>
> *What is the basic literal sense of things?* (The newspaper version.)
> *What emotions are involved both for the characters in the story and for you, the reader?*
>
> The combination of those questions is the *meaning*.

AVOID SUMMARY

You must absolutely avoid talking about the newspaper version only. Doing that amounts to a summary. The ETS readers *do not want to read a summary of the passage*. Discuss the way emotions are involved in the story and focus on the feelings the language produces, and you'll be discussing meaning in the right way.

THE MODIFIED CLASSIC ESSAY QUESTION

Your AP exam may very well have the classic question on it almost word for word, but probably not. What you will probably see is a modified classic essay question. There is an endless number of modifications that ETS can throw at you, but they do nothing more than focus the subject of the second part of your writing. The beginning remains the same. You want to talk about what meaning you found in the poem or passage and then use that as a foundation to discuss the topic ETS has specifically asked for in the question.

Typically, instead of being asked about how the author conveys the overall meaning of the poem or passage, you're directed to a specific element of the poem or passage and asked, "How did the author convey his meaning about that element?" Let's look at an example. (P.S. You don't need the actual passage to understand our discussion of the question here.)

> Read the following passage carefully. Write a well-organized essay that discusses the interrelationship of humor, pity, and horror in the passage.

This seems like a simple enough question—until you try to answer it. How do you go about discussing the interrelationship of humor, pity, and horror? Most students start out something like this:

> "The story X by writer Z mixes humor pity and horror in an interesting way. It begins with a father meeting his son. The father seems like a funny guy because of things he does, but then we see that he is actually a person who arouses our pity because he goes to far, so far in fact that the father becomes almost horrible."

The student who writes this response knows he's basically flailing. He's just trying to answer the question without looking like someone who's insane or can't write in English. If the student uses reasonable examples, writes with some organization and only a few grammatical errors, then the student will get a five, a "limbo" score, not passing, not failing.

But the student who understands that this question is a modified form of the classic question and knows how to use the Idea Machine will break it down:

What does the passage mean? What was I supposed to get from it? What did I get from it? Okay, I got that the passage was about a father and son and that the son feels his father is basically embarrassing. Yeah, that sounds about right. Now, let's see, how does the author get that across using humor, pity, and horror?

Notice how this student has taken the question, turned it into the classic question, and simply used the modification to focus on the point to be developed. The student began by describing the meaning of the story. ("The son feels his father is basically embarrassing" is the meaning. Remember the meaning doesn't have to be a complicated or super-deep insight.) Then this student asked himself, *how does the author get that across using humor, pity, and horror?* This student's opening is going to look something like this:

> In story X, writer Z shows us a son confronted by the embarrassing spectacle of his father. By shifting the son's perspective of his father from humor, pity, and horror, we see and feel the son's fluctuating, uncertain responses to his father's vulgarity and ignorance.

This student is writing about something and it shows. She's on the way to a score of at least seven, and if the essay stays this clear and focused, it's going to be a score of nine. Do you see how slight an alteration has been made between this response and the one that came before it? Yet there's a world of difference. The first student rephrased the question without really saying anything, and then began to work his way through the points ticking them off . . . humor, then pity, then horror. The second student began by answering the implied question in every essay: *What does this story mean?* Then she began to show how the author brought that meaning across.

The best part is that the second essay is easier to write than the first one. It's easier to write an essay about something than nothing. Writing a bogus essay is like trying to wind up a ball of string with nothing to wrap it around. The second essay is going to wrap itself neatly around the core of the story's meaning—the son's uncertain embarrassment at his father's behavior.

NO FEAR!
Sometimes the questions can be fairly intimidating. But don't let them throw you. Remember to use the Idea Machine. **What does the passage mean? How does that meaning come across?**

Once you've got that under your belt you can think about how to focus on the points in the poem. Let's look at an example:

> Read the poem below carefully. Notice that the poem
> is divided into two stanzas, and that the second
> stanza reapplies much of the first stanza's imagery.
> Write a well-organized essay in which you discuss
> how the author's use of language, including his use of
> repetition, reflects the content and tone of the poem.

That's a hair-raising question, not because it's actually super-hard, but because it's so scary-looking it could mess with your confidence. Again, you should look at it and remember that, as always, *it's just a modified version of the classic essay question*. Your first task is to get at the author's meaning. **What does the author want you to get from the whole poem?** Once you've answered that for yourself, you can think about how the author got that across with repeated imagery. In fact, this question almost organizes itself once you look at it that way. Your first paragraph would say something about what you get from the whole poem. Your next paragraph would talk about the language of the first stanza and what it means. Then you would write about the second stanza and what it means. Your conclusion would look back at the poem and summarize what you said.

A GREAT START

The key to a great essay is a great start. The key to a great start is having an overall conception of what you're doing. We've shown you how to address the meaning (literal and emotional) of the poem right from the beginning, and that you then have to address the "how" of the author's method. Taken together, these things form your opening. They form the central *idea* around which you will write—the idea you will explain and support. If you're already a sharp, sensitive reader, following these instructions will lead you to high-scoring essays.

Sounds easy in principle. But are you ready? Let's go back to that tough, intimidating question we just looked at in the No Fear section with the poem that goes with it. We'll use our approach to come up with a good first paragraph for a high-scoring essay. Then we'll show you two powerful tools you can use to open up a passage and get the kinds of ideas that blow AP Readers away.

DYLAN THOMAS' "IN MY CRAFT OR SULLEN ART"

Read the poem below carefully. Notice that the poem is divided into two stanzas, and that the second stanza reapplies much of the first stanza's imagery. Write a well-organized essay in which you discuss how the author's use of language, including his use of repetition, reflects the content and tone of the poem.

In My Craft or Sullen Art

In my craft or sullen art
Exercised in the still night
When only the moon rages
And lovers lie abed
(5) With all their griefs in their arms,
I labor by singing light
Not for ambition or bread
Or the strut and trade of charms
On the ivory stages
(10) But for the common wages
Of their most secret heart.

Not for the proud man apart
From the raging moon I write
On these spindrift pages
(15) Nor for the towering dead
With their nightingales and psalms
But for the lovers, their arms
Round the griefs of the ages,
Who pay no praise or wages
(20) Nor heed my craft or art.

—Dylan Thomas

So, where do you begin? Well, before you begin to consider the repetition mentioned in the essay instructions, get the answers to the questions that let you write a classic essay. Use the Idea Machine.

What does the poem say, literally? That shouldn't be too tough to answer roughly, even if you don't know *exactly* what Dylan Thomas is trying to say. Put it in your own words. What does the poet say about his "craft or sullen art"? Take a moment to think about it, then read on.

You should have come up with something like this: "Dylan Thomas explains that he isn't writing for money or fame but for lovers, who don't even care about his writing."

Okay, now what is the feel of the poem? What emotions are conveyed? Is there an overall emotion? Again, think about it a moment before you read on.

It's a tougher question, isn't it? You probably went back to the poem to look at it again, thinking, "Just what emotion was I supposed to get? There's something there, but what?"

You might have picked up on a few things: pride, grief, loneliness, perhaps futility, and also perhaps the opposite of futility—a sense of total purpose. The poem has a truly complex emotionality to it. Don't let that scare you off; it only gives you more to write about.

What is the meaning of the poem for your AP essay? Take your literal sense and your emotional sense, and combine them:

> Dylan Thomas' "In My Craft of Sullen Art" explores the pride, grief, loneliness, futility and yet sense of total purpose that come from the author's struggle to write not for fame or for wealth but for "the lovers, their arms round the griefs of ages."

So far so good. But don't think we're finished. This is just the answer to question number one of the Idea Machine—what does the poem mean? If you're particularly astute, you may even notice that we haven't completely answered that question, we've only said what Thomas "explores." We haven't come out and taken a stand on exactly where Thomas's exploration has led him. Don't worry. You don't have to try to pin everything down all at once. If this were an assignment due at the end of the week you'd want to write a rough draft so that you could revise carefully later. Here on the AP test, you don't have the opportunity for careful revision. You don't have to write a perfect essay. The Readers don't expect you to, not even for a score of nine. Just stay with our method: What does the work mean, and how does the author achieve his effects?

So there's still the second part of our two-part approach to consider: How does the author achieve his effects? Perhaps in answering that question we can take more of a stand. How does Thomas bring his emotions into his sense of what writing means to him and (because the essay instructions demand we consider it) what does the repetition have to do with it?

How indeed? Thomas gets his message across in so compact a fashion you may feel a little lost and overwhelmed, you might want to say to the Reader, "He does it by, uh, writing the poem." Hey, remember you're just trying to write a 40-minute essay on a poem you've never seen before. The readers don't expect perfection or profound originality. They want to see you focus on saying *something*, and then they want you to say it as clearly as you can. In brief, they want to see you confidently develop your ideas as best you can.

Here's how we'd complete our opening statement and answer the question of how Thomas explores his sense of what, to him, it means to write:

> Dylan Thomas' "In My Craft or Sullen Art" explores the pride, grief, loneliness, futility and yet sense of total purpose that come from the author's struggle to write not for fame or for wealth but for "the lovers, their arms round the griefs of ages." Thomas gives us an image of himself, laboring alone "by singing light" and contrasts this with an image of self-contained completeness, of lovers wrapped in each other's arms, oblivious to all the world and even to his poetry. By repeating these images, and key words like "moon," "rage," and "grief," he emphasizes the power of his emotions and the intensity of his need to define himself and the purpose of his art.

This puts our essay off to a great start. Of course, you might have had different ideas and you undoubtedly would have phrased your ideas another way even if you saw exactly what we saw in the poem. You might even have written two or three better sentences—although you wouldn't have had to in order to score well. This brings up our next point.

DON'T WORRY ABOUT BEING WRONG

There are many other things you might have said about the Dylan Thomas poem. It all depends on what you got from it. Don't worry about interpreting a poem or passage badly. Any interpretation that isn't completely insane is fine. Really. The readers want to see you say something and develop it. They want to see how the literary work you've been asked to write about acted on your imagination and how well you've managed to convey those impressions you've received.

IMAGERY AND WORDS

Speaking of *imag*ination, notice what we've done in the "how" part of our opening paragraph about the Dylan Thomas poem. We've discussed imagery.

We chose to mention the contrasting images of the author working alone and of the lovers in their self-enclosed togetherness. You might have chosen something else. The point to remember is: *It's always a safe bet to talk about imagery.* The most important, most open-ended, most easily discussable aspect of a poem is almost always the imagery.

In writing (as opposed to cinema or theater or painting) an image is made of words. Is that obvious? Yes it is. But just because it's obvious doesn't mean all students pay attention to that important fact. On the AP essays your job is to discuss writing. Remember then, whenever you're discussing the imagery in a passage you're discussing words. If a word sticks out as unusual or particularly vivid, think about it. Ask yourself, why did the author use *just* that word? What effect does that word have? If you can think of something to say about the words an author has used to create an image and the specific effect those words have, by all means put it in your essay. You'll have the AP Readers eating out of your hand.

Notice that in our sample opening we zeroed in on the two most striking word choices in the poem. *Rage* and *grief*. It's odd (and poetic) to say lovers have their arms around their griefs. And when was the last time you saw the moon raging? A lot of students run from unusual language like that. They think the poet is just being a typical psychotic artist who can't really be understood, or that they'll misinterpret the phrase anyway and look dumb. But when you see unusual usages like that, consider them. Why that word? What does that word do to the feel of the piece? Thinking that way, you'll jog ideas loose and come up with the material that makes for great AP essays. Notice also that both *rage* and *grief* have strong emotional content. Writing about the emotional content is the best way to let the reader know you're really reading, and not enacting some dry, mechanical exercise.

OPPOSITION

If you've been following our discussion so far, you should see that we think you need to be able to get ideas from the text you're working with, so that you have ideas for your essay. Considering imagery and word choice is a good start, but there's one more concept we want you to think about as you read. This concept should really help you find the ideas that you need to write a great essay.

How can you get to the heart of what you read on the AP English Test? How can you find something interesting and important to say about a passage quickly? What do you look for to see what makes a passage or a poem "tick?"

The answer is *opposition*.

Attune your reading to seeing opposition and you'll open up AP passages like cans of sardines. You'll have something around which to center your discussion of the way an author uses language and imagery and tone to make her point.

Some people call opposition *conflict*, but we think that's too narrow a term. *Conflict* sounds like two people having a fight. Don't be crude. Be subtle. Be devious. Opposition is everywhere in good writing, and the passages on the AP test will always be good. Seek out opposition, count on it being there and look for it, because opposition leads you to the important parts of a passage or poem.

SO, WHAT'S OPPOSITION?

Opposition is any pair of elements that contrast sharply. Opposition might be as blatant as night and day. Or it might be less obvious: a character who's naive and a character who's sophisticated. Opposition might be found in a story that begins with a scene in a parlor but ends with a scene around a campfire, which would be the opposition of indoors and outdoors. It would be easy to miss if you weren't looking for it. Opposition can often be found between the author's style and his subject. For example, a cerebral, intellectual style that's heavy on analysis in a story about a hog farmer would be opposition; your essay would want to address why the author wrote that way, and what effect it has on the story. Keep an eye out for any elements that are in contrast to each other: they'll often lead you to the heart of the story.

Let's look at that Dylan Thomas poem again. Notice what we went after in our opening paragraph: the image of the author working alone, and the image of lovers in each other's arms. That's an opposition. Do you see it's not exactly a conflict? It's a pairing of images whereby each becomes more striking and informative when placed against the other. Doesn't that pair of images seem central to the poem? Doesn't it seem there's something to talk about there? What exactly it means is open to interpretation, and that's exactly what you should do when you see elements opposed to each other: *interpret*. Don't worry about getting it right; there is no single right answer. The AP reader will see that your searching intelligence has found the complexity of the material and is making sense of it. That's exactly what the reader wants you to do. (And it's what very few students know to do.)

Opposition creates tension and mystery. What's the most mysterious line in "In my Craft or Sullen Art"? We think it's, "And the lovers lie abed/With all their griefs in their arms." That line alone has an opposition: if they're lovers, why do they have their griefs in their arms?

So your job is to figure out what Thomas means by that. The answer is: Nothing simple, but something you can write about. Realize that you don't have to resolve opposition. You don't have to interpret that line (or the poem) in a final way that makes absolute perfect sense. It's a poem, not a riddle.

Our opening paragraph mentioned a third opposition: Thomas's sense of futility, and his sense of total purpose. The sense of futility in the poem comes from the statements that the lovers "pay no praise or wages", nor do they heed Thomas's "craft or art." Describing how Thomas gets across his deep sense of purpose is more difficult, even though it is the stronger of the two impressions. In many ways the entire poem is about conveying the sense of purpose Thomas feels when writing poetry. An AP essay won't get to them all; it shouldn't try to. But you can be sure we'll mention that repetition plays a part.

We found these things because we looked for the oppositions. Some oppositions are obvious—like a frog in a bus station—they catch your attention immediately and make you wonder what's going on. Good writers toss boldly mismatched things together all the time. But good writers also work with quiet oppositions that aren't nearly so easy to spot. If you aren't paying attention you'll feel what's going on without realizing where it's coming from. Many literary oppositions come from within one character. The character who wants two totally opposite things at the same time is a classic case of opposition, as is the character who badly wants something that he just isn't cut out for. Another important opposition is *tone*. Some writers will write about the silliest thing possible in a deadly serious way. (This is generally done to make a situation funnier.) Still another opposition, one that is often handled with supreme delicacy and with seemingly infinite repercussions, is *time*. Writers will often let the past stand in opposition to present. The story of a once proud family that has fallen on hard times is an example of a plot that uses the changes time brings to develop oppositions.

We could come up with hundreds of specific examples of oppositions in literature, but those examples won't do you any good if you haven't read the works referred to. Our point here is to give you a tool with which to generate ideas for your AP essays.

You're probably still a little unclear as to how to apply this concept of oppositions to a short AP essay, but don't worry. The samples and examples in chapter 9 will take you through several AP passages and point out how you might use oppositions to find ideas (and boost your essay scores into the eights and nines).

AFTER THE FIRST PARAGRAPH—DO AN ESSAY CHECK

Look back at our overall approach to the essay section and you'll see that the second to last point is the recommendation to do an essay check. That sounds fancy, but all it means is that you should think, briefly, about the points you need to make in your essay.

The time to do this thinking is after you've written that first paragraph. The first paragraph comes from using the Idea Machine: discussing the meaning of the passage or poem (remember, the newspaper version plus emotion) and beginning to talk about how the author gets her point across. This gives you a first paragraph that establishes the foundation the rest of your essay will build on. If it's hyperfocused, it will already set out the overall points you intend to cover, but even if it just gives you a general platform on which to build you've got plenty, enough to put you miles ahead of the majority of other (flailing) students. The essay check is just a spot check, a place to pause and make sure you're on the right track and haven't forgotten anything important. When you've finished your first paragraph stop and ask yourself:

—What points does my first paragraph indicate I'm going to cover?
—Do those points address the specifics the essay question calls for?
—What order am I going to put my points in?

When you've decided what order to put your points in, get back to writing. It shouldn't take more than a minute. The least important part of the check is deciding what order to put your points in. It's the closest thing to an outline you need to do, and don't overdo it. As long as you've paused to think about addressing the question it makes sense to form a rough plan of how you'll proceed. But the idea is to make it easier for you to write, not to suffocate your writing. Be flexible. If it's convenient to change the order of your points as you write, change them. If you think of new things to say, say them.

DON'T CRAMP YOUR STYLE

As you write, you'll notice things that you hadn't seen at first. These are things that will depart from your original ideas and take you in unexpected directions. Should you include these things? **YES!**

Many, many students are intimidated by the test. They think their writing has to be truly organized and tight. These students end up writing crabbed-up, short, dry, little essays. Essays that receive a score of five. Go with the flow. It is impossible to write a tight, well-organized essay in 40 minutes—*impossible*. As long as your ideas have some faint connection to the question ETS has asked, include them. Write a great first paragraph that sets you out in the right direction and then loosen up—you'll score high.

DEVELOPING YOUR ESSAY

Once you've finished your first paragraph and your essay check, it's time to develop your essay. Because when it comes to development, each essay is unique. The best way to study development is through examples. The next chapter is devoted to sample essays; we'll show you how to put our method (and your ideas) into practice.

SUMMARY

- If you can get off to a good start, you're more than halfway to a great score.

- Use our approach
  —Note the time. Remember, 40 minutes per essay.
  —Start with either the poetry or the prose passage. Save the open essay for last.
  —Skim the passage.
  —Read the passage carefully. This should take about five minutes.
  —Use the Idea Machine to create your first paragraph. This should take between five and ten minutes.
  —After you've written your first paragraph, do an Essay Check.
  —Support and develop the points you made in your first paragraph. You should have roughly 25 minutes left to complete your essay.

- Don't write an outline

- **Use the Idea Machine:**
  —What is the meaning of the work?
    Meaning is literal meaning plus the emotions the work evokes.
  —How does the author get that meaning across?
    important images
    specific words or short phrases
    opposition

- The Idea Machine is the tool that helps you to apply your skills specifically to a 40 minute essay.

- Any student who can write a five-scoring essay can write a seven-scoring essay or better.

- Understand the question and how to turn the question into an *essay idea*.

- There is a single, classic essay question that ETS uses time after time:

    > Read the following work carefully. Then write a well-organized essay in which you discuss the ways by which the author conveys her meaning. Be sure to consider such literary elements as diction, imagery, structure, and point of view.

- The AP essay questions never directly asks what the poem or passage means. *But they all want you to answer that question.*

- You probably won't see the classic question word for word; you'll see a modified version that asks you to focus on a specific element or two from the passage.
- Don't worry about being wrong. Any interpretation that isn't completely insane is a good one.
- Unusual language and imagery is a great place to find essay ideas.
- *Opposition* is created when any pair of elements in a story or poem contrast sharply or subtly.
- Look for elements that are in opposition. They'll lead you to the heart of the passage and give you material for the kinds of ideas that make AP Readers give out nines.
- Go with the flow. It is impossible to write a tight, well-organized essay in 40 minutes. Write a great first paragraph that sets you out in the right direction, and then loosen up.

9

Sample Prose and Poetry Essays

Here's a poem you've seen before, this time with an essay question. Read the question and the poem and think about how you might write a response.

SAMPLE ESSAY ON POETRY — ROBERT BROWNING'S "MY LAST DUCHESS"

ESSAY — (SUGGESTED TIME — 40 MINUTES)

Read the following poem carefully, and then write a well-organized essay in which you discuss the author's use of language to convey his themes. As you read and interpret the poem, keep in mind the following background information: The poem is in the form of a monologue delivered by the Duke of Ferrara, who is negotiating the dowry arrangements of his pending betrothal to a count's daughter.

The Duke's previous wife, his "last duchess," has died recently under mysterious circumstances. The implication is that she was murdered at the Duke's bidding.

My Last Duchess

FERRARA:

That's my last duchess painted on the wall,
Looking as if she were alive. I call
That piece a wonder, now: Frà Pandolf's hands
Worked busily a day, and there she stands.
Will't please you sit and look at her? I said
"Frà Pandolf" by design, for never read
Strangers like you that pictured countenance,
The depth and passion of its earnest glance,
But to myself they turned (since none puts by
The curtain I have drawn for you, but I)
And seemed as they would ask me, if they durst,
How such a glance came there; so, not the first
Are you to turn and ask thus. Sir, 'twas not
Her husband's presence only, called that spot
Of joy into the Duchess' cheek: perhaps
Frà Pandolf chanced to say, "Her mantle laps
"Over my lady's wrist too much," or "Paint
"Must never hope to reproduce the faint
"Half-flush that dies along her throat": such stuff
Was courtesy, she thought, and cause enough
For calling up that spot of joy. She had
A heart—how shall I say?—too soon made glad,
Too easily impressed; she liked whate'er
She looked on, and her looks went everywhere.
Sir, 'twas all one! My favor at her breast,
The dropping of the daylight in the West,
The bough of cherries some officious fool
Broke in the orchard for her, the white mule
She rode with round the terrace—all and each
Would draw from her alike the approving speech,
Or blush, at least. She thanked men—good! but thanked
Somehow—I know not how—as if she ranked
My gift of a nine-hundred-years-old name
With anybody's gift. Who'd stoop to blame
This sort of trifling? Even had you skill
In speech—which I have not—to make your will
Quite clear to such an one, and say, "Just this
"Or that in you disgusts me; here you miss,
"Or there exceed the mark"—and if she let
Herself be lessoned so, nor plainly set
Her wits to yours, forsooth, and made excuse,
—E'en then would be some stooping; and I choose

> Never to stoop. Oh sir, she smiled, no doubt,
> Whene'er I passed her; but who passed without
> Much the same smile? This grew; I gave commands;
> Then all smiles stopped together. There she stands
> As if alive. Will't please you rise? We'll meet
> The company below, then. I repeat,
> The Count your master's known munificence
> Is ample warrant that no just pretense
> Of mine for dowry will be disallowed;
> Though his fair daughter's self, as I avowed
> At starting, is my object. Nay, we'll go
> Together down, sir. Notice Neptune, though,
> Taming a sea-horse, thought a rarity,
> Which Claus of Innsbrück cast in bronze for me!

DISCUSSION

This poem should look familiar; we've asked you to read it once before. We hope that between that first time and this time, you've developed your AP test reading skills.

There is a great deal to say about this work; it is one of the most famous and most studied poems of the nineteenth century. The point here is to figure out what *you* might have to say about this poem in order to write an essay that answers the question ETS has given you. Let's use the Idea Machine, the simple orderly process that you should apply to every AP essay.

First, tackle the question. It is the classic AP essay question. That makes our lives a little easier; the Idea Machine will work perfectly here.

> What's the literal meaning of the poem?

Here's a quick summary of what you should have in your mind after reading the poem: The Duke of Ferrara talks to his visitor and shows his visitor the portrait of his "last duchess." He describes the strange look of pleasure the portraitist has captured. This leads Ferrara to discuss how annoying he found his former wife. She was too easily pleased. All sorts of things made her happy. Ferrara disliked the joy she received from other people and the simple things in her life. He felt this showed she did not truly appreciate the honor of being his wife. Because he could never descend so low as to discuss his displeasure, "he gave orders" and "all smiles stopped together." Then he discusses his upcoming marriage. He expects a good dowry. The monologue ends with his changing the subject and pointing out another work of art he owns.

Before we go on, notice how fundamentally boring the preceding paragraph is. It's a summary. When the AP question instructions tell you to avoid summary, this is what they mean. And regardless of whether the question tells you explicitly to avoid summary or not, avoid it. Nothing looks more commonplace or mechanical than a simple retelling of the passage. Stretch out that summary paragraph above a few more lines, quote a line or two from the poem, and you have the essay that many students write. It would receive a maximum score of four. Let's continue with the Idea Machine:

> What feelings do you get from the poem?
>
> What do you think the author is trying to inspire in the reader?
>
> What is the overall effect of the poem?

Hmm. This one is isn't so easy. Ferrara is extremely creepy. Something awful has happened. But what does it mean? Is the point just to show us a scary man? That sounds pretty lame. (By the way, if to you the poem seemed a terrifying portrait of a repellent, cold-hearted, arrogant, murderous snake of a Duke, that's the essay you would write. There's plenty to support it. If it were well-written, you would score an eight.)

Only for a nine do you need to go any deeper—but why not write nine-scoring essays if you can? Let's see, Ferrara feels evil. That sounds better: evil is a more interesting concept than simple terror. What's more, Ferrara is a particular kind of evil. He is cold-hearted, arrogant, and utterly self-righteous. He probably doesn't even think of himself as evil. In fact, you can be sure he thinks himself a great man. That's interesting, too. Ferrara thinks he's great but he's not. Hmm.

Any other feelings? Other emotional reactions? Well, what about the Duchess? Don't you feel sorry for her? She sounds like a pleasant, happy creature. She probably never knew what terrible trouble she was in. She rode a white mule around the castle, smiling . . . how was she to know the Duke would have her killed for smiling so much? See, we're getting something here.

Now let's get to the second part of the Idea Machine—how does the author get the meaning across? To do that, let's consider imagery and oppositions, see if we can refine things, and create that great first paragraph.

The most colorful imagery in the poem has to do with the Duchess (the "spot of joy" upon her check, the "faint half-flush that dies along her throat"). Then there are all the images of things that made the Duchess happy: the favor, the sunset, a bough of cherries, and the white mule.

Oppositions? We could really go crazy here; the oppositions are everywhere. But they aren't obvious, so you need to make a point of looking for them. Did you notice any when you read the poem? If not, go back to the poem now and take another look. Ask, "what elements are contrasted against each other?"

Foremost and central to the whole poem is the opposition of the Duchess and the Duke. How could two people be more different? She is happy, innocent, and full of blushing life and joy. When was the last time Ferrara blushed? Has he ever? He's so bloodless that he can admit to having the Duchess killed ("I gave commands;\Then all smiles stopped together") and a few seconds later talk about getting married again, and then point out, "Oh yes, isn't that a lovely bronze sculpture there in the niche on the stairs." This guy has no soul!

Finding the central opposition can lead you to the other contrasts and details that percolate below the surface of the poem and give it its power. The Duchess is dead, "yet looking as if alive." The Duke is alive, but by failing to appreciate his Duchess, and by failing to appreciate anything but his own glorious self, he seems a walking dead man. Notice how the entire poem takes place indoors. Maybe it's just us, but we see the hushed interior of a Northern Italian castle with cold and damp rising from the stone floors, dark tapestries and heavy curtains, and an aura of solemn grandeur. Where do these images come from? They come from completing the contrast with the Duchess. Notice how the images the poem gives of the Duchess are outdoorsy and natural: the cherry bough, the sunset, and the white mule. The Duchess is natural, light, and warm. The Duke, her opposite, must just as surely be solemn and cold. The Duchess loves life and people, but notice Ferrara's love of dead things, of objects and of "his 900-years old name"; indeed, although the living Duchess disgusted Ferrara, he admires her portrait. Notice too Ferrara's sudden enthusiasm for the sea-horse bronze. Control stirs Ferrara's feelings, self-control above all, but also the control over nature an artist shows in capturing life in dead materials, in oil-paint or bronze.

When you first read the poem, did you wonder about the final image, the bronze of Neptune and the sea-horse? It jumps out and seems important, ending the poem. Does it make more sense now? The Duke sees himself as Neptune taming a sea-horse. He thinks of himself as a god of enormous power taming the wild, strange, and beautiful creatures of nature, like the Duchess. Of course the reality is that the Duke is just a man, in fact more like a selfish child, narrow-minded and vain, whose power is merely ownership and who destroys what he cannot control. The final image is actually an ironic one.

We came to all these things by thinking about the imagery in the poem and by looking for oppositions. But, hey, we also had all the time we needed and we've had some practice at this kind of thing before. So . . .

RELAX

Are you supposed to get all this in one or two readings with the test-gun pointed at your temple and two more essays to write before you can go home? Of course not. We wanted to show you how much there is to unearth in a typical AP passage or poem, and how much our techniques can dig up for you. All you'd need to see about this poem on the actual test is that the opposition of the Duke and Duchess is at the heart of the poem. If you saw that, and looked for the ways Browning got it across, you'd find enough to write a great essay.

A GREAT BEGINNING

You should be ready to formulate your opening. Here's an example:

> "My Last Duchess," even the title is chilling isn't it? "My last Duchess," as though this human being were disposable, replaceable, not really a human being at all but an object. And of course that is all that remains of the Duchess, an object: her portrait.

Is this good writing? No. It won't win any prizes, that's for sure. But for the AP English Literature Test, it's well on its way to a score of nine—an *easy* nine. Anything close to this will blow your reader away. Let's take it apart for a moment, and then we'll finish the essay.

The beginning paragraph is a first stab at talking about meaning. We wanted to start with something more original than, "In 'My Last Duchess' by Robert Browning . . . ." Starting that way is okay, and if the rest of your essay is good you'll score high, but the readers like to see you try something a little more daring, so we tried. We connected the title to a feeling—the overall feeling of the poem—and it seemed to work. We connected the image of the portrait to the idea that the Duchess is just an object. This justifies our effort at an original beginning. The reader would be impressed that you so quickly arrived at a main (but by no means obvious) point of the passage.

Unfortunately, we ran out of steam before we could satisfy the overall goal of our beginning: to get at the meaning of the poem (literal and emotional), and explain how Browning gets it across.

KEEP GOING

No problem, we'll just start a new paragraph and go for it again. Even though we're starting another paragraph, in reality we're still working on our opening. If it takes two or three short paragraphs to lay the foundation of your essay, fine.

Since our first little introductory paragraph began with such originality, we can begin our second paragraph, "Browning's poem," without fear of seeming dull or mechanical. We'll start describing (*not summarizing*) what Browning's poem is and what it does: It's a portrait, a double portrait (whenever you can show that an author does two things at once, you're good to go). We can't stop there though. We've got to say what it's a portrait *of*. We might have said any number of things: a portrait of an evil man, or a portrait of an unhappy marriage. We decided to stick with the central contrast of opposites: the poem is a portrait of the Duke created by talking about the Duchess. Great—again we're talking about two things at once.

> Browning's poem itself is a portrait, a double portrait. Ferrara, through discussing the remarkabley life-like painting of his wife paints a picture in words not only of his wife, but of himself. Its as though he is every thing his wife is not. Browning lets Ferrara talk and everything that Ferrara says about his wife and her portriat tells us something about him as well.

Great—now let's do an essay check. Is our opening complete? No. We still haven't said enough about how Browning shaped the poem, and we haven't addressed our specific intention of writing about Browning's language. We need to commit ourselves to a statement about how Browning shapes imagery. What comes next is the most "mechanical" part of our opening, but it's necessary and will launch us into the rest of the essay:

> Through this one-sided dialog (for really Ferrara seems to be talking not so much to his listener as to the past and the Duchess and himself) and through his careful control of the Duke's language and imagery Browning gives us a picture of a man driven to destroy what he could not control.

There. We've said something. We've sketched the meaning of the poem and said that through controlling the Duke's language, Browning shows us a man who destroys what he cannot control. It's a fantastic start. Now it's time to check again, (yep, we got our great start!) and pause briefly to consider what points we'll make, and how we'll address the specifics of the ETS question.

AND GOING

What's left? Let's see, it looks like we're pretty thin on specifics, particularly concerning the controlled language part of the question. We should support that with examples from the passage. Good examples from the passage are key. We said there's no checklist the readers use, but if there is one thing they all look for, it's good examples from the passage. Looking over our beginning, it seems we've *talked* about Browning's use of language and structure, but we haven't *shown* it. So that's our job now: to support what we've said with good examples. That's our plan.

Hey, what about the misspellings and grammatical errors in our opening? Aren't they going to lower the essay score? No. In fact, the writing above is clean by AP standards. The readers expect mistakes and are forgiving of those you do make. *Notice that the first two sentences do not contain any obvious errors*. Remember to take care to start out with two clean initial sentences. Make no mistakes in the first two sentences and you establish to your reader that you can write under ordinary circumstances; the readers understand that the test is not an ordinary circumstance.

Forgiving does have its limits, though: prolly you willn't score so good and high ritin like this way on you're Apey test.

Here's the rest of our essay:

> What was it the Duke could not control? His wifes smiles. This is the first thing that Ferrara point out in the portrait: "the depth and passion of her earnest glance," the "spot of joy on her throat," and above all her smiles, the smiles she gave to everyone: "Who passed without much the same smile?" These smiles drove the Duke to cold Fury. and to murder— "all smiles stopped together." Why? Because the smiles were common, given to everyone. Ferrara couldn't stand that "the gift of his nine-hundred hears old name" alone" did not control and command his wife. It's wonderful how Browning paints this portrait of this sinister man through discussing his wife. Imagine, the examples Ferrar gives of his wife's faults! They look like qualitites to any normal person. She delights in a "bough of cherries" some fool broke off for her. "The daylight dropping in the West"

and "The white mule she rode with round the terraces"—what delightful simple pleasures. What a quick portrait of a natural happy young girl" and how quickly it shows us the darkness and solitude of Ferrara, with his curtained portraits. Browning shows that he has one this battle. The poor innocent Duchess has been frozen into a picture of herself. The sneering Duke has captured her and stopped her smiles. But it also seems the Duke has missed the point of living.

That's the essay's finish. Pretty awful, huh? But with the first paragraph it would be given a nine, the top score. Why?

First, as we said, the AP Readers are forgiving of some mistakes. The opening of the essay lets the readers know that the grammatical errors of the second half were the result of working under time pressure, and not the result of not knowing how to write. Second, the essay continues to make good points. It talks about the language and imagery of the poem and uses well chosen examples to support its points about the language and imagery. We went on a writing-roll about the smile. We probably overdid it. So what? It's an insight into the poem; that makes it worth saying. The readers want to see your ideas. By making those insights clear and obvious to the reader, you make it easy for the reader to give you a high score.

Is this a well-organized essay? Not by classroom standards, but by AP standards it is. The essay begins with a clear direction, first discussing the overall impact of the poem, and then saying that this impact derived from Browning's controlled use of language to portray the Duchess and the Duke. The rest of the essay, in a slightly scattered fashion, provided examples of the contrasting images that Browning created. For a first draft in just 40 minutes top to bottom, the essay is admirable, and as we said before, a nine.

In fact, here's a piece of happy news: Browning's poem is at the difficult end of the spectrum of work you'll see on the AP test. You may see a poem as challenging as "My Last Duchess," but certainly nothing harder. And keep in mind that what you find difficult, everyone else finds difficult as well.

SAMPLE ESSAY ON PROSE—FROM MALCOLM LOWRY'S *ULTRAMARINE*

Let's look at another sample. If you've got paper and pencil handy, try the question below and time yourself. At the very least, before you go to our sample essays (we've written two sample responses to this passage, one great and one fair) think about your first paragraph and try writing it in your head. But you really should practice writing a whole essay, timed.

ESSAY—(SUGGESTED TIME—40 MINUTES)

Read the passage below carefully. Write a well-organized essay that discusses the author's use of the resources of language to dramatize the speaker's experiences of life at sea as well as to dramatize the character of that speaker.

The passage is drawn from the novel *Ultramarine* by Malcolm Lowry. The novel concerns the story of an educated, English, upper-class, nineteen year-old boy, who for the sake of experience takes a job as deck-hand upon a tramp-steamer bound for Asia. The passage is one of several interior monologues the boy, Dana Hilliot, engages in as he thinks of the girlfriend, Janet, he has left back in England.

Puella mea[1] . . . No, not you, not even my supervisor would recognise me as I sit here upon the number six hatch drinking ship's coffee. Driven out and compelled to be chaste. The whole deep blue day is before me. The breakfast dishes must be washed up: the forecastle and the latrines must be cleaned and scrubbed—the alleyway too—the brasswork must be polished. For this is what sea life is like now—a domestic servant on a treadmill in hell! Labourers, navvies, scalers rather than sailors. The firemen[2] are the real boys, and I've heard it said there's not much they can't do that the seamen can. The sea! God, what it may suggest to you! Perhaps you think of a deep gray sailing ship lying over in the seas, with the hail hurling over her: or a bluenose skipper who chewed glass so that he could spit blood, who could sew a man up alive in a sack and throw him overboard, still groaning! Well, those were the ancient violences, the old heroic days of holystones; and they have gone you say. But the sea is none the less the sea. Man scatters even farther and farther the footsteps of exile. It is ever the path to some strange land, some magic land of faery, which has its extraordinary and unearthly reward for us after the storms of ocean. But it is not only the nature of our work which has changed, Janet. Instead of being called out on deck at all hours to shorten sail, we have to rig derricks, or to paint the smokestack: the only thing we have in common with Dauber, besides dungarees, is that we still "mix red lead in many a bouilli[3] tin." We batter the rusty scales off the deck with a carpenter's maul until the skin peels off our hands like the rust off the deck . . . . Ah well, but this life has compensations, the days of joy even when the work is most brutalising. At sea, at this time, when the forecastle doesn't need scrubbing, there is a drowsy calm there during the time we may spend between being roused from our bunks and turning out on deck. Someone throws himself on the floor, another munches a rasher; hear how Horsey's limbs crack in a last sleepy stretch! But when bells have gone on the bridge and we stand by the paintlocker, the blood streams red and cheerful in the fresh morning breeze, and I feel almost joyful with my chipping hammer and scraper. They will follow me like friends, throughout the endless day. Cleats are knocked out, booms, hatches, and tarpaulins pulled away by brisk hands, and we go down the ladder deep into the hold's night, clamber up along the boat's side, where plank ends bristle, then we sit down and turn to wildly! Hammers clap nimbly

1 My girl, (Latin).
2 The men that tend the steam engines and boilers of the ship.
3 bouillion

against the iron, the hold quivers, howls, crashes, the speed increases: our scrapers flash and become lightening in our hands. The rust spurts out from the side in a hail of sharp flakes, always right in front of our eyes, and we rave, but on on! Then all at once the pace slackens, and the avalanche of hewing becomes a firm, measured beat, of an even deliberate force, the arm swings like a rocking machine, and our fist loosens its grip on the slim haft—

And so I sit, chipping, dreaming of you Janet, until the iron facing shows, or until eight bells go, or until the bosun comes and knocks us off. Oh, Janet, I do love you so. But let us have no nonsense about it.

DISCUSSION

Did you practice writing the essay on this passage? Did you time yourself? If so, great; if not, we hope you at least read the passage carefully and thought about how you would go about writing your first paragraph.

Oddly enough, writing about prose can actually be more difficult than writing about poetry. Poetry often presents many difficulties to the reader, difficulties caused by the density and complexity of poetic language. Those same difficulties, once interpreted, give you material to write about.

Prose, however, presents the opposite problem. In general, assimilating the passage is not much of a problem, finding something worth saying presents more of one.

As always, start out with the classic question and let the Idea Machine guide your thinking process. Of course, make sure that you allow the actual ETS question to focus the development of your essay, and also note the time so that you don't go overboard and come up short on the last essay.

Below you'll find two responses to the passage. One is excellent, and one is mediocre. We'll discuss both responses after the samples are given. By the way, in these two essays we've taken out the annoying errors of diction and spelling that creep into every student's essay. We want you to read the essays for what they say and how they say it without distracting errors. The sentence construction reflects student writing, but in reality, both essays would have more language mistakes.

SAMPLE RESPONSE TO *ULTRAMARINE*—ESSAY 1

In the passage, Malcolm Lowry effectively uses the resources of language to create an interior monologue (a mental speech) to dramatize the adventures a young English boy has aboard a ship, and shows the character of the boy, Dana Hilliot, as well. He uses vivid imagery and many details from the boy's life to show who Hilliot is and what he thinks, and captures the different rhythms of life aboard a ship.

First Hilliot thinks that no one, "not even my supervisor would recognise me . . ." This shows that Hilliot thinks that he has changed and that life at sea has changed him. But he's happy, he likes the change, as he says, "The whole deep blue day is before me." But there are many conflicting feelings in Hilliot as he sits and drinks his coffee. For he quickly screams out, "this is what sea life is like now—a domestic servant on a treadmill in hell!" This shows the conflict that Hilliot undergoes. He doesn't know whether he thinks life at sea is great or a stinking hell. Lowry shows this by switching all the time between images that are pleasant, and images that are full of misery and despair and heartbreak. He really misses Janet and it shows. A sailor's life is lonely, and Lowry shows that. Lonely and boring sometimes, as hard as that may be to believe. But the boredom is broken up by danger and hardship. "We batter the rusty scales of the deck with a carpenter's maul until the skin peels off our hands like the rust off the deck . . ." is an example of the hardship. But immediately, the conflict shows up again. The very next sentence is, "Ah well, but this life has compensations, the days of joy even when the work is most brutalising."

Through it all though, Hilliot thinks of Janet. He begins thinking of her "Puella mea . . . ." which is Latin for "my girl" and ends saying "Oh, Janet, I do love you so." This tells us a great deal about Hilliot. He misses his girlfriend and is probably homesick for England too. These are normal reactions for the character of a young Englishman far from home, and by framing the story between these statements Lowry shows that the character of Dana Hilliot hasn't changed as much as he thinks it has. Hilliot is still a lonely young man with a great deal to learn.

SAMPLE RESPONSE TO *ULTRAMARINE*—ESSAY 2

Who hasn't dreamed of throwing everything away and running off to sea? And yet very few people actually do run off to sea, probably because, at least in part, they realized (around the time they're packing all those wool sweaters into a duffle bag) that life at sea isn't just dropping anchor at exotic ports and gazing at the moon setting over the Indian Ocean. It's a hard, dangerous life. Better unpack the sweaters.

The passage shows the inner thoughts of one young man who actually did run off, and as he sits and thinks of the life he's leading and the life he's left behind, we get a picture of what a young sailor's life is really like. We get something else as well, a detailed portrait of a young, confused man, Dana Hilliot, and all the swirling emotions that he carries in his young heart. Hilliot is lonely, defiant, excited, bored, romantic, and cynical all at once.

The passage begins, "Puella mea . . ." Although that's Latin for "my girl," the translation isn't so important as the fact that it's Latin. Right from the beginning, Lowry shows us a fish out of water. Dana's educated, but how many of Dana's shipmates speak Latin? Probably none. Dana talks about how unrecognizable he's become. Maybe he really is unrecognizable to his old friends, but it's more likely that he can't recognize himself. He's gotten more than he bargained for, "this is what sea life is like now—a domestic servant on a treadmill in hell!" This is one of the recurring themes of the passage. Hard, dull, work. Polishing brass. Chipping paint. Scrubbing and cleaning. It isn't a very romantic scenario. This theme tells us not just about sea-life, but about Dana. He must have been pretty naïve to not know that a sailor works from daybreak into the night, and it's all manual labor.

Lowry gives us a picture of the wild, terrifying, intense life that Dana thought he was going to lead. He describes it to his girlfriend, to correct her and tell her the truth, but you can be sure that these were Dana's ideas of life at sea before he came to the ship. "Perhaps you think of a deep gray sailing ship lying over in the seas, with the hail hurling over her: or a bluenose skipper who chewed glass so that he could spit blood . . . ." Well, Dana has learned that it isn't anything like that at all. His romantic dreams have been squashed, all except the sea. He still finds poetry in the sea. It is "ever the path to some strange land, some magic land of faery. . . ." This is the beauty that Dana really got on board for.

The passage then takes us even deeper into Dana's character. In the beginning, he talked about how horrible it was to be just a lackey, scrubbing decks. As he thinks deeper though, we see a real change in him. He loves the moments of calm, and is such a sensitive experiencer of the life around him that he even notes the way one of his fellows' joints crack, but the amazing thing is that he's learned to love the work. He describes it with relish, "I feel almost joyful with my chipping hammer and scraper. They will follow me like friends . . . . The rust spurts out from the side in a hail of sharp flakes, always right in front of our eyes, and we rave, but on on!" The work, the hard relentless work, is the real adventure, and in those words "on on!" you can hear almost hear Dana's amazement at the fact that he can do it, he can keep going on.

In the end Dana's loneliness, cut off from his familiar life, returns him to being a moody "Romeo," dreaming of his girlfriend, imagining sweet-talking her. It wells up in him with the line, "Oh, Janet, I do love you so." But then comes the very last line of the passage, another abrupt change, "But let us have no nonsense about it." He's still a young person, pouring out his love to his girlfriend but then a second later he's pretending to be a tough guy, a sailor, who wants "no nonsense." By putting these lines, one after the other, Lowry shows Dana in the midst of growing up, and pretending to be more hardened than he is.

DISCUSSION OF SAMPLE RESPONSES 1 AND 2

It shouldn't be too difficult to tell which of these is the better of the two responses. Essay 1 is clearly an average response. It shows an intelligent student struggling to write a response about a passage he didn't get much from. Notice the mechanical repetition of the question, and the mechanical, plodding way he works through the passage, not so much interpreting it as summarizing. He did manage to address the question somewhat, and did pull together a few simple insights into the passage. He would receive a score of five. Not a terrible score by any means, but you can do better.

The biggest mistake the author of the first essay made was to choose to emphasize the life-at-sea aspect of the question. Unless an author is just setting the stage for what is to come, or planting some enormous symbol, almost every sentence in a novel or a story is intended to reveal character. This is especially true of the kind of masterful writers you'll be dealing with on the AP exam. When you read prose on the AP test always *ask yourself what the sentences tell you about the people* in the passage. In the Lowry passage, everything Dana thinks tells us something about Dana. The first student missed most of the psychological details of the passage and ended up floundering.

The author of the second essay worked with the Idea Machine. She asked herself about both the literal and emotional content of the passage. She kept an eye out for strong imagery and evidence of opposites. In doing so she saw that the passage was filled with conflicting images. Dana loves Janet, but then wants "no nonsense." Dana thinks the work is beneath him ("domestic servant"—Dana's the kind of kid who's used to having servants, not being one) and makes his shipboard life hell, but at the same time he realizes that when he's lost in the physical frenzy of the labor, he finds the work exhilarating. The author of the second essay tried to put these oppositions together in a meaningful way. Most important, she knew to focus on character. By tying everything back to Dana's character she assured herself of a high score. In fact, the second essay would be scored a nine. The top score.

Also notice that the second passage does not begin with the typical restatement of the question. That doesn't mean that a reader would look at essay 2's beginning and think, "Oh my, what an original opening—this essay gets a high score." A nice opening isn't enough. You still have to write the essay.

But, the reader would think, "Hmm, this kid isn't writing like a robot . . . now if she can show me she understood the passage and communicate her understanding with anything like the flair of this opening, I'll give her a high score." In other words, yes, your opening can be a little stiff and dull (yes, you can paraphrase the question if you want to) if you write an otherwise good, insightful essay, but an original, interesting opening is the icing on a cake. If the cake tastes terrible the pretty decorations don't help; but if the cake's tasty then marvelous icing makes it seem even better. So if you can write an interesting opening without wasting a lot of time, by all means do so.

SUMMARY

- Avoid summary.
- Get a feel of the passage.
- Notice imagery.
- Notice oppositions.
- Your essay doesn't have to be great. An AP essay that scores a nine might not even be an A paper in English class. Of course not. It's a 40-minute essay on a story or poem you've never seen before.
- Whenever possible, show your verbal flare.
- If your first paragraph runs out of steam don't worry about it. Start a new paragraph and try again. Keep writing.
- Your first two sentences should be free of error, but nobody writes an error-free paper. That doesn't mean be careless and sloppy. It means write as well as you can and don't worry about mistakes.
- If the question gives you the opportunity, write about character. The writing in AP passages almost always says something about character. This is especially true when a character speaks, or in a first-person narration.
- A nice opening is icing on the cake.

10
THE OPEN ESSAY

HOW DO YOU PREPARE FOR AN ESSAY ON *ANYTHING*?

The open essay is usually the last of the three essays on the AP test. Unlike the prose or poetry essays, the open essay does not give you a text to work with; you must write an essay on a given theme provided using support drawn from your own reading.

The open essay is generally considered the most difficult of the three essays. This is false; the open essay scores break down the way the prose and poetry essays break down. Most students' scores are bunched up at the middle, with a small percentage of scores at the upper and lower ends of the scale. All the same, the open essay is the most dreaded and anticipated portion of the AP exam. It isn't worth any more than the other questions, but unlike the rest of the test, the open essay question feels like the one you *have to* study for. At the same time it's the question that most students feel like they *haven't* studied for, at least not enough, not as much as the kid next to them.

We hope we've proven that you can and should study for the rest of the test. We hope we've shown you that knowing what you're doing on the essay section is *the way* to shoot your scores through the roof. Now, what about the open essay—how do you prepare for it?

The answer is simple. Use all the techniques we've already described for writing the prose and poetry essays. Use the Idea Machine to direct your thoughts and answer the classic question as you go about answering the specifics of the ETS question. The open essay is no different from the other essays. There's just one more bit of preparation you need: *two well-chosen works of literature that you know backward and forward.*

WHAT ETS REALLY WANTS FROM YOUR OPEN ESSAY

You can, should, and *must* prepare a work for the open essay. But what if the open essay question asks for a theme that the work you've prepared doesn't address? Don't worry. ETS isn't trying to persecute you. (Although it does feel that way sometimes.) Follow our instructions and you'll be prepared.

What ETS would really like to do is say, "Write an essay about any literary work that you enjoyed. We just want to see how well you can write on a longer work that you've read and studied." Unfortunately, they can't ask you that directly because there would be no way to stop students from writing essays ahead of time (or having dear Aunt Toni, the Pulitzer prize-winning novelist, write an essay ahead of time) and memorizing them. The open essay question is just a way of making sure that the student hasn't prepared the whole essay in advance.

However, ETS has nightmares about asking open essay questions that are too restricted. They won't ask a question that points to just a handful of literary works, for example. They won't ask for an essay about "a character who may or may not be insane and who sees ghosts that may or may not be there." A few hundred students would get nines by writing about Henry James' *The Turn of The Screw*. A few thousand would struggle to make this question make sense for *Hamlet* or *Macbeth*. The rest would just stare at their hands and cry.

ETS goes out of its way to make sure the open essay question is truly open and provides an opportunity for a student who has read challenging literary works to write a good essay.

Let's look at the kinds of themes the open essay question asks for.

SAMPLE THEMES FOR THE OPEN ESSAY

- Discuss the function of a character who does not appear or appears only briefly in a novel or play, and yet is a significant presence in the work.

- Discuss the function of a character who serves as the main character's sympathetic listener, or confidant(e).

- Discuss a scene or character that provokes "thoughtful laughter."

- Discuss a novel or play in which much of the "action" occurs internally, within the consciousness of a character or characters in the work.

- Discuss the use of contrasting settings in a novel or play.

- Discuss parent-child conflict in a novel or play.

As you can see, these themes are broad, and any one of them can be applied to thousands of literary works. At the same time, these themes are specific enough that you couldn't just go ahead and write an essay ahead of time, as not every work applies to each theme equally well. The key to a great open essay is having the right work for the theme, and knowing it cold.

So what works should you study?

PREPARING FOR THE OPEN ESSAY

To be really ready for the open essay, you should know at least two works truly well. At least one should be a longer work that you've studied in class. We'll call this the *primary* work. The second work is a safeguard. We'll provide you with a list of short *secondary* works which are useful for the AP test.

THE PRIMARY WORK

Have a primary work which you know well.

Your primary work should be fairly hefty. One of Shakespeare's plays or a thick complex novel will do. The full-length works of the following authors are all good choices: Jane Austen, Emily or Charlotte Brontë, Charles Dickens, Thomas Hardy, George Elliot, Fyodor Dostoyevsky, and Thomas Mann. The object in choosing your primary work is to come up with a novel or play so rich in incident and form that no matter what the open essay question asks, you have something to say.

CHOOSE A WORK YOU ALREADY KNOW (AND LOVE)

You've already studied some literary works in school. Pick one (or maybe two) and go over your notes. Read the book again, or at least spend a few hours looking it over thoroughly. Pick your favorite work, the one you liked best. If you fell in love with Shakespeare's *Hamlet*, great, use *Hamlet*. If you felt sleepy every time the word Shakespeare was mentioned but thought Dostoyevsky's *Crime and Punishment* might change your life, then that's the work to use.

There are just a couple of exceptions to the favorite work rule. Do not pick a short story or poem. The ETS open essay questions, as a rule, say, "Choose a play or a novel: Do not choose a poem or short story." There have been very few exceptions to this rule, and the exception is that they'll allow epic (that is, long) poetry. Now, if your favorite work of literature is really-honestly-no-kidding-I-loved-it Milton's *Paradise Lost* or Spenser's *The Faerie Queene* . . . well, okay, you can prepare those novel-length poems for the open essay, but you'd still be better off with a novel. (In fact, if those are your favorites you're doomed to become an English professor anyway. Don't even try to fight it. In fact, better tell your parents now so they can get used to the idea.) Short stories are wonderful to read but useless for the AP exam. ETS just won't let you use them. They don't want students preparing to write essays on short stories; they think it's too easy.

If you don't have a usable favorite work, or are for any reason undecided about what to choose for your primary work, we highly recommend Shakespeare's plays, particularly *Hamlet*, *A Midsummer Night's Dream*, *King Lear*, and *The Tempest*. All of these plays are intricately plotted, all contain elements of comedy and tragedy, and all are incredibly rich in the kind of material about which open essays are written. The object in choosing your primary work is to find a work which can support any number of questions, and Shakespeare's works fit that bill better than any others of comparable length. As tough as Shakespeare's plays can be to read, they are considerably shorter than say, *Crime and Punishment* or *David Copperfield*. If you decide to go with Shakespeare you could easily prepare to write about two plays in the time it takes to prepare a longer novel. Just remember, we said we *recommend* Shakespeare. If you already know the work of another writer better, by all means prepare something else. But remember that we strongly recommend using a book you've already studied in class.

SUGGESTIONS FOR PRIMARY WORKS
Here are some other books we think make for good primary works. But hey, this list is not even close to complete! If you happen to know and love another long work inside and out—that's fine.

Emma by Jane Austen
Jane Eyre by Charlotte Brontë
Wuthering Heights by Emily Brontë
Don Quixote by Miguel Cervantes
Bleak House by Charles Dickens
David Copperfield by Charles Dickens
Great Expectations by Charles Dickens
A Tale of Two Cities by Charles Dickens
Crime and Punishment by Fyodor Dostoyevsky
Invisible Man by Ralph Ellison
The Sound and the Fury by William Faulkner
Tess of the D'Urbervilles by Thomas Hardy
The Scarlet Letter by Nathaniel Hawthorne
Their Eyes Were Watching God by Zora Neale Hurston
Sons and Lovers by D. H. Lawrence
The Magic Mountain by Thomas Mann
One Hundred Years of Solitude by Gabriel Garcia Marquez
Moby Dick by Herman Melville
The Catcher in the Rye by J.D. Salinger
The Grapes of Wrath by John Steinbeck
Of Mice and Men by John Steinbeck
Anna Karenina by Leo Tolstoy
The Adventures of Huckleberry Finn by Mark Twain

THE SECONDARY WORK
The secondary work is your just-in-case work, and perhaps a bit more. The question may just not fit any aspect of your primary work. You need to have something prepared for that situation. You don't want to be stuck trying to remember some book you haven't looked at since ninth grade. The other reason to prepare a secondary work is simply to have more options. If the question fits your secondary work perfectly you'll want to use it. Prepare your secondary work well, and, in effect, you have two primary works. With well-chosen and well-prepared primary and secondary works you would have to be extremely unlucky to find yourself faced with an open essay question that did not fit either work.

CHOOSE SOMETHING DIFFERENT FROM YOUR PRIMARY WORK
Ideally, you want your secondary work to be as different as possible from your primary work. If you pick *Hamlet* as your primary work, you don't want to pick another Shakespearean tragedy starring a messed-up, confused, violent hero. In other words, don't pick *Macbeth*. You'd be much better off picking a comedy such as *A Midsummer Night's Dream*. Even better would be to pick a twentieth century comic novel like *Catch-22* or *The Great Gatsby* (which, although not a comedy, has

many comic touches). If you pick an extremely male-oriented work for your primary work, say *Moby Dick* (are there *any* women in *Moby Dick*?), then Kate Chopin's *The Awakening* makes an excellent choice for a secondary work, as would Henry James' *The Turn of the Screw*, both of which feature female main characters.

SUGGESTIONS FOR SECONDARY WORKS

We've put together a list of secondary work books. These are all short novels, novellas, and plays which are acceptable to the AP Readers. Some works are not acceptable. Writing about Star Trek episode 19 will result in a low score, as will writing about a Danielle Steele or a Stephen King novel. Don't push it. You may think William Gibson's *Neuromancer* is a great book. The AP committee probably won't be impressed, and they'll downgrade your score.

The books on the list below were chosen according to the following guidelines: They're all recognized classics that the AP Readers will highly approve of. They're all short. Most importantly, they're all works that have been perfect fits with many open essay questions.

We strongly recommend studying at least one of the works listed below. If you've read one of these works in class (and there's a good chance you have), by all means look it over and prepare it for the AP exam. An * means that the work is most highly recommended reading for the exam. Those asterisked items are the AP open essay superstars. Pick one and you won't go wrong.

Finally, if you really don't feel comfortable with any of the longer works that you studied in class, or if you're thinking of taking the AP exam without having taken an AP course, or if you, well, slacked off in class—don't try to prepare a longer work for the AP exam. Go straight to the list below and knock off two or three or four titles (remember, these are short works). You'll be prepared.

Novellas and Short Novels:

The Awakening by Kate Chopin*

Heart of Darkness by Joseph Conrad*

Notes from the Underground by Fyodor Dostoyevsky

The Great Gatsby by F. Scott Fitzgerald*

The Old Man and the Sea by Ernest Hemingway

The Turn of the Screw by Henry James*

Death in Venice by Thomas Mann

Ballad of the Sad Café by Carson McCullers

A Sentimental Journey by Lawrence Sterne

The Death of Ivan Ilyich by Leo Tolstoy

Candide by Voltaire

Plays:

Waiting for Godot by Samuel Beckett

A Man for All Seasons by Robert Bolt

The Cherry Orchard by Anton Chekhov

The Seagull by Anton Chekhov

Uncle Vanya by Anton Chekhov

Medea by Euripides*

A Doll's House by Henrik Ibsen*

Hedda Gabler by Henrik Ibsen*
The Crucible by Arthur Miller
Death of a Salesman by Arthur Miller
Emperor Jones by Eugene O'Neill
Hughie by Eugene O'Neill
Long Day's Journey Into Night by Eugene O'Neill
Antigone by Sophocles*
Oedipus Rex by Sophocles*
A Streetcar Named Desire by Tennessee Williams
The Glass Menagerie by Tennessee Williams

WHAT DOES PREPARE THE WORK MEAN?

We keep telling you to *prepare* your primary and secondary works. What does this mean? It means two things:

- Study the work as thoroughly as you can.
- Write a first paragraph based on the classic question for each work you prepare.

STUDYING YOUR PRIMARY AND SECONDARY WORKS

Study the works you've chosen. You can't do too much.

The bare-minimum preparation would be to review the works the night before the test, making sure you know the main characters' names and the plot lines. That's truly minimal though; you ought to do more.

- **Reread your primary and secondary works within four weeks of the test.** You want to have each one fresh in your mind.
- **Work from critical editions.** The books you should prepare for the AP test are the kinds of works that have been studied and restudied over the years. Because of this, while you can easily find your chosen texts in small inexpensive reading editions, you can also find them in larger, critical editions that contain full introductions, notes, and sometimes appendices containing background material, biographical information, and samplings of past critical commentary. Whenever possible use these fuller editions. Read as much of the supplementary material as you can stand (we hope you'll find it fascinating, of course). No AP reader is going to downgrade your essay because the points you make about *Moby Dick* seem influenced by the opinions of D.H. Lawrence and Charles Olson. On the contrary, they'll think you're a genius. One student in a thousand actually bothers to read literary criticism about the book she prepares, but here's hoping you're that one in a thousand.

To sum it up again: **Know as much as you can about the works you prepare.** Of course, you've got other things going on in your life; just do as much as you can. Pick books you honestly like: The studying you do will be interesting and rewarding and will seem less like work.

WRITE THE FIRST PARAGRAPH OF THE OPEN ESSAY AHEAD OF TIME

The second part of preparing your works for the open essay is writing the first paragraph to your open essay a couple of nights before the test. How sick and crazy are we? How much work do we expect you to do for one silly essay on one test? Hey, we're talking about maybe 30 minutes, max. Skip one *Gilligan's Island* rerun and you're finished.

Sometime before the test, you should practice beginning an AP essay. The open question is your best place to practice. Ask yourself the classic question, "What literary devices (imagery, tone, point of view, plot, etc.) does the author use to convey his themes?" Answer the question using the Idea Machine. What did the work mean? What was the emotional content of the work? How was all that achieved? Because you're dealing with a longer, complicated work, the answers here will take some deep thought. How do you summarize the impact (not the story, not the blow by blow plot) of *Hamlet* or *David Copperfield* in just one paragraph? Well, you won't know how until you try, and practicing is great discipline for the AP test. You won't actually use your open essay first paragraph on the actual test, so don't try to memorize it. You will find that having done this, you'll cruise when it comes time to write for the test because you'll know just how to go about answering the question.

SUMMARY

- When writing the open essay use all the techniques we've already described for writing the prose and poetry essays.

- Don't worry about having to face an open question that doesn't apply to the works you've prepared. ETS tries to make its open essay questions broad enough that you won't be lost . . . as long as you have *something* prepared.

- Prepare a primary and a secondary work.

- If you've studied Shakespeare in class (and enjoyed it), we strongly recommend using a Shakespeare play as your primary work. His plays are chock full of the material open essays use.

- Choose a work that you've already studied in class.

- Have at least one secondary work.

- Our list of secondary works suggests novellas and plays that have proven useful on many AP open essays in the past.

- Your secondary work should be as different as possible from your primary work. For example, if your primary work is a Shakespearean tragedy, pick a modern comic novella for your secondary work.

- Stick with accepted classics for your primary and secondary works.

- If possible, reread your primary and secondary works within four weeks of the test. Otherwise, at least skim the book and look over any class notes you have. (Use critical editions if you can find them.)

- Write a sample first paragraph of the open essay ahead of time. It's great practice.

11

A Tiny Grammar Review with Sample Questions

HOW MUCH GRAMMAR DO YOU NEED TO KNOW FOR THE AP TEST?

There are usually three or four questions on basic grammar. That's one grammar question or fewer per passage, so grammar is not a big deal on the multiple-choice section. The samples we provide in chapters 5 and 6 should give you a good idea of what the grammar questions are like, especially the question on the poetry passage. Because there are so few grammar questions, we don't recommend you spend a lot of time studying grammar. You'd be far better off working on writing timed essays or reading some difficult poetry.

MASTER SENTENCE I

Here's a great simple sentence to memorize for basic grammatical relations:

Sam threw the orange to Irene.

Okay, it isn't poetry, but this sentence clearly shows the basic grammatical relationships you need to concern yourself with on the AP test.

- *Sam* is the subject.
- *The orange* is the direct object.
- *Irene* is the indirect object.

Notice that in this sentence, the direct object is in fact an object (an orange). The orange is thrown to Irene, the indirect object. In other words, the indirect object receives the direct object. It's pretty simple.

MASTER SENTENCE II

There are two more sentence elements you should understand: the phrase and the clause. Here's a model sentence that should help you keep clear on their definitions.

Feeling generous, Sam threw the orange to Irene, who tried to catch it.

The heart of the sentence is still *Sam threw the orange to Irene*. Subject, verb, direct object, and indirect object all remain the same. But we've added a phrase to the beginning of the sentence, and a dependent (also called *subordinate*) clause to the end. Both phrases and dependent clauses function as modifiers. *Feeling generous*, a phrase, modifies *Sam*; *who tried to catch it*, a clause, modifies *Irene*.

The difference between clauses and phrases is simple:

> A clause has both a subject and a verb.
>
> A phrase does not have both a subject and a verb.

Because a clause has both a subject and verb, a clause is always close to being a sentence of its own. The dependent clause, *who tried to catch it*, could be turned into a complete sentence by replacing *who* with *Irene* or *she*.

The hallmark of a phrase is its lack of a subject or verb (or both). Phrases obviously cannot stand alone. *Feeling generous* needs the addition of both a subject, *Sam*, and a verb, *was*, in order to become the sentence *Sam was feeling generous*.

Our model sentence contains another clause besides the dependent clause we've already mentioned. The other clause is *Sam threw the orange to Irene*. Since it has both a subject and a verb it must be a clause. Notice that it doesn't need any changes in order to stand alone as a complete sentence: that makes it an *independent* clause.

GLOSSARY OF BASIC PARTS OF SPEECH

You also need to know the basic parts of speech. The last time you studied this was probably sometime in sixth grade. We're not trying to be insulting, but we've provided a review just in case you're rusty:

Noun A person, place, or thing (or an abstraction—for example, *strength* and *determination* are nouns).

Verb An action.

Adjective A word that modifies a noun.

Adverb A word that modifies a verb, an adjective, or another adverb. In the phrase *the profoundly nasty little poodle*, *nasty* and *little* are adjectives, but *profoundly* is an adverb, as it modifies the adjective *nasty*.

Preposition Words such as *of*, *by*, *to*, *in*, and *from*.

Prepositional phrase A phrase that begins with a preposition and which serves to modify another sentence element, usually another noun. In the sentence, *Sue ate a piece of pie*, the prepositional phrase *of pie* modifies the noun *piece*.

Pronoun A word such as *he*, *she*, *it*, or *them*, which replaces a noun.

Antecedent The word that precedes a pronoun and to which the pronoun refers. (In the sentence *The profoundly nasty little poodle snapped viciously at Francine's ankles but she managed to kick it away*, the pronoun *it* takes as an antecedent the word *poodle*.)

AND NOW THE BAD NEWS

You probably think that you're sure to answer all the grammar questions on the test correctly, since this stuff is a piece of cake.

Actually the *grammar* part is easy, but the *questions* aren't.

The reason we don't think you should bother studying much grammar for the AP test (unless the stuff you read above is totally new to you) is that ETS uses grammar as just another way to test reading comprehension. The grammar is seldom the hard part. ETS likes to ask grammar questions about tangled up sentences which, if you didn't quite get what you were reading, you'll have trouble with despite knowing darn well what nouns, modifiers, or clauses are).

SAMPLE GRAMMAR QUESTIONS

Try these for hideous, but excellent, practice. They're harder than real AP questions, but not by much.

```
        Nature's most secret steps
        He like her shadow has pursued, wher'er
        The red volcano overcanopies
        Its fields of snow and pinnacles of ice
Line
 (5)    With burning smoke, or where bitumen lakes
        On black bare pointed islets ever beat
        With sluggish surge, or where the secret caves
        Rugged and dark, winding among the springs

        Of fire and poison, inaccessible
(10)    To avarice or pride, their starry domes
        Of diamond and of gold expand above
        Numberless and immeasurable halls,

        Frequent with crystal column, and clear shrines
        Of pearl, and thrones radiant with chyrsolite.
```

1. The subject of the sentence above is

    (A) Nature's (line 1)
    (B) steps (line 1)
    (C) He (line 2)
    (D) volcano (line 3)
    (E) caves (line 7)

The answer is (C). Believe it or not, pull all the fancy window dressing off of this rococo verse and you get the sentence *He has pursued her*. Or, slightly more accurately, *He has pursued her (Nature's) most secret steps in the vicinity of the following places: volcanoes, secret caves, and bitumen lakes*. Nasty, eh?

Try this one:

> There's a certain Slant of light,
> Winter Afternoons—
> That oppresses, like the Heft
> Of Cathedral Tunes—
>
> *Line*
> *(5)* Heavenly Hurt, it gives us—
> We can find no scar,
> But internal difference,
> Where the meanings, are—
>
> None may teach it—Any—
> *(10)* 'Tis the Seal Despair—
> An imperial affliction
> Sent us of the Air—
>
> When it comes, the Landscape listens—
> Shadows—hold their breath—
> *(15)* When it goes, 'tis like the Distance
> On the look of Death—

2. In line 5, *it* refers to

    (A) cathedral tunes
    (B) love
    (C) slant
    (D) despair
    (E) God

The correct answer is (C). Asking what a pronoun refers to is an ETS favorite. The *slant of light* is the antecedent. Do you see that this isn't so much a question of grammatical analysis as it is a comprehension question? If you thought, *it* refers to *light*, and were confused when you didn't see *light* among the answer choices, realize that the prepositional phrase *of light* modifies *slant*.

SUMMARY

- Don't sweat grammar for the AP English Test. It isn't worth many points.
- Grammar questions on the AP English Test are usually disguised comprehension questions, that is, the grammar part of the question isn't terribly difficult, but comprehending the sentence well enough to answer the question is.
- Know the terms *antecedent* and *subject of the sentence*.

Part IV

The Princeton Review AP English Literature and Composition Practice Test 1

ENGLISH LITERATURE AND COMPOSITION

SECTION I

Time—1 hour

Directions: This section consists of passages drawn from literary works and questions about those passages' style, form, and content. Read each prose selection or poem carefully and choose the best answer to each of the subsequent questions on the passage. Remember to completely darken the corresponding oval on your answer sheet. (Also, be sure to take extra care on those questions that contain the words NOT, LEAST, or EXCEPT.)

Questions 1–15. Choose your answers to questions 1–15 based on a careful reading of the following passage.

Of Seeming Wise

It hath been an opinion, that the French are wiser than they seem, and the Spaniards seem wiser than they are. But howsoever it be between nations,
Line certainly it is so between man and man. For as the
(5) Apostle saith of godliness, Having a show of godliness, but denying the power thereof; so certainly there are, in point of wisdom and sufficiently, that do nothing or little very solemnly. It is a ridiculous thing, and fit for a satire to persons of judgment, to see what
(10) shifts these formalists have, and what prospectives to make superficies to seem body, that hath depth and bulk. Some are so close and reserved, as they will not show their wares, but by a dark light; and seem always to keep back somewhat; and when they know
(15) within themselves, they speak of that they do not well know, would nevertheless seem to others, to know of that which they may not well speak. Some help themselves with countenance and gesture, and are wise by signs; as Cicero saith of Piso, that when he
(20) answered him he fetched one of his brows up to his forehead, and bent the other down to his chin. Some think to bear it by speaking a great word, and being peremptory; and go on, and take by admittance, that which they cannot make good. Some, whatsoever is
(25) beyond their reach, will seem to despise, or make light of it, as impertinent or curious; and so would have their ignorance seem judgment. Some are never without a difference, and commonly by amusing men with a subtilty, blanch the matter. Generally, such men
(30) in all deliberations find ease to be of the negative side, and affect a credit to object and foretell difficulties; for when propositions are denied, there is an end of them; but if they be allowed, it requireth a new work; which false point of wisdom is the bane of business. To
(35) conclude, there is no decaying merchant, or inward beggar, hath so many tricks to uphold the credit of their wealth, as these empty persons have, to maintain the credit of their sufficiency. Seeming wise men may make shift to get opinion; but let no man choose them
(40) for employment; for certainly you were better take for business, a man somewhat absurd, than over-formal.

1. The overall point of the passage is that
   (A) some people habitually pretend to possess knowledge that they do not have, and such people should be avoided
   (B) at some point everyone pretends to possess knowledge; this pretension is ridiculous, but forgivable
   (C) if one learns the signs, one can spot those that pretend to have wisdom they do not actually possess; this is a valuable skill because those that seem to be wise are often the least wise of people
   (D) only fools pretend to have wisdom they do not actually possess
   (E) people that are overly concerned with dressing, behaving, and speaking formally are worse than absurd

2. In the third sentence of the passage (lines 3–5) the author
   (A) compares godliness and wisdom in order to emphasize the importance of the former
   (B) avows that faith is more important than simple wisdom
   (C) asserts the existence of those who know less than they seem to through an analogy to those who seem to be faithful but are not
   (D) suggests that a solemn but false indication of possessing knowledge is as evil as seeming to be religiously faithful without having true belief
   (E) proposes that just as some make no outward show of piety but are inwardly faithful, some make no show of wisdom but are actually very wise

GO ON TO THE NEXT PAGE

3. By "formalists" the author means

    (A) people overly concerned with proper manners
    (B) people whose concern with their physical appearance makes them humorously vain
    (C) an English religious sect of the sixteenth century that followed a strictly formal code of behavior
    (D) a philosophical school that accords reality to the outer form of people, things, and ideas
    (E) those people who make a deliberate show of certain characteristic behaviors without feeling the motivation those appearances imply

4. The term "dark light" is an example of

    (A) onomatopoeia
    (B) apostrophe
    (C) oxymoron
    (D) zeugma
    (E) hyperbole

5. Which of the following is an example of being "wise by signs," as indicated in line 19?

    (A) Understanding things only when they are pointed out to one directly
    (B) Agreeing with what one does not understand
    (C) Disagreeing with a superficial point in a larger argument
    (D) Making facial expressions indicative of deep thought
    (E) Speaking in such a way as to seem learned

6. In the sentence beginning in line 21, "Some think to bear it" the author discusses

    (A) those who vehemently object to points that in reality they understand poorly, if at all
    (B) those who adopt a dismissive air to points they do not actually possess the knowledge to judge
    (C) those who use erudite vocabulary in order to disguise their lack of knowledge
    (D) those who pretend to be weighed down with such heavy thoughts that they can respond only in monosyllables
    (E) those who quickly change the subject when points they don't understand are discussed

7. Lines 29–34 suggest that one of the motives of those who seem to be wise is

    (A) intellectual laziness
    (B) vanity
    (C) stupidity
    (D) a desire to please
    (E) stubbornness

8. Which of the following best describes the structure of the passage?

    (A) A general proposition is made, specific historical examples are investigated in detail, and the proposition is then summarized and reaffirmed in a conclusion in the form of advice.
    (B) An analogy is made between nations and men. The analogy is supported by specific examples and then reaffirmed in the conclusion.
    (C) An assertion is made. Logical arguments for the assertion's validity are presented. The truth of the assertion is reaffirmed.
    (D) A generalization is offered. The generalization is refined until a specific point is determined which is then supported by somewhat contradictory examples. The conclusion then restates the original generalization in the form of advice.
    (E) An assertion is made for the existence of a type. The characteristics of the type are presented in a series of generalized examples. In conclusion, the type is summarized.

GO ON TO THE NEXT PAGE

9. Which of the following approaches to debate does the author maintain is most often shared by those who would seem wise?

   (A) Nit-picking at the details of an otherwise sound argument
   (B) Saying very little with a facial expression that suggests deep thought
   (C) Feigning a lack of interest that suggests the point at hand is too obvious for comment
   (D) Agreeing as though in perfect confidence to points one doesn't understand
   (E) Disagreeing with what one doesn't understand in order to forestall any further intellectual challenge

10. Which one of the following adjectives best characterizes the passage?

    (A) Satirical
    (B) Pedantic
    (C) Contemptuous
    (D) Farcical
    (E) Introspective

11. It can be inferred from the passage that the author intended at least in part to write for

    (A) university academics interested in learned discourse
    (B) people seeking advice on practical concerns
    (C) those who at times displayed the characteristics of the seeming wise
    (D) the amusement of the aristocracy
    (E) fellow writers that might study the author's style and literary method

12. In line 23, those who "take by admittance, that which they cannot make good"

    (A) confess to slight misunderstandings in order to disguise their complete ignorance
    (B) gain entry into areas where they do not belong
    (C) let others endow them with what they do not possess
    (D) take pains to agree with incorrect statements in order to render the discussion meaningless
    (E) allow others to agree with statements they know to be false

13. In the passage the author makes a comparison between

    (A) those who truly possess knowledge and those who lack it
    (B) the faithful and the wise
    (C) those who are overly polite and those who lack knowledge
    (D) those who disguise their lack of money and those who disguise their lack of knowledge
    (E) those who are vain despite their ridiculous garments and those who pretend to possess knowledge despite being entirely ignorant

14. As used in line 13, "as they will not show their wares" is an example of

    (A) double entendre
    (B) antithesis
    (C) aphorism
    (D) metaphor
    (E) synaesthesia

15. The passage contains elements of

    I. Didacticism
    II. Humorous irony
    III. Metaphysical speculation

    (A) I only
    (B) II only
    (C) III only
    (D) I and II
    (E) I, II, and III

Questions 16–29. Choose your answers to each of the following questions based on careful reading of the following poem by Christina Rossetti.

Passing away, saith the World, passing away:
Chances, beauty and youth sapped day by day:
Thy life never continueth in one stay.
Line Is the eye waxen dim, is the dark hair changing to gray
(5) That hath won neither laurel nor bay?
I shall clothe myself in Spring and bud in May:
Thou, root stricken, shalt not rebuild thy decay
On my bosom for aye.
Then I answered: Yea.

(10) Passing away, saith my Soul, passing away:
With its burden of fear and hope, or labor and play;
Hearken what the past doth witness and say:
Rust in thy gold, a moth is in thine array,
A canker is in thy bud, thy leaf must decay.
(15) At midnight, at cockcrow, at morning, one certain day
Lo the bridegroom shall come and shall not delay:
Watch thou and pray.
Then I answered: Yea.

Passing away, saith my God, passing away:
(20) Winter passeth after the long delay:
New grapes on the vine, new figs on the tender spray,
Turtle calleth turtle in Heaven's May.
Tho' I tarry, wait for Me, trust Me, watch and pray.
Arise, come away, night is past and lo it is day,
(25) My love, My sister, My spouse, thou shalt hear Me say.
Then I answered: Yea.

16. How many "speakers" does the poem directly present?

   (A) one
   (B) two
   (C) three
   (D) four
   (E) five

17. "Laurel" and "bay" are allusions to

   (A) flowers highly prized for their rarity which bloom briefly and beautifully and then die
   (B) spices which add flavor to food and, metaphorically, to life
   (C) leaves traditionally woven into wreaths to honor poets
   (D) traditional symbols for Homer and Ovid respectively
   (E) traditional symbols for true faith and pious conduct respectively

18. Lines 6–7 suggest that

   (A) the principal narrator is faced with a choice between the afterlife that true faith offers, or the physical corruption that awaits the unbeliever
   (B) although the World has regenerative powers, the principal narrator of the poem does not
   (C) paradoxically, life can sometimes emerge from death
   (D) there is a natural cyclical pattern of renewal that the principal narrator has forsaken
   (E) the principal narrator is gravely ill and certain to die before the spring

19. Which of the following lines contains an image NOT echoed closely elsewhere in the poem?

   (A) Line 6
   (B) Line 7
   (C) Line 13
   (D) Line 14
   (E) Line 21

20. Which of the following choices best characterizes the speaker's attitude in each of the poem's three stanzas respectively?

   (A) Realization of death's inevitability; fear of physical decay; passive acceptance of what cannot be escaped
   (B) Nostalgia for the earthly world that must be left behind; fear of physical decay; welcome acceptance of the afterlife
   (C) Realization that death will come before one's ambitions have been achieved; dismay over the visible signs of physical decay; supplication for the healing powers of divine intervention
   (D) Sorrow and mild surprise at the arrival of early death; deepening awareness of death's certainty; hopefulness for a place in the afterlife
   (E) Acknowledgment of death's inevitability; understanding of the need to prepare oneself; gladness at the prospect of union with the divine

GO ON TO THE NEXT PAGE

21. In the context of the poem "A moth is in thine array" (line 13) is intended to imply that
    (A) the narrator's attire is being eaten by moths
    (B) the narrator's body is being consumed by cancer, or a cancer-like disease
    (C) the narrator's soul contains a destructive element which, unless the narrator takes some action, will render it unworthy of the afterlife
    (D) the narrator's soul is corrupted with sin that only death can purge
    (E) the narrator's body is being gradually destroyed by the silent and natural processes of life

22. Taken together lines 7 and 8 provide an example of
    (A) apostrophe
    (B) doggerel
    (C) enjambment
    (D) mixed metaphor
    (E) simile

23. In the third stanza "winter" can be taken to represent:
    (A) long disease
    (B) earthly life
    (C) the coldness of the grave
    (D) spiritual despair
    (E) aging and loss of vigor

24. Which of the following statements most accurately characterizes the relationship of the imagery in the third stanza to that of the first and second stanzas?
    (A) The third stanza weaves together the wedding-day imagery of the second stanza and the springtime imagery of the first stanza thereby reconciling those earlier stanzas' differing views.
    (B) Through its imagery the third stanza further develops the themes which had been advanced by the first stanza and questioned by the second stanza.
    (C) The third stanza echoes much of the first two stanza's imagery, but recasts that imagery so that what earlier had been likened to decay is instead characterized as renewal.
    (D) By echoing the imagery of the earlier stanzas the third stanza reaffirms and repeats the views advanced by those stanzas.
    (E) By introducing the terms "love" and "sister" the third stanza continues the progression by which each stanza proposes its own unique central metaphor around which to further the poem's exploration of the themes of death and renewal.

25. Lines 15 and 16 suggest that
    (A) the principal narrator's final hour will come, despite the small uncertainty of knowing exactly what hour that will be
    (B) the bridegroom mentioned in line 16 will arrive at three distinct times
    (C) the hour when a deadly illness first infects the principal narrator cannot be avoided
    (D) a mysterious and evil stranger will arrive at some time between midnight and morning
    (E) the principal narrator's soul prophesies that she will eventually meet the man who will become her beloved husband

GO ON TO THE NEXT PAGE

26. In context, the word spray (line 21) most nearly means

    (A) tree
    (B) blanket
    (C) a small branch
    (D) a liquid mist
    (E) a holy spirit

27. The grammatical subject of the sentence that begins at line 24 is

    (A) "Arise"
    (B) "night is past and lo it is day,"
    (C) "My love, My sister, My spouse,"
    (D) "thou"
    (E) "Me"

28. The poet Tennyson disliked the sound created by the overuse of sibilants in a line, or several lines, of verse. On those grounds, which of the following lines would Tennyson have been most likely to object?

    (A) Line 10
    (B) Line 11
    (C) Line 14
    (D) Line 15
    (E) Line 17

29. In Line 25 the word thou is

    (A) a once-standard usage of the informal second-person singular
    (B) a once-standard usage of the formal second-person singular
    (C) a once-standard usage of the informal third-person singular
    (D) a once-standard usage of the formal third-person singular
    (E) an idiomatic usage of the formal second-person singular particular to the English of the King James Bible

GO ON TO THE NEXT PAGE

Questions 30–40. Choose answers to questions 30-40 based on a careful reading of the passage below. The selection in part discusses Romantic poet John Keats' "Ode on a Grecian Urn," particularly that poem's famous closing lines: "Beauty is truth, truth beauty,—that is all/Ye know on earth, and all ye need to know." The blank in line 30 represents the omission of a word which will be the subject of a later question.

The question of real importance is not whether Eliot, Murry, and Garrod are right in thinking that "Beauty is truth, truth beauty" injures the poem. The question of real importance concerns beauty and truth (5) in a much more general way: What is the relation of the beauty (the goodness, the perfection) of a poem to the truth or falsity of what it seems to assert? It is a question which has particularly vexed our own generation to give it I. A. Richards's phrasing, "it is the (10) problem of belief."

The "Ode," by its bold equation of beauty and truth, raises this question in its sharpest form—the more so when it becomes apparent that the poem itself is obviously intended to be a parable, on the nature of (15) poetry, and of art in general. The "Ode" has apparently been an enigmatic parable, to be sure: one can emphasize beauty is truth and throw Keats into the pure-art camp, the usual procedure. But it is only fair to point out that one could stress truth is beauty, (20) and argue with the Marxist critics of the 'thirties for a propaganda art. The very ambiguity of the statement, "Beauty is truth, truth beauty" ought to warn us against insisting very much on the statement in isolation, and to drive us back to a consideration of the (25) context in which the statement is set.

It will not be sufficient, however, if it merely drives us back to a study of Keats's reading, his conversation, his letters. We shall not find our answer there even if scholarship does prefer on principle investigations of (30) Browning's _____ question, "What porridge had John Keats?" For even if we knew just what porridge he had, physical and mental, we should still not be able to settle the problem of the "Ode." The reason should be clear: our specific question is not what did (35) Keats the man perhaps want to assert here about the relation of beauty and truth; it is rather: was Keats the poet able to exemplify that relation in this particular poem? Middleton Murry is right: the relation of the final statement in the poem to the total context is all-(40) important.

Indeed, Eliot, in the very passage in which he attacks the "Ode" has indicated the general line which we are to take in its defense. In that passage, Eliot goes on to contrast the closing lines of the "Ode" with a line (45) from King Lear, "Ripeness is all." Keats's lines strike him as false; Shakespeare's, on the other hand, as not clearly false, and as possibly quite true. Shakespeare's generalization, in other words, avoids raising the question of truth. But is it really a question of truth (50) and falsity? One is tempted to account for the difference of effect which Eliot feels in this way: "Ripeness is all" is a statement put in the mouth of a dramatic character and a statement which is governed and qualified by the whole context of the play. It does (55) not directly challenge an examination into its truth because its relevance is pointed up and modified by the dramatic context.

Now, suppose that one could show that Keats's lines, in quite the same way, constitute a speech, a (60) consciously riddling paradox, put in the mouth of a particular character, and modified by the total context of the poem. If we could demonstrate that the speech was in "character," was dramatically appropriate, was properly prepared for—then would not the lines have (65) all the justification of "Ripeness is all?" In such case, should we not have waived the question of the scientific or philosophic truth of the lines in favor of the application of a principle curiously like that of dramatic propriety? I suggest that some such principle (70) is the only one legitimately to be invoked in any case. Be this as it may, the "Ode on a Grecian Urn" provides us with as neat an instance as one could wish in order to test the implication of such a maneuver.

30. Based on its style and content the passage is most likely taken from

(A) a letter exchanged between poets regarding the value of Keats's poetry
(B) an early nineteenth-century critical appreciation by a friend of John Keats
(C) a nineteenth-century treatise on poetic technique
(D) a twentieth-century critical study of the structure of poetry
(E) a twentieth-century literary essay examining the relationship of the work and the biography of John Keats

31. Which of the following correctly completes the blank in line 30?

    (A) paradoxical
    (B) naive
    (C) perceptive
    (D) foolish
    (E) ironic

32. The third paragraph emphasizes which of the following assertions?

    (A) To understand what is meant by "Beauty is truth, truth Beauty" one must consider the social and personal context surrounding Keats at the time he composed the lines.
    (B) In order to pass a meaningful critical judgment upon the final lines of "Ode on a Grecian Urn" one must consider how those lines mesh with the entire poem.
    (C) The meaning of the final lines of "Ode on a Grecian Urn" cannot be exactly deciphered, which is as Keats perhaps intended.
    (D) It does not matter what Keats the man wanted to say, but only what Keats the poet wanted to say.
    (E) The relation of beauty and truth is exemplified by the context of the final statement of the poem.

33. Which of the following best describes the third paragraph?

    (A) It develops the thesis set forth in the second paragraph by focusing the problem onto more manageable areas than the necessarily vague concepts "beauty and truth."
    (B) It injects a much needed note of levity by poking fun at the scholarly pretensions of poet Robert Browning.
    (C) It reaffirms the recommendation of the second paragraph after first identifying and repudiating a misinterpretation of the author's initial recommendation.
    (D) It redirects the assertion of the second paragraph away from a consideration of isolated lines toward the all-important concept of the total poem.
    (E) It proves that "Beauty is truth, truth beauty" can be understood by consideration of the context of those lines within the larger "Ode."

34. Based on the second paragraph, with which of the following statements would the author be most likely to agree?

    (A) The "Ode" was in some part written to offer symbolic instruction about the essence of poetry and art.
    (B) The "Ode" is a poetic type of riddle.
    (C) The purpose of Keats' poem was to pose questions, not to provide answers.
    (D) The meaning of Keats' lines can be found through a combination of the views of the "pure-art camp" and the Marxist critics of the "'thirties."
    (E) Both the "pure-art camp" and the "Marxist critics of the 'thirties" are correct in their assessment of the final lines of the "Ode." This ambiguity is what makes the poem an enigmatic parable.

GO ON TO THE NEXT PAGE

35. Which of the following asks a question most similar to that posed in lines 5–7?

   (A) How can we know whether a poem is beautiful before we know if it is true?
   (B) Does the truth of the claims a poem makes affect the poem's artistic merit?
   (C) Is it more important for a poem to be beautiful than it is to be true?
   (D) Can a poem deal in unpleasant, even "ugly" truth and still be a good poem?
   (E) Are truth and beauty truly equivalent, or is the phrase simply "poetic?"

36. Based solely on the passage, it is certain the author disagrees with which of the following statements?

   (A) The lines "Beauty is truth, truth beauty that is all/ye know on Earth and all ye need to know" need not be understood in terms of Keats' own belief in the sentiment these lines express.
   (B) The lines "Beauty is truth, truth beauty that is all/ye know on Earth and all ye need to know" are effective even when one considers what Keats actually meant to say.
   (C) The lines "Beauty is truth, truth beauty that is all/ye know on Earth and all ye need to know" are effective only when considered in the context of the total poem.
   (D) The lines "Beauty is truth, truth beauty that is all/ye know on Earth and all ye need to know" do not mar the perfection of Keats' Ode.
   (E) The lines "Beauty is truth, truth beauty that is all/ye know on Earth and all ye need to know" are best understood independently of the poem from which they are drawn.

37. The thesis the author prepares to explore is

   (A) In the context of the poem, a consideration of the last lines of "Ode on a Grecian Urn" as a character's speech shows the lines to be dramatically prepared for as well as provides a test-case for this type of analysis.
   (B) Keats' "Ode on a Grecian Urn" is as great a masterpiece as Shakespeare's King Lear.
   (C) If "Ode on a Grecian Urn" is read as a dramatic monologue delivered by a character not unlike Shakespeare's King Lear it takes on richer meaning.
   (D) According to the principle of dramatic propriety a character's speeches, no matter how ambiguous or paradoxical can be justified by the total context of the play or poem.
   (E) The only principle that may be legitimately invoked concerning "Ode to a Grecian Urn" is that of dramatic propriety.

38. In lines 21–23 the author makes a distinction between two questions in order to

   (A) highlight the extremely subtle difference between what an author says, and what an author intends to say
   (B) contrast the flaws of an obsolete critical method with the virtues of the author's own method
   (C) reveal the similarities in the methods of otherwise widely differing critical approaches
   (D) emphasize that he intends to examine not what exactly the poet meant to say, but whether the poem itself has been crafted into a harmonious embodiment of the poet's ideas
   (E) underscore the point that a critic must possess a thorough understanding of a poet's biographical situation and beliefs in order to begin to analyze a poem with any fidelity to the author

GO ON TO THE NEXT PAGE

39. In the sentence "Keats's lines strike him as false; Shakespeare's, on the other hand, as not clearly false, and as possibly quite true," the comma immediately following "Shakespeare" is

   (A) an error
   (B) necessary both to bracket the prepositional phrase "on the other hand" and to indicate the omission of the words "lines strike him"
   (C) necessary to bracket the independent clause "on the other hand"
   (D) necessary to bracket the dependent clause "on the other hand"
   (E) an optional comma used here for effect

40. The sentence that begins "In such case, should" (lines 65–70) contains an example of which one of the following?

   (A) A simile
   (B) An epic question
   (C) A rhetorical question
   (D) A metaphor
   (E) Onomatopoeia

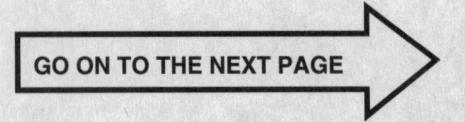

GO ON TO THE NEXT PAGE

Questions 41–55. Read the poem below carefully then choose answers to the questions that follow.

    Mother, picked for jury duty, managed to get through
    A life of Voltaire in three volumes. Anyway, she knew
    Before she half-heard a word, the dentist was guilty.

Line As a seminarist whose collar is his calling
(5) Chokes up without it, baring his naked neck,
    The little furtive dentist is led across the deck
    Mounts the plank, renders a nervous cough.
    Mother frowns, turns a page, flick a fly-speck
    With her fingernail. She will push him off!
(10) Call to her, Voltaire, amid the wreck
    Of her fairmindedness; descended from a line
    Of stiff physicians; dentists are beyond
    The iron palings, the respectable brass plate,
    Illegible Latin script, the chaste degrees.
(15) Freezing, she acknowledges the mechanic, welder, wielder
    Of pliers, hacker, hawker, barber—Spit it out, please.
    Worst of all, this dentist advertises.

    Gliding through Volume II with an easy breast stroke,
(20) Never beyond her depth, she glimpses him,
    Formerly Painless, all his life-like bridges
    Swept away; tasting brine as the testimony
    Rises: how he chased his siren girl receptionist,
    Purse-lipped, like a starlet playing nurse
(25) With her doll's kit, round and round the little lab
    where full balconies of plaster teeth
    Grinned at the clinch.

    New musical chimes

    Score their dalliance as the reception room fills.
(30) Pulling away at last from his mastic Nereid,
    He admits a patient; still unstrung,
    Stares past the tiny whirlpool at her, combing
    Her silvery hair over his silver tools, runs the drill—
    Mark this!—the drill through his victim's tongue.
(35) Mother took all his easy payments, led the eleven
    Crew-members, docile, to her adamantine view:
    He was doomed, doomed, doomed, by birth, profession,
    Practice, appearance, personal habits, loves . . .
    And now his patient, swollen-mouthed with cancer!

(40) Doves

    Never cooed like Mother pronouncing sentence.
    She shut Voltaire with a bang, having come out even,
    The last page during the final, smiling ballot,
    The judge, supererogated, studying the docket
(45) As Mother, with eleven good men in her pocket
    And a French philosopher in her reticule, swept out.

    Nice Mrs. Nemesis, did she ever look back
    At love's fool, clinging to his uneasy chair,
    Gripping the arms, because she had swooped down,
(50) And strapped him in, to drill him away, then say,
    "Spit out your life, right there."

    Imposing her own version of the Deity
    Who, as the true idolaters well know,
    Has a general practice, instructs in Hygiene &
(55) Deportment,
    Invents diseases for His cure and care:
    She knows him indispensable. Like Voltaire.

41. Overall, the Mother's attitude toward the trial related in the poem shows her to be

(A) interested in seeing that all the relevant facts be uncovered and considered
(B) completely unaware of the duties imposed upon her by her situation
(C) believes that those brought to trial are almost always guilty
(D) unconcerned with taking her responsibilities as a juror too lightly
(E) one who considers herself above the law

42. The phrase "Half-heard" serves to

(A) characterize the Mother as elderly
(B) reinforce the fact that the Mother pays as much attention to reading as the trial
(C) show that the Mother does not hear well
(D) emphasize the speed with which the Mother reaches her decision
(E) suggest the very quiet tone in which the guilty dentist speaks

43. In the second stanza, the dentist is most directly stated to be

(A) a man suffering from a terminal illness
(B) a fly-speck
(C) a seminarist
(D) a man who will be made to "walk the plank"
(E) a victim of circumstances over which he has had no control

44. Which of the following best conveys the meaning in context of (lines 15–17) "Freezing, she acknowledges the mechanic, welder, wielder/ Of pliers, hacker, hawker, barber?"

   (A) The Mother thinks of other tradesman she dislikes as much as she does dentists
   (B) The Mother thinks of professions similar to dentistry
   (C) The Mother thinks of the diverse and distasteful aspects of the dentist's profession
   (D) The Mother thinks of trades which, like dentistry, she recognizes as necessary although disagreeable
   (E) The Mother thinks of the control typically male professions exert upon her and how in this instance the tables are turned

45. The phrase, (line 18) "the dentist advertises" principally suggests:

   (A) the dentist is unscrupulous
   (B) the dentist is not professionally qualified
   (C) the dentist's lack of skill causes him to constantly seek new clientele
   (D) the dentist is a newcomer to the area
   (E) the dentist offends the Mother's sense of propriety

46. The poem states or implies which of the following?

   I. To a large degree the Mother finds the dentist guilty because he is a dentist
   II. The jury finds the dentist guilty
   III. The dentist should be found innocent

   (A) I only
   (B) II only
   (C) III only
   (D) I and II only
   (E) I, II, and III

47. In the fourth stanza, the dentist is portrayed as:

   (A) Comically lecherous
   (B) Brutally vicious
   (C) Calculatingly criminal
   (D) Timidly amorous
   (E) Angrily frustrated

48. The phrase "tasting brine" indicates the dentist's

   (A) desire for the trial to be over quickly
   (B) anger at the falsehoods offered as testimony against him
   (C) shame at the revelations of his unprofessional behaviour
   (D) fear of being imprisoned for his acts
   (E) sense of the growing likelihood of a guilty verdict

49. Which one of the following is used as a metaphor for reading:

   (A) Dreaming
   (B) Walking
   (C) Conversing
   (D) Swimming
   (E) Flying

50. Which stanza suggests that the Mother's treatment of the dentist could be seen as "poetic justice?"

   (A) 4
   (B) 5
   (C) 6
   (D) 7
   (E) 8

51. "Nice Mrs. Nemesis" is an example of:

   (A) Understatement
   (B) Hyperbole
   (C) Ironic diction
   (D) Personification
   (E) Onomatopoeia

GO ON TO THE NEXT PAGE

52. The poem's final stanza suggests which of the following?

   I. the mother's vision of God is deeply held but unsophisticated
   II. the mother believes that God's views are similar to those of Voltaire's
   III. the mother believes that God shares her belief in the need for social decorum

   (A) I only
   (B) II only
   (C) III only
   (D) I and III only
   (E) II and III only

53. Grammatically "Swept out" in line (46) takes as its subject:

   (A) The judge (line 44)
   (B) Mother (line 45)
   (C) eleven good men (line 45)
   (D) French philosopher (line 46)
   (E) her reticule (46)

54. The Mother disapproves of the dentist for all of the following reasons except:

   (A) His religious beliefs
   (B) His profession
   (C) His affair with his assistant
   (D) His demeanor
   (E) His mistreatment of a patient

55. Which one of the following choices best describes the poet's attitude toward the Mother's jury service?

   (A) Frustrated anger
   (B) Anxious shame
   (C) Scornful displeasure
   (D) Cold indifference
   (E) Amused ambivalence

STOP
END OF SECTION I
IF YOU FINISH BEFORE TIME IS CALLED, YOU MAY CHECK YOUR WORK ON THIS SECTION. DO NOT GO ON TO SECTION II UNTIL YOU ARE TOLD TO DO SO.

ENGLISH LITERATURE AND COMPOSITION

SECTION II

Total Time—2 hours

Question 1

(Suggested time—40 minutes. This question counts as one-third of the total essay score.)

The passage that follows is a fictional treatment of the young Lee Harvey Oswald, who as an adult would assassinate President John F. Kennedy Jr. Read the passage carefully. Then write a well-organized essay concerning the methods by which the author has portrayed the subject and the substance of the portrait itself. Be sure to consider such literary elements as diction, imagery, and point of view.

He returned to the seventh grade until classes ended. In summer dusk the girls lingered near the benches on Bronx Park South. Jewish girls, Italian girls in tight skirts, girls with ankles bracelets, their voices (5) murmurous with the sound of boys' names, with song lyrics, little remarks he didn't always understand. They talked to him when he walked by making him smile in his secret way.

Oh a woman with beer on her breath, on the bus (10) coming home from the beach. He feels the tired salty sting in his eyes of a day in the sun and water.

"The trouble leaving you with my sister," Marguerite said, "she had too many children of her own. Plus the normal disputes of family. That meant I (15) had to employ Mrs. Roach, on Pauline Street, when you were two. But I came home one day and saw she whipped you, raising welts on your legs, and we moved to Sherwood Forest Drive."

Heat entered the flat through the walls and (20) windows, seeped down from the tar roof. Men on Sundays carried pastry in white boxes. An Italian was murdered in a candy store, shot five times, his brains dashing the wall near the comic-book rack. Kids trooped to the store from all around to see the traces of (25) grayish spatter. His mother sold stockings in Manhattan.

A woman on the street, completely ordinary, maybe fifty years old, wearing glasses and a dark dress, handed him a leaflet at the foot of the El steps. (30) Save the Rosenbergs, it said. He tried to give it back thinking he would have to pay for it, but she'd already turned away. He walked home, hearing a lazy radio voice doing a ballgame. Plenty of room, folks. Come on out for the rest of this game and all of the second. It (35) was Sunday, Mother's Day, and he folded the leaflet neatly and put it in his pocket to save for later.

There is a world inside the world.

He rode the subway up to Inwood, out to Sheepshead Bay. There were serious men down there, (40) rocking in the copper light. He saw, beggars, men who talked to God, men who lived on the trains, day and night, bruised, with matted hair, asleep in patient bundles on the wicker seats. He jumped the turnstiles once. He rode between cars, gripping the heavy chain. (45) He felt the friction of the ride in his teeth. They went so fast sometimes. He liked the feeling they were on the edge. How do we know the motorman's not insane? It gave him a funny thrill. The wheels touched off showers of blue-white sparks, tremendous hissing (50) bursts, on the edge of no-control. People crowded in, every shape face in the book of faces. They pushed through the doors, they hung from the porcelain straps. He was riding just to ride. The noise had a power and a human force. The dark had a power. He (55) stood at the front of the first car, hands flat against the glass. The view down the tracks was a form of power. It was a secret and a power. The beams picked out secret things. The noise was pitched to a fury he located in the mind, a satisfying wave of rage and (60) pain.

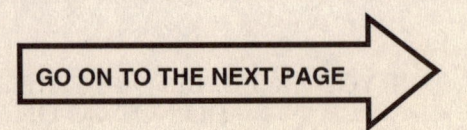

Question 2

(Suggested time—40 minutes. This question counts as one-third of the total essay score.)

Read the following poem carefully. Considering such literary elements as imagery, diction, and tone, write a well-organized essay that examines the author's vision of Miss Blount in the countryside.

Epistle to Miss Blount
on her leaving town, after the coronation

As some fond virgin, whom her mother's care
Drags from the town to wholesome country air,
Just when she learns to roll a melting eye,
Line And hear a spark[2], yet think no danger nigh;
(5) From the dear man unwilling she must sever,
Yet takes one kiss before she parts forever:
Thus from the world fair Zephalinda[3] flew,
Saw others happy, and with sighs withdrew;
Not that their pleasures caused her discontent;
(10) She sighed not that they stayed, but that she went.
She went to plain work, and to purling brooks,
Old-fashioned halls, dull aunts, croaking rooks:
She went from opera, park, assembly, play,
To morning walks, and prayers three hours a day;
(15) To part her time ëtwixt reading and bohea[4],
To muse, and spill her solitary tea,
Or o'er cold coffee trifle with the spoon,
Count the slow clock, and dine exact at noon;
Divert her eyes with pictures in the fire,
(20) Hum half a tune, tell stories to the squire;
Up to her godly garret after seven,
There starve and pray, for that's the way to heaven.
Some squire, perhaps, you take delight to rack,
Whose game is whist, whose treat a toast in sack;
(25) Who visits with a gun, presents you birds,
Then gives a smacking buss, and cries—"No words!"
Or with his hounds comes hollowing from the stable,
Makes love with nods and knees beneath a table;
Whose laughs are hearty, though his jests are coarse,
(30) And loves you best of all things—but his horse.
In some fair evening, on your elbow laid,
You dream of triumphs in the rural shade;
In pensive thought recall the fancied scene,
See coronations rise on every green
(35) Before you pass the imaginary sights
Of lords and earls and dukes and gartered knights
While the spread fan o'ershades your closing eyes'
Then gives one flirt, and all the vision flies.
Thus vanish scepters, coronets, and balls,
(40) And leave you in lone woods, or empty walls!

So when your slave[5], at some dear idle time
(Not plagued with headaches or the want of rhyme)
Stands in the streets, abstracted from the crew,
And while he seems to study, thinks of you'
(45) Just when his fancy points your sprightly eyes,
Or sees the blush of soft Parthenia rise,
Gay[6] pats my shoulder, and you vanish quite;
Streets, chairs, and coxcombs, rush upon my sight;
Vexed to be still in town, I knit my brow,
(50) Look sour, and hum a tune—as you may now.

—Alexander Pope

[2] A man-about-town
[3] A playful name for Miss Blount
[4] A fashionable and expensive tea
[5] Pope refers to himself here
[6] the author's friend, John Gay

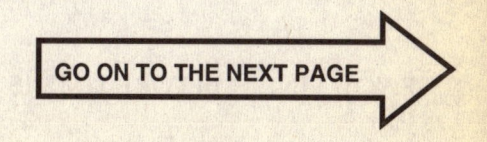

Question 3

(Suggested time—40 minutes. This question counts as one-third of the total essay score.)

In some works of literature the insanity (or a period of insanity) of a main character plays a central role. Choose a novel or play of literary merit and write a well-organized essay in which you discuss the mental illness of a central character and the specific ways in which that character's mental illness relates to the larger themes of the work. Avoid plot summary.

You may select a work from the list below, or you may choose to write upon another work of comparable literary merit.

The Idiot
Moby-Dick
The Turn of the Screw
As I Lay Dying
I Know Why the Caged Bird Sings
Hamlet
King Lear
Invisible Man
Native Son
Medea
A Fan's Notes
Heart of Darkness
Nausea
Crime and Punishment
Waiting for Godot

Man's Fate
The Duchess of Malfi
Wuthering Heights
The Iliad
Hunger
Catch-22
Miss Lonelyhearts
Marat/Sade
Old Goriot
Under the Volcano
The Scarlet Letter
Long Day's Journey Into Night
One Flew Over the Cuckoo's Nest
The Yellow Wallpaper

STOP
END OF SECTION II
IF YOU FINISH BEFORE TIME IS CALLED, YOU MAY CHECK YOUR WORK ON THIS SECTION.

PART V

Answers and Explanations— Practice Test 1

QUESTIONS 1–15

The passage, "Of Seeming Wise," is by Francis Bacon (1561–1626) from his collection *Essays*. Bacon is considered the first English essayist. A true polymath, Bacon, besides writing the tremendously popular *Essays*, also wrote important works of general philosophy, philosophy of science, political science, and law. On the down side, he was a thoroughly corrupt politician/lawyer who managed to get sent to the Tower of London for taking large and frequent bribes while serving as a judge.

In terms of the test, you should realize that the passage is not a particularly difficult one by the standards of sixteenth-century writing—which is not to say that the passage is easy. Sixteenth-century writing is understandably challenging to a twentieth-century reader. The point to take is this: if the passage gave you trouble, you should brush up on your skills with sixteenth- and seventeenth-century writing, especially poetry. There will definitely be a sample of writing from this period on your test and it will most likely be poetry, which is usually more challenging than prose. Even if you breezed through the passage, it can't hurt to practice your skills reading some John Donne, Andrew Marvel, or John Milton (well, okay, maybe the Milton hurts a little). If you can read those guys' verse with any confidence you can rest assured you're in good shape for the multiple-choice section of the AP test.

On this passage, the questions required that you make your way through the difficulties of Bacon's language, achieving comprehension of the broad outline of his meaning, the details of his points, and the critical but humorous aspect of his tone. Bacon's overall message is the (not especially surprising) fact that there are men who pretend to be wise. The pleasure of the piece is in Bacon's sharp observation of tricks by which the "seeming wise" fake out the unwary. (And is there really any one of us who's never nodded and "oh yessed" his way through a conversation he didn't understand?) The tone aims at social improvement but stays light, probably because vanity skewered is almost unavoidably comic.

Finally, it's important to note that the *content* is ironic, not the tone. This last point will be discussed in greater detail in the explanation to question 15.

1. **The correct answer is (A).** You may have read answer choice (A) which is a straightforward phrasing of the passage's thesis and thought "oh, that's the answer" and then puzzled over the other choices wondering if you'd missed something. Perhaps (C), or (D) seemed awfully close to correct as well? You needed to see that (A) summarizes the point without straying into comments that can't be justified. It isn't so much a matter of seeing that (A) is correct as seeing that the other four choices are incorrect. (B) suggests that everyone sometimes puts on the airs of the "seeming wise"; however much this may or may not be true, the statement is not the overall point of the passage, nor even in the passage. It cannot be the answer. (C) has similar troubles. The emphasis the answer puts on spotting the "seeming wise" is wrong, and, moreover, the author never says that these fakers are actually the "least wise" of people. In (D), the emphasis is off. The passage is less about trying to paint the "seeming wise" as foolish—Bacon takes that as a given—than about describing them so that the reader can avoid being *fooled by* them. Nevertheless, this answer might have given you trouble. Remember, when you're deciding between two similar answers, compare them and ask yourself: what's different?

    Choice (E) is a trap for those who were completely thrown off by Bacon's use of the word "formal," and thought the passage had more to do with physical appearance than behavior.

2. **The correct answer is (C).** To answer this question, you should have gone back to the passage and reread the lines cited plus a little before and after. Even if the analogy seemed somewhat unclear all this question really called for was a general comprehension of the

entire passage. Remember, keep your answers consistent with the main point of the passage unless you have an extremely good textual reason not to. Given that requirement, the only answer that would make sense is (C). (D) may have given you some trouble, but you could eliminate it because it introduces the topic of evil, a subject which is not found in lines 3–5 or anywhere in the passage.

3. **The correct answer is (E).** "Formalist" refers to those who take the manner (the form) of something, without anything to back it up. This is certainly not a usage that exists in present day English, but in the context of the passage the meaning should have become clear. Here, the wrong answer choices reflect traps for students who struggled with the language of the passage and so were led toward other more vaguely familiar applications of the word "formal." Or, the wrong answers could also pose problems for students who are suggestible and over-think, or have a misplaced respect for the test writers. Remember, if an answer *seems* ridiculous, it undoubtedly *is* ridiculous. So don't fall into the incredibly common standardized-test trap of thinking: "Geez, that answer choice seems so insane I must have missed something." Choice (C), for example, is designed to make some poor stressed-out student think back to a half-remembered philosophy class . . . "formalists . . . formalists . . . that rings a bell . . ." and by the time she's done she has to reread the passage just to make sure it isn't the right answer. At best this is a waste of time, and at worst you can end up taking a relatively normal reading of a line and turn it into a confusing nightmare. This is especially easy to do with verse. Don't get suckered.

4. **The correct answer is (C).** This is a literary term question, pure and simple. If you knew the terms you were golden. Always use as much process of elimination as you can and guess. The definition of each answer choice is given in our glossary of terms on page 195.

5. **The correct answer is (D).** This question requires that you return to the passage and read enough of the material surrounding the phrase "wise by signs" to see that it refers to "countenance and gesture." In other words, "wise by signs" refers to how one looks, specifically, one's facial expressions and gestures. The incorrect choices, although supported by the passage as means of seeming wise (except for choice (A), which is simply wrong) are not related to being "wise by signs." Remember, always go back to the passage when you are given line numbers and read the citation as well as a little before and after. You may occasionally find that you could have answered the question without referring to the passage, but so what? It is much more important to avoid careless errors. Finishing early isn't worth one point.

6. **The correct answer is (B).** The form of this question is almost identical to that of question 5, and, not surprisingly, your technique should be the same. As in question five, the incorrect choices refer to points made earlier or later in the passage, not at the line specified. The correct answer adequately expresses the sense of "bearing a great word," and being "peremptory," which mean, essentially, acting as if all is so perfectly obvious it can be accepted or rejected without further discussion. "Peremptory" describes a manner which is offensively decisive, final, and absolute. The incorrect answers refer to tricks for seeming wise that occur elsewhere in the passage or not at all.

7. **The correct answer is (A).** This is the last of the little series of questions, beginning with question 5, that asked about the various ruses used by the "seeming wise." Here you needed to understand that "for when propositions are denied, there is an end of them; but if they be

allowed, it requireth a new work; which false point of wisdom is the bane of the business" means that these fake-wise types want to put an end to difficult discussions before they have to expend more intellectual energy, and the last thing they want to do is think. "Intellectual laziness" is convenient shorthand for this trait. The other choices again apply to the "seeming wise" but not to the lines specified.

8. **The correct answer is (E).** In structure questions you want to move through the answer choice making sure that each element in the choice is present in the passage. For example, in (A), you would begin with "a general proposition is made." Yep, so far so good. Then comes "specific historical examples are investigated." Well, examples are given, sure, but they aren't specific historical examples. Scratch (A). Remember, partly wrong is *all* wrong. You may have liked the phrase "a conclusion is given in the form of advice" and crossed off answers that didn't contain it. This is not the way to work. Yes, the conclusion does contain advice, but it also makes a summary statement. Answer choice (E) has nothing wrong in it. Remember, when you get stuck because nothing seems perfect, look for the answer that is least wrong.

9. **The correct answer is (E).** Don't freak out if you run into a question that sends you right back to a line you've already looked at. This question sends you right back to lines 29–34 (from question 7) where the general trait of disagreement was discussed. Students often think they must have screwed up somewhere when they hit a question that seems similar to one that came before. In fact, it's a sign that you're on the right track. The passages on the AP English Literature and Composition Test tend to be well focused. As a result, some overlap in questions is common. The danger sign is when your answers have nothing to do with one another, or are contradictory. Remember, Consistency of Answers is the general rule. The wrong answers all refer to traits that poseur pundits (we're getting tired of saying "seeming wise" all the time) sometimes exhibit, but not to the common trait.

10. **The correct answer is (A).** The passage is satirical. You may have gotten this question right but not with much confidence, or perhaps you got the question wrong because the passage didn't fit your conception of satire. Many of us today, when we use the word *satire*, mean *parody*, something that takes on a well-known style and then pokes fun at its subject through exaggeration and skewed content. In general, we are used to seeing satire enacted. When a character behaves in a fashion that is both ridiculous and readily identifiable, especially when the character has no self-conscious sense of being ridiculous, that's satire. But this is only one type of satire, called indirect satire. The other broad category of satire is formal satire. Bacon's "Of Seeming Wise" is 100 percent formal satire, which can be defined as follows: The formal satire aims at pointing out (and even correcting) a foolish flaw commonly seen in people. It approaches its task wittily in direct address to the reader or listener.

    There are other finer distinctions to be made within the category of satire (Juvenalian satire, Horatian satire) but you don't have to worry about them. In fact, you don't need to worry about the distinction between the formal and the indirect types so long as you can recognize both as satire.

11. **The correct answer is (B).** This is an inference question. Remember, an inference question does not mean you are supposed to go hunting for something that isn't there. If you do, you'll find it—in the wrong answer choices. When ETS asks for an inference they mean that something in the passage strongly indicates something else. In question 11, you needed to

see the advice offered at the passage's end, that "seeming wise" types should not be taken for "business" (by "business" Bacon means the entire spectrum of public life, not just shopkeeping or finance). This advice directly implies that Bacon feels his writing has a practical application. It isn't just writing for the sake of writing.

Answer choice (E) is an excellent example of the kind of inference you want to *avoid*. In general, literary writers have a strong sense of the eyes of other writers upon them. If you recognized the passage as Bacon and knew that the passage is an example of one of the first true essays written in English, you might have thought that Bacon must have known he was doing something really new, at least in English, and that other writers would take an interest in this new form. All true, and nicely logical, *but it isn't in the passage*. The outside knowledge you might possess about a passage can be an invaluable aid to *understanding* the passage. It can always be used to eliminate answers. If you saw an answer and thought, "Bacon would never say that," you could eliminate it with confidence. But the passage itself, and nowhere else, is the place to look for answers, *especially* on inference questions.

12. **The correct answer is (C)**. Here your task was to demonstrate your comprehension of line 23 with a paraphrase. Bacon's usage of "admittance" is unusual, which is precisely why the test writers have asked this question. It can be figured out by its context or, even better, by using process of elimination. Since this clause follows a semicolon it must be closely linked to the preceding clause. Given that, choice (A) would come out of left field. It must be wrong. Choice (B) is for those students who are really stuck and just grasping at the most familiar use of admittance. The second half of choice (D) should look extremely suspicious. Even if you didn't have a solid grasp of exactly what Bacon was saying, it should have been evident he wasn't saying that. Choice (E) suggests that the "seeming wise" actually know things to be false; it implies that they have evil intentions. This reading would be terribly inconsistent with the passage. Notice that choice (C) is perfectly consistent. The entire passage describes people who, through a variety of tricks, get others to believe their that empty heads are actually filled with knowledge.

13. **The correct answer is (D)**. The traps to avoid here were (A) and (B). Although it would seem a reasonable thing to do, the author never compares those who possess knowledge and those who don't. Remember, you must stay within the confines of the passage. Concerning (B), many students look back to the early analogy drawn between pious hypocrites and wisdom fakers. Simply put, this is not a comparison between the faithful and the wise, but between the faithless and the ignorant. Still, it feels close. Some students just bubble it in and move on. Don't *ever* put down an answer without reading all the choices. The comparison that (C), the correct answer, refers to is found in lines 35–38. The "decaying merchant" and "inward beggar" refer to people who use little deceits in order to appear to have more than they actually do, exactly like the "seeming wise." In the former case, they lack money; in the latter, wisdom.

14. **The correct answer is (D)**. There are a few terms on the AP English Literature and Composition Test that you simply must know. They show up on test after test. Metaphor and simile are the most important of these. Be able to recognize them and to distinguish between the two.

15. **The correct answer is (D)**. When presented with a I, II, III question, be sure to use process of elimination. It was probably easiest to say that choice III was not in the passage. Metaphysical speculation would mean wondering about the intrinsic nature of the soul, or offering a definition of the essence of justice. Nothing like this occurs in the passage and you could have easily eliminated choices (C) and (E). Next, you might have reasoned that humorous irony is certainly present. (The subject itself is ironic. Irony is a famously difficult concept to pin down. It can be quite obvious or extremely subtle. We provide an extended definition of irony in the glossary; please refer to it if you had trouble seeing this passage as ironic.) This would have allowed you to eliminate answer choice (A) since it does not contain selection II. Even if you could go no further (suppose for example you didn't know what didacticism means), you would be left with a fifty-fifty chance and *must* guess. Of course, if you studied our literary terms section (page 195) you would know that didacticism—instructiveness or guidance—is present in the Bacon essay. That would leave only (D), the correct answer.

QUESTIONS 16–29

The passage is by Christina Rossetti (1830–94), and was written when she was in her early thirties. The poem's spiritual, death-haunted theme is typical of Rossetti, who was beset with ill-health her entire—yet relatively long—life.

The Rossetti's, Christina and her brothers William Michael and Dante Gabriel, were at the center of an influential mid–nineteenth-century arts movement called the Pre-Raphaelite Brotherhood. Pre-Raphaelite painting and writing was concerned with medieval themes, with romance (often tinged with self-destruction or death), nature, nostalgia, and vivid imagery and color.

Christina's brother, Dante (arguably the leader of the Pre-Raphaelite movement) is guilty of one of the truly cheese-ball acts of literary narcissism. When Dante Gabriel Rossetti's wife died, the painter-poet buried the manuscripts of several of his poems in the casket with her. Ah, love. Seven years later he decided maybe it wasn't such a good idea and had the mess dug up so he could get his poems back. The last laugh, however, is on Dante, whose literary reputation is waning, whereas, after years spent in her brother's shadow, Christina Rossetti has acquired a growing respect from the literary world.

The poem on the test (like almost everything Christina Rossetti wrote) is a meditation on the transience of life and the inevitability of death. When, in the third stanza, God promises to come for the poet when her hour arrives, the poem becomes an avowal of faith.

While the bulk of the poem's meaning is accessible to most readers, the questions asked on the test lay several traps for the unwary. When reading and interpreting poetry, be on guard against making assumptions that can't be justified. Several questions have incorrect choices that suggest the principal narrator is on her deathbed. You should not reason that the poem's intense contemplation of death indicates the poet is gravely ill or about to die; it is an unwarranted assumption.

Another difficulty you face when answering the questions on the Rossetti passage is that the questions ask about some of the poem's subtler points. There are several questions, for example, about the important shift in the recurrent nature imagery that occurs in the poem's final stanza. Complications also rise from the presence of more than one speaker in the poem.

There is a longstanding tradition in English poetry of conversing with the spiritual forces of the cosmos and oneself. It may seem a hopelessly old-fashioned device, but poets up to the present day continue to create interesting and important works using this convention. The Rossetti poem, however, not only has the speaker in dialogue with the metaphysical world, but in the second stanza takes matters a degree further by having the Soul speak with the voice of the past. Following the line "Hearken what the past doth witness and say:" the Soul presents what the past has to say about human mortality. You needed to understand that in this stanza the past is *not* being directly presented as a speaker, in fact the past is probably not even being quoted; the Soul is interpreting the past for the benefit of the principal narrator. This is a tangled piece of rhetorical construction and causes most students some problems.

Overall, the passage, taken together with its questions, is at the difficult end of the spectrum of work you will see on the AP English Literature and Composition Test.

16. **The correct answer is (D).** As noted in the general notes to the passage, this is a tough question. Most students choose answer choice (E), five. But the past is not a speaker. The past is being interpreted for the principal narrator by the Soul. Another choice that sophisticated readers sometimes pick is (A), one. The reasoning behind choosing (A) is usually that only the poet is speaking; the Soul, World, and God represent elements and ideas within the poet. In this reading, the poem is a kind of internal monologue in which the poet sorts out her feelings about death and the afterlife. This interpretation is absolutely plausible (Rossetti certainly did not intend for you to think she had actually held a conversation with the World or with God). The problem is that it is an *interpretation*. The question asks, "How many speakers does the poem present?" The emphasis is on what the poem presents, not what the poem might suggest. The question is not asking for an interpretation but simply for what the poem presents. It presents four speakers.

    One more note: if you got questions 13, 14, 15, and 16 correct you'd have four *D*'s in a row on your answer sheet. Some students freak when they see the same letter more than twice in a row. Don't think about it. Don't look for weird hidden meanings in the bubbles. Please don't start to think things like, "hey, I haven't put down a (B) in 13 questions . . . *I'm going down in flames!*" Just ignore the bubbles (but be sure to darken them in completely).

17. **The correct answer is (C).** This is one of the relatively rare knowledge questions on the test. You either know it or you don't. Eighty to ninety percent of the test is about your ability to understand the material you read, both the details and the larger picture. But there are some facts which ETS feels they can expect you know. They expect you to know the basic terminology of literary criticism and form (i.e. simile, metaphor, sonnet, couplet etc.) and they occasionally ask about those literary historical references a broadly read individual should recognize. This question is an example of the latter.

    In Ancient Greek and Roman society a garland of laurel and bay leaves was awarded in recognition of triumph in sports, war, or poetry. The original "Gold Medal" of the Olympics was a laurel wreath, as is that wreath you always see framing Julius Caesar's bald pate. The reason the answer specifically mentions poets is that laurel (bay is a variety of laurel) was the symbolic flower of Apollo, patron God of poetry. Even today, when a person is honored as the national poet their title is *poet laureate*. Speaking of honors, graduation from college with a bachelor's degree will mean that you have earned your bacc*alaureate*, a term derived from the medieval university tradition of crowning graduates with laurel.

18. **The correct answer is (B).** The lines in question here, "I shall clothe myself in Spring and bud in May:/ Thou, root stricken, shalt not rebuild thy decay," contrast the cyclical progress of the seasons with the linear trajectory of human life. Line 7 is a troublemaker line for many students, who frequently pick-up on "root-stricken" as indicating that the principal narrator is deathly ill. What root-stricken refers to is the fundamental presence of death in human life. The author and humans in general are "root-stricken" in the sense that death is immanent in us from the beginning, or to use another plant metaphor: We carry the seed of death within us from conception.

19. **The correct answer is (C).** The incorrect answers all make use of imagery that draws on living things, especially plants, and of the changing seasons. In line 13, the image of "Rust in thy gold" is the one image of the poem that draws neither on the seasons nor on living things.

20. **The correct answer is (E).** In this question the key was to use process of elimination, reading each answer choice carefully for what makes it *wrong*. An answer that gets the meaning of two out of three stanzas correct is still all wrong. In these kinds of questions, pay close attention to the wording of the answer choices. In (B), for example, you should reason that stanza 1, "nostalgia for the earthly world that must be left behind" is close enough to leave alone, and "welcome acceptance of the afterlife" for stanza 3 is substantially correct. However, "fear of physical decay" for stanza 2 is only half-correct. Physical decay is certainly contemplated, but fear is much too strong a term. This makes the answer wrong. Cross it off. Working this way you should find yourself, without too much trouble, left only with the correct answer, (E).

21. **The correct answer is (E).** The question shouldn't have given you too much trouble. You were asked, essentially, what "a moth in thine array" is meant to signify metaphorically. The image is yet one more description of the natural aging process. The incorrect choices offer various misreadings, either seeing illness where none is present, or spiritual anxieties that neither the line in question, nor the poem as a whole, is concerned with.

22. **The correct answer is (C).** This is another terminology question. If it gave you any trouble you should refer to our section on literary terms for the AP English Literature and Composition Test. Also, remember to use process of elimination to get rid of those answers you are sure are wrong and guess with what's left. No blanks!

23. **The correct answer is (B).** This is a question than many students get wrong. Always return to the passage. The third stanza presents a dramatic reversal in the poem's meaning and direction by refiguring imagery from the previous stanzas with an antithetical meaning. In the first two stanzas, Spring and all the imagery of Spring is used to represent youth, energy, and life. You might easily think then that winter, as Spring's opposite, represents (E) aging and loss of vigor, or perhaps (C) the coldness of the grave, that is, death itself. But the question asks for the meaning of winter in the *third* stanza. In this stanza God says that now "winter passeth after the long delay." What follows are images of spring now clearly tied to death and the afterlife. Spring in the final stanza is a metaphor for the joy of reunion with God. In the final stanza, God offers death as a joyous spring-like occasion. It is earthly life, separate from the Maker, which is the long winter.

24. **The correct answer is (C).** As with all questions with longer answers you must read carefully and eliminate when an answer is partially correct. Partially correct means all wrong. Otherwise, the reasoning behind this question is fully covered in the explanation to question 23.

25. **The correct answer is (A).** Understanding the lines in question is less a matter of the lines themselves than letting them make sense in the overall context of the poem. If you understood the bulk of the poem, then this shouldn't have been a difficult question. If the poem itself gave you trouble, this question might have as well. The incorrect choices offer various misreadings and over-interpretations.

26. **The correct answer is (C).** One of the easiest questions on the test. This is essentially a vocabulary question, but chances are you were unfamiliar with the passage's usage of the word "spray." It was a matter of figuring out the meaning from context. None of the incorrect answers makes sense in context except possibly (A), and we hope that between (A) and (C), you chose (C).

27. **The correct answer is (D).** You are certain to see a question (or two or three) like this on your test. If you got this question wrong, brush up on your skills with our section on Grammar for the AP English Literature and Composition Test (page 123). As outlined in that section, the best way to figure out the construction of the kind of sentence ETS likes to ask about is to rewrite the sentence (in your mind—you shouldn't need to actually write it down) into a more natural form. The sentences ETS chooses are never straightforward "subject, verb, direct-object, indirect object" sentences like "Jack threw the ball to me." The sentence that begins line 24 "Arise, come away, night is past and lo it is day, My love, My sister, My spouse, thou shalt hear me say," should be re-written:

> "Thou shalt hear me say, 'Arise, come away, night is past and lo it is day,
> My love, My sister, My spouse.'"

Notice we've put quotation marks around what God reports he will say. This is how the sentence would normally be punctuated. Written this way, it should be no problem to see that "Thou" is the grammatical subject.

28. **The correct answer is (A).** This question was a snap if you knew what sibilants are. The test writers, however, not wanting to make this question purely vocabulary, left you a way out if you didn't know the definition of "sibilants" The question specifies that excessive sibilants produce a possibly undesirable *sound*, undesirable at least to the delicate sensibilities of Tennyson. Based on this you might have looked over the answer choices for lines that contained a noticeable sonic effect. By restricting your search to sound and not worrying about metaphor or any other such rhetorical devices, the repeated *s*'s of line 10 should have been evident. None of the other choices contain any heavy sound effects. (A) would have been your best guess and worth a point. Sibilants are *s*, *sh*, and *z* sounds, as in, *Mississippi Sal scarfed azure pizza in his shuttered cell*.

29. **The correct answer is (A).** Although this looks like a grammar question, it is more of a fact question. The question tests whether you are familiar enough with older forms of English to avoid the popular misconception that "thou" is a formal manner of address. You also needed to know that "thou," like "you," is second person singular, but most students know this grammatical point, especially those who have studied a foreign language.

"Thou" is an obsolete form, parallel to the formal "you" but used to address familiar persons on an equal or lower station. "You" was reserved for situations that called for more politesse. The misapprehension that "thou" is formal comes from its conspicuous place in the King James Bible, where, as it happens, most people encounter the word for the first time. The misunderstanding arises from the fact that when people in the Bible call upon God, they address Him as "thou." Surely if anyone merits formal address it's God. But, on the contrary, it is in order to indicate the deep intimacy of their relationship with Him that the Hebrews and early Christians of the Bible use "thou" to address God.

QUESTIONS 30-40

The passage is by critic Cleanth Brooks. Brooks was a leading member of the "New Critics," an influential school of literary criticism that flourished in the United States and England from the 1930s through the 1960s. The New Criticism was never as monolithic as some of its detractors have claimed. Important New Critics like Brooks, William Empson, and Robert Penn Warren, had numerous differences and each was a highly idiosyncratic (and successful) writer. But they did share some common assumptions about literary criticism. Uppermost was their belief that a work of literature should be interpreted through the words on the page. The author's psychological imperatives and historical situation were to be considered only slightly if at all (in general not at all.) The test's passage highlights this feature of New Critical thought, most obviously in the paragraph that cites Browning's ironic question, "What porridge had John Keats?"

Another feature of New Criticism is it's emphasis on "close reading." That is, New Critics were famous (or infamous) for spending pages discussing a single line, sometimes even a single word, of a poem. This was probably the inevitable result of an approach that limited one's discussion solely to the text, treating the author as little more than a name at the bottom of the page. But while sometimes excessive and dubiously reasoned, close reading, at its best, in the hands of critics like Brooks or Empson, could sometimes produce ten pages of illuminating thought about a single line.

Since 1960, English and American literary criticism has come increasingly under the influence of continental European modes of thought. The European critics (led by French scholars such as Barthes, Foucault, Derrida, and Kristeva) have literary criticism take on broader issues of language and society while holding itself to a kind of philosophical rigor. Against this very different current of thought, New Criticism has fallen by the wayside. Nevertheless, most contemporary scholars agree that New Criticism, especially when applied to poetry, the form to which it is best suited, has produced exciting and original commentary.

The passage is, of course, non-fiction, which is mildly unusual for the AP English Literature and Composition Test. But past AP Literature tests have sometimes included non-fiction passages, and you shouldn't be thrown off if you see something like this on the test you take. This passage would be right at home on the Language and Composition Test, so if you're wondering what sort of stuff shows up on the Language test, this is a very good example. But keep in mind that the questions would emphasize structure and technique more.

If you were unfamiliar with Keats's "Ode on a Grecian Urn" you might have felt this passage was somewhat unfair: How are you supposed to understand a passage and answer questions about a poem you haven't read or can't remember? Well, there's no doubt you would have felt more comfortable answering the questions on this passage if you knew Keats's great Ode, but realize the questions focused on the passage's general argument, not on details of Keats's poem. Knowing the Ode wasn't necessary to understanding the passage and even less to answering the questions. But this brings up an important point. Confidence plays a large role in standardized test taking, and test taking in general. Don't let unfamiliar or difficult passages rattle you. Chances are if a question or even a whole passage seems tough (or even impossible), you aren't alone—tens of thousands of other AP students across the country feel the very same thing. If you keep this in mind and don't get rattled, a hard passage could work to your *advantage*: while your peers experience mental meltdown you're just working away knowing that you'll float to the top of the curve.

30. **The correct answer is (D).** It would have speeded up your elimination of answers to know that when the author mentions Eliot he means T.S. Eliot, the modernist poet and critic. You would have been able to scratch out the answers that place the passage in the nineteenth century; Eliot was active as a poet and critic in the first half of the twentieth century. But the

AP English Literature Test is above all a comprehension test, and this question was actually a disguised comprehension question. You didn't need any special knowledge about the names mentioned in the passage. You needed to understand that the passage is drawn from a larger work that uses Keats's poem to test certain means of looking at poetry in general. This focus becomes most apparent in the last line of the passage, where the author writes: "Be this as it may, the 'Ode on a Grecian Urn' provides us with as neat an instance as one could wish in order to test the implication of such a maneuver." This line should make it clear that the true subject of discussion is less Keats's poem than the trying out of a means of interpretation. The correct answer does *not* mention Keats. Many students cross out (D) for this reason. Those students get the question wrong. A better way to work was to cross out those answers which contained something wrong. Choice (A) was simply ridiculous. The passage is nothing like a personal letter, nor does it question the value of Keats's poetry. (Keats's best poems, particularly the Odes, are as unassailable as Shakespeare's work.) In choice (B), again the emphasis is incorrectly on Keats, and you should have recognized the style of the passage as distinctly twentieth century, certainly not *early* nineteenth century. Choice (C) emphasizes poetic technique, yet nowhere in the passage is the nitty-gritty of poetic composition discussed—eliminate. Choice (E) emphasizes the life and work of Keats. This is precisely the critical approach the author explicitly rejects. This leaves only choice (D), the correct answer.

31. **The correct answer is (E).** Here you needed to realize that the blank in the passage precedes a *deliberately* and *obviously* foolish question. Filling the blank with the word "foolish" would indicate that Browning didn't realize his question was silly. Assuming Browning was sane—a safe assumption—that couldn't be the case. All the same, nine out of ten students pick (D), foolish, here and get the question wrong. Of the choices given, (E) is the only possible choice. When a statement is made that intentionally calls attention to its foolishness, that statement is ironic.

32. **The correct answer is (B).** The correct answer nicely paraphrases the sense of the third paragraph. The incorrect choices make, in one way or another, a garble of the paragraph. Choice (A) speaks for the importance of biographical understanding, which is exactly what the author is arguing against. Choice (C) mentions a point discussed in the second paragraph, not the third. Choice (D) makes of a mess of a key sentence by repeating the word "want" where the author discussed what was "exemplified." Choice (E) passes judgment, whereas in the passage the question of whether or not Keats's last lines are successful is still in dispute.

33. **The correct answer is (C).** This was a plain old hard question. Understanding the answer choices was a reading comprehension question in itself. Well, you want every point you can get, but don't think that means you should or are going to get every question right. The proper technique here, as with any question you are less than 100% sure of, was to go through the choices one phrase at a time and eliminate what you found to be wrong. If you kept your concentration and eliminated well you should have been left with the right answer. For example, choice (D) might have tempted you if you were looking for correct answers: "all-important concept of the total poem" probably sounded pretty good. Looking for what is wrong however, you would have noticed that the answer's description of the second paragraph is way off the mark, and eliminated it.

34. **The correct answer is (A).** The question relied on your ability to understand what the author meant by "it becomes apparent that the poem itself is obviously intended to be a parable, on the nature of poetry, and of art in general." A parable is a story that offers symbolic instruction. By saying that the Ode is "an enigmatic parable, to be sure," the author indicates that just what symbolic instruction Keats intended is open to interpretation, but Choice (B) takes this reading too far by suggesting that the poem is a riddle. Choice (C) is similar to choice (B), and wrong for the same reasons. Choice (D) uses words from the paragraph to say things the passage never came close to stating. Like choice (D), choice (E) uses phrases from the passage. Its point may be more reasonable than (D)'s but it too is not found in the paragraph.

35. **The correct answer is (B).** Here your task was to paraphrase a difficult, abstractly phrased question. A good technique would have been to rephrase (and simplify) the question in your own words. For example: What is the relation of the goodness of poem to its truth or falsity? Having done this you should see that the question is asking about the relationship of a poem's truth to the quality of the poem. Most simply, the question is: Does a poem have to be true to be good? Notice that most of the wrong answers use the proper terms—truth, beauty—but misplace the emphasis. For example, choice (C) asks which is more important, truth or beauty? You should have been able to see that the relationship of truth to beauty, not their relative importance, was at issue.

36. **The correct answer is (E).** Questions where you're looking for what *isn't* right are real mind-benders, and students miss them all the time. They seem easy enough in principle, but when it comes to actually doing them under time pressure and with all the other stresses of taking the test it sometimes seems like you can actually feel your brain getting crisped. Take these questions *slowly*, and concentrate. What usually happens is you're fine through the first choice or so but then the strain of making sense of ETS's gobbledy-gook language gets to be too much and you lose it.

    There are two key words in the question. The first, of course, is "disagrees," but another key word is "certain." You must look for what the passage shows the author to be definitely against. Don't get caught up in wondering if he *might* or *might not* disagree. You need to find what he definitely disagrees with. We mentioned this earlier but it's worth repeating here: on "opposite" type questions, don't use process of elimination unless you absolutely have to—just look for the right answer. Choice (E) is correct because he thinks the lines *cannot* be understood independently of the poem. The incorrect choices all offer ideas with which the author agrees *or* which are uncertain (that is, ideas where it isn't certain he disagrees). He might disagree, maybe we have a strong hunch he'll disagree, but that isn't enough. We've got to be certain.

37. **The correct answer is (A).** This question called on your ability to see where the passage was headed. You should have seen two points: First, the author was preparing to support the last two lines of the poem by treating them as character's speech rather than as the testimony of Keats. Second, the author intends this defense to provide a test-case example of the value of his method of treating poems as akin to dramatic monologues.

    When the answer choices are longish, as they are for this question, remember to beware of the "little" words. What seems like a plausible answer often falls apart when you take that answer word by word and phrase by phrase. Choice (E), for example, might have been tempting. If you looked at the word "only," however, you would have changed your mind. Does the author really suggest that dramatic propriety is the *only* principle that can be applied to "Ode on a Grecian Urn"? No. He says that he thinks it is the only principle to apply when considering the appropriateness of the last two lines, but that is much more specific. (E) is also wrong because a further discussion of this point is not where the passage is headed.

38. **The correct answer is (D).** Here your task was to understand the author's use of the questions in lines 21–23. The point was to emphasize that the author does not believe understanding Keats's intent reveals much about the poem. He wants to look at what Keats actually wrote and consider whether it hangs together with the unity of a true work of art. The correct answer paraphrases this idea well.

39. **The correct answer is (B).** This question brings up a fairly uncommon grammatical point, but assuming you knew the comma was mandatory (and eliminated (A) and (E) from your choices) all you really needed to be able to do was identify "on the other hand" as a phrase and not a clause. This would have eliminated (C) and (D).

    The correct answer mentions the often unnoticed use of a comma to mark omissions. Here's an example: John's coat was black; Jim's, blue. As you know, a semicolon joins related sentences. That is, what follows a semi-colon should be a complete sentence. In our example "Jim's, blue" certainly doesn't look like a complete sentence, but it is in fact legit. The comma represents the omission of "coat was."

40. **The correct answer is (C).** This is a straightforward literary term question. If you had any trouble with it, refer to our glossary of terms on page 195.

QUESTIONS 41–55

The passage is the poem "A Long Line of Doctor's" by contemporary American poet Carolyn Kizer. Overall, the questions shouldn't have caused you too many problems as long as you had a working sense of the general content of the poem and kept the poem's main idea in mind.

Essentially, the poem describes a character called Mother (we shouldn't presume that the poem is in fact about Kizer's mother, the poem might narrate an entirely fictional trial and fictional people) who serves on the jury at the trial of a dentist. The Mother takes a strange and not particularly honorable approach to her duties; she simply finds the dentist guilty from the moment she lays eyes on him, and so pays as much attention to the book she's reading as to the trial itself. If you got this much from the poem you would be off to a good start. Using POE carefully should have solved most (or all) of your problems.

41. **The correct answer is (D).** This question called for you to interpret the answer choices carefully. You needed to pay strict attention to the wording of the choices. Choice (A) should have been an easy first elimination. It describes an attitude completely opposite to that of the Mother's. The other three incorrect answers were a little bit tricky. In (B), was she "completely unaware?" Take the statement literally. Does she not know that she will be called upon to deliver a verdict? Of course she does. She may be unaware of some of the ethical duties imposed on her, but that doesn't make her "completely" unaware. Eliminate (B). Similarly, in (C), just because the Mother judges the dentist according to her own rather than legal standards we can't assume that she would face every jury situation this way, nor in fact does she hold the Dentist's status as accused against him. She just doesn't like creepy little dentists. (E) shouldn't have been too tough to eliminate. The Mother certainly considers herself superior to the dentist (and probably a lot of other people as well) but how she feels the law applies to her we don't know. Eliminate. This leaves only (D). Yes, it's fair to say that

the Mother takes her responsibilities too lightly, and her certainty about the whole affair tells us that she is has no doubts about her fitness as a juror.

42. **The correct answer is (B).** This should have been a piece of cake. You needed to not read too much into the phrase "half-heard." Don't let the answer choices' power of suggestion steer you down false paths. The Mother half-hears because she's reading. If the poet wanted to suggest age or poor hearing she would have returned to those ideas to make them clearer. Here, she wants to reinforce the impression that the Mother has made up her mind so fully that she barely bothers with the details of the trial.

43. **The correct answer is (D).** This is an extremely tricky question. Many students pick answer choices (B) or (C). But the dentist is not said to be a seminarian (a clergyperson.) The dentist is uncomfortable like a priest without the white collar of that profession. The rest of the stanza relates the courtroom to a ship. (e.g. the "plank," the "deck.") The dentist isn't compared to a condemned sailor, but is described as though he is one when the Mother pushes the fly-speck from the page, and says "she will push him off." This refers to the way in which she will push him from the plank. It also suggests that she thinks of him as easily dismissed and insignificant as a fly, and perhaps as repulsive. But the poet does not describe the dentist as a fly-speck. Choice (E) may or may not be true, but it is found neither in the stanza, nor in the poem. Only (D) is correct.

44. **The correct answer is (C).** Here you needed to understand that the poem is about the Mother and the dentist, not about other people. That is, you needed to stay with the main idea. The phrase in question refers only to the dentist, in fact choice (C) summarizes it nicely. The dentist is the "hacker, wielder of pliers" etc. Yes, some of the items in the list are a bit confusing, but use your imagination. How is the dentist a "barber"? Well, think of the hydraulic chair you have to sit in, or the bib the dentist pulls around your neck: aren't those things reminiscent of being in a barber-shop?

45. **The correct answer is (E).** Here you needed to stay with the main idea and not get drawn toward a silly answer. Throughout the poem the Mother feels herself to be superior to dentists in general and to this dentist in particular. The Mother is a tremendous snob; she considers dentists low-lifes. Advertising is just one more thing that her-kind-of-people just don't do. You might have had some difficulty if you didn't know the word "propriety." It refers to what is proper or polite. POE should have led you to the right answer anyway however, so long as you saw that other answers all involved reading much too deeply into the passage.

46. **The correct answer is (D).** This is a super POE question and it should have been pretty easy. Choices I and II should have been obvious. The Mother finds the dentist guilty because he is a dentist and she persuades the rest of the jury that the dentist is guilty. Using POE you are then down to just choices (D) and (E). So, does the poem imply that the dentist should have been found innocent? Not at all. All it implies is that the dentist is an unattractive creep who drilled a patient through the tongue. Does this make him guilty? Who knows. Innocent? Again: who knows. We're never told with what exactly the dentist has been charged.

47. **The correct answer is (A).** ETS has a way of sneaking a good bit of vocabulary into the test, and this question is a good example. It is also a good example of a question that lends itself to POE and the principle of half-bad = all-bad. You didn't have to know what lecherous meant in (A) to say that the dentist could be seen as comically chasing his assistant round the

chair while molded plaster teeth grin from the shelves, and there's something sickly funny too about his being so out of it with love that he drills right through a patient's tongue. So if you didn't know what lecherous meant you'd leave (A) for a guess. For (B) to be correct the dentist would had to have deliberately drilled through his patient's tongue. That's wrong, so eliminate (B). For exactly the same reason eliminate (C), the dentist was not calculating. In (D) you find more vocab. What's amorous? If you know great, but you don't need to know to eliminate the choice. You could eliminate by simply using the half-bad = all-bad principle. Is the dentist timid? No. He chased his assistant around the chair. He sounds more like a maniac. Eliminate (D). (*Amorous* means seeking—amore—that is, love and sex.) Finally there's (E). The dentist drilled his patient's tongue in a moment of dreamy contemplation, not anger. Eliminate (E). Thus, using POE, we're left with only (A). So what does lecherous mean? Well, essentially, it means: lustful, with strong overtones of slime.

48. **The correct answer is (E).** The phrase "tasting brine" continues the doomed-sailor-forced-to-walk-the-plank metaphor of the second stanza. Again vocabulary helps: "brine" is sea-water. The dentist has begun to realize that things are not going well, that he will be found guilty. Metaphorically then, he will walk the plank and end up with a mouthful of sea-water. It's worth pointing out how nicely Kizer sets this image of "tasting brine." It refers back to the earlier sailor metaphors, but it also works as a fresh rephrasing of a stale idea: that one finds a bitter taste in one's mouth in the face of unpleasant prospects. Along similar lines and just because artistry is worth pointing out wherever you find it, note Kizer's use of the word "rises" in the phrase "as the testimony rises." It's an unusual striking verb in this context, but perfectly suited to the moment. "Rises" implies increase in sound and in passion. It is also the verb of choice to refer to deepening water, as in a rising tide—or even more appropriately—to the effect an approaching storm has on the seas, as in the seas' rise. In the poem, Kizer has found a use for "rise" where all three meanings—increasing sound, increasing emotion, rising (metaphorical) water—come into play. Does seeing this specifically help you answer question 8? Not really. But we wanted to point out the kind of sensitivity to language you want to develop in order to fully appreciate poetry (and everything else you read). Developing a keen ear for language brings pleasure and success far beyond the AP test (although it brings that too).

49. **The correct answer is (D).** The key to this question was to go back and find where the poem attaches a metaphor to reading. The question gives no line reference, but you shouldn't have had too much trouble spotting line 19, where the mother reads with "an easy breaststroke." (Of course, to do this you needed to have an idea of what a metaphor is. We've mentioned it a couple of times already, but here it is again: make sure you can define the terms simile and metaphor, and make sure you can tell the difference between them. Both concepts are defined in our glossary of literary terms.) This was a very easy question so long as you went back to the passage. The disastrous mistake was to not go back to the passage and try to figure out the answer based on memory and common sense. Even if you didn't get the question wrong you'd actually end up wasting time, and you'd probably get it wrong.

50. **The correct answer is (D).** This is primarily a term question but you could have arrived at a correct guess without knowing that "poetic justice" refers to punishment that reflects the crime. (For example, a counterfeiter buys an expensive old painting with bogus money only to discover later that the painting is a forgery.) In the seventh stanza the poet describes the dentist now in the position of a patient, gripping the arms of his chair and being most

uncomfortably drilled. This sort of reversal also falls under the category of poetic justice. If you were unfamiliar with the term poetic justice you could have arrived at a perfectly good guess by reading the question carefully. It refers to the "Mother's treatment" of the dentist. In which stanza is the mother most directly involved with the dentist himself (and not simply the legal process)? In the seventh stanza, where she "strapped him in, to drill him away." This should have made (D), the most attractive guess. *Guess*. By the way, there's another more technical definition of poetic justice, which ETS will probably not use. We cover that definition, as well as the one above, in our glossary.

51. **The correct answer is (C).** There's our old friend irony again. In the phrase "Nice Mrs. Nemesis" the irony is not very delicate, in fact it has almost become irony's nasty little brother sarcasm. To answer this question it helped a great deal to know that a "nemesis" is an arch-enemy. (In the poem, Kizer actually refers to the Greek goddess, Nemesis, who represented righteous anger.) If you knew that a nemesis is an arch-enemy, or even just something negative (which you could have figured out from context) you could have reasoned that "Nice Mrs. 'something nasty'" contains the kind of contradiction that makes for irony. Barring that, you should have worked with the terms you knew and used POE to eliminate. All the terms in the answer choices are covered in our glossary of terms.

52. **The correct answer is (D).** These I, II, III questions are made for POE. After reading through the selection items you should have gone back to the final stanza and reread it. Then look at the items again. Which choice is easiest to decide upon? Choice II should look weird—eliminate it. The stanza discusses the Mother's idea of God; Voltaire is an afterthought, and all that's said is that she finds him "indispensable." What Voltaire's views are the poem doesn't say (and ETS does not expect you to know Voltaire's philosophy). With item II gone, choices (B) and (E) are gone as well. What about item III? Social decorum refers to polite behavior. In the last stanza the mother mentions that God instructs in "hygiene and deportment," that is, in necessary social graces. Item III is a keeper. Even if you didn't know what decorum meant, which makes more sense: the Mother believes God agrees with her, or disagrees? If you got the general drift of the poem you should know that the Mother thinks God shares her views. Keeping item III means you can eliminate (A). All that's left are choices (C) and (D). Okay, let's look at item I. Here you needed to read closely. She says God is "indispensable." That's good enough to justify the "deeply held" part of item I. What about "unsophisticated." Is it a sophisticated conception of the Divine to think that God cares about hygiene? Not really. Furthermore, Kizer's comparison of the Mother to "true idolaters" reinforces the unsophisticated idea. Does the Mother think she's unsophisticated? Not at all! She thinks she's hot-stuff reading Voltaire and all! But the question doesn't ask what the Mother thinks of herself. It asks about what the poem says about her. In the final stanza Kizer has some fun at the Mother's expense. Item I is a keeper, which makes the right answer (D).

53. **The correct answer is (B).** This should have been a truly easy grammar question. In fact, it really isn't a grammar question at all, just a disguised comprehension question. Basically it asks, who "swept out?" The answer is Mother. You should have gone back to the poem and read the sentence carefully. ETS likes to ask grammar, or pseudogrammar questions like this one, when the elements in question are widely separated. In this instance, the only difficult aspect of the question is that several words intervene between "Mother" and "swept-out." Don't let that throw you. Subject and verb do not have to come close to one another.

ETS likes it when they don't. You've probably also been taught that modifiers should be placed next to the word(s) they modify. That's true, but ETS likes to ask questions about sentences that are exceptions to that rule.

54. **The correct answer is (A).** The lines "He was doomed, doomed, doomed by birth, profession,/ Practice, appearance, personal habits, loves . . . / And now his patient swollen-mouthed with cancer!" gave this question away. All you had to do was to work through the choices using those lines to eliminate (remember this is an EXCEPT question!) In the end, all you are left with is the correct answer. The dentist's religious beliefs are never mentioned.

55. **The correct answer is (E).** This is a tone question. As you read the poem you probably found yourself thinking the Mother is being pretty harsh and unfair condemning a man for being a dentist. And it's true. By conventional ethical standards the Mother has behaved abominably. Kizer knows it but never passes judgement. Mostly Kizer has fun with the situation. She's impressed with the Mother's strength (and arrogance) even as she calls upon Voltaire to rescue the "wreck of [the Mother's] fairmindedness." Kizer's sympathetic to the Mother, but not entirely so, not when she refers to the Mother as "Nice Mrs. Nemesis" and not when she relates the Mother's vision of the deity. These things are lightly critical. The whole thing is softened by the fact that the dentist does sound like a creep who deserves what he gets, so the Mother's cavalier attitude doesn't have tragic consequences. All of this adds up to (E), amused ambivalence. The situation might have been shocking, but Kizer prefers to see the underlying humor in the clash of the Mother's sense of snooty proper conduct, the dentist's low-life self-presentation, and the irony that neither of them are actually conducting themselves well. The incorrect choices all call up emotional states that are too extreme to be justified, and should have been pretty easy to eliminate so POE should have gotten you the right answer even if the term "ambivalence" in choice (E) puzzled you.

Part VI

The Princeton Review AP English Literature and Composition Practice Test 2

ENGLISH LITERATURE AND COMPOSITION

SECTION I

Time — 1 hour

Directions: This section consists of passages drawn from literary works and questions about those passages' style, form, and content. Read each prose selection or poem carefully and choose the best answer to each of the subsequent questions on the passage. Remember to completely darken the corresponding oval on your answer sheet. (Also, be sure to take extra care on those questions that contain the words NOT, LEAST, or EXCEPT.)

Questions 1–15. Choose your answers to questions 1–15 based on a careful reading of the following passage.

An Invective Against Enemies of Poetry

With the enemies of poetry I care not if I have a bout, and those are they that term our best writers but babbling ballad-makers, holding them fantastical fools, that have wit but cannot tell how to use it. I (5) myself have been so censured among some dull-headed divines, who deem it no more cunning to write an exquisite poem than to preach pure Calvin or distill the juice of a commentary in a quarter sermon. Prove it when you will, you slow-spirited Saturnists, that (10) have nothing but the pilferies of your pen to polish an exhortation withal; no eloquence but tautologies to tie the ears of your auditory unto you; no invention but "here it is to be noted, I stole this note out of Beza or Marlorat"; no wit to move, no passion to urge, but (15) only an ordinary form of preaching, blown up by use of often hearing and speaking; and you shall find there goes more exquisite pains and purity of wit to the writing of one such rare poem as *Rosamund* than to a hundred of your dunstical sermons.

(20) Should we (as you) borrow all out of others, and gather nothing of ourselves our names should be bafful'd on every bookseller's stall, and not a chandler's mustard pot but would wipe his mouth with our waste paper. "New herrings, new!" we must (25) cry, every time we make ourselves public, or else we shall be christened with a hundred new titles of idiotism. Nor is poetry an art whereof there is no use in a man's whole life but to describe discontented thoughts and youthful desires; for there is no study (30) but it doth illustrate and beautify.

To them that demand what fruits the poets of our time bring forth, or wherein they are able to prove themselves necessary to the state, thus I answer: first and foremost, they have cleansed our language from (35) barbarism and made the vulgar sort here in London (which is the fountain whose rivers flow round about England) to aspire to a richer purity of speech than is communicated with the commonality of any nation under heaven. The virtuous by their praises they (40) encourage to be more virtuous; to vicious men they are as infernal hags to haunt their ghosts with eternal infamy after death. The soldier, in hope to have his high deeds celebrated by their pens, despiseth a whole army of perils, and acteth wonders exceeding all (45) human conjecture. Those that care neither for God nor the devil, by their quills are kept in awe.

Let God see what he will, they would be loath to have the shame of the world. What age will not praise immortal Sir Philip Sidney, whom noble Salustius (50) (that thrice singular French poet) hath famoused; together with Sir Nicholas Bacon, Lord Keeper, and merry Sir Thomas More, for the chief pillars of our English speech. Not so much but Chaucer's host, Bailly in Southwark, and his wife of Bath he keeps (55) such a stir with, in his *Canterbury Tales*, shall be talked of whilst the Bath is used, or there be ever a bad house in Southwark. Gentles, it is not your lay chronographers, that write of nothing but of mayors and sheriffs and the dear year and the great frost, that (60) can endow your names with never-dated glory; for they want the wings of choice words to fly to heaven, which we have; they cannot sweeten a discourse, or wrest admiration from men reading, as we can, reporting the meanest accident. Poetry is the honey of (65) all flowers, the quintessence of all sciences, the marrow of wit and the very phrase of angels. How much better is it, then, to have an elegant lawyer to plead one's cause, than a stutting townsman that loseth himself in his tale and doth nothing but make (70) legs; so much it is better for a nobleman or gentleman to have his honor's story related, and his deeds emblazoned, by a poet, than a citizen.

GO ON TO THE NEXT PAGE

1. In the first paragraph, preachers are accused of all the following EXCEPT

   (A) plagiarism
   (B) stupidity
   (C) dullness
   (D) eloquence
   (E) laziness

2. "Saturnist" (line 9) means

   (A) astrologer
   (B) nymphomaniac
   (C) depressed and depressing person
   (D) pagan
   (E) foolishly optimistic person

3. Lines 20–27 argue that

   (A) poets must take second jobs to make a living
   (B) most people don't respect poets
   (C) there are too many poets
   (D) poets have to work hard to present consistently fresh material
   (E) poetry books are never bestsellers

4. "New herrings, new!" (line 24)

   (A) refers to an implied comparison between the writers of new poems and the sellers of fresh fish
   (B) suggests that poetry is slippery and hard to catch the meaning of, like fish
   (C) implies that poetry is just another commodity
   (D) implies that poetry grows stale rapidly, like fish
   (E) compares poetry to rotten fish

5. In lines 34–39 London is described as:

   (A) flooded
   (B) a damp, rainy city
   (C) the main influence on the English language
   (D) a cultural garden
   (E) an important port city

6. The main idea of lines 39–48 is

   (A) People are motivated by concern for their reputations.
   (B) Poetry is fair to the virtuous and the evil alike.
   (C) Poetry is inspirational.
   (D) Poetry is most attractive to atheists.
   (E) Poets are very judgmental.

7. Who is Salustius (line 49)?

   (A) a French poet
   (B) Sidney's *nom de plume*
   (C) the Roman god of poetry
   (D) the King of England
   (E) the Wife of Bath

8. What is Bath?

   (A) a state of sin
   (B) a character in Chaucer
   (C) a married man
   (D) a poet
   (E) a town and spa in England

9. In the last paragraph, poets are said to be like

   (A) lawyers
   (B) mayors
   (C) chronographers
   (D) townsmen
   (E) angels

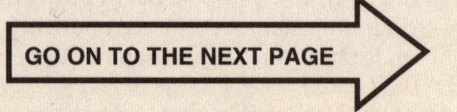

10. Line 10 is an example of

    (A) metaphor
    (B) onomatoepeia
    (C) paradox
    (D) alliteration
    (E) apostrophe

11. In line 2, what is the referent of "those"?

    (A) poets
    (B) the author
    (C) ballads
    (D) poems
    (E) poetry's enemies

12. What are "divines" (line 6)?

    (A) preachers
    (B) great writers
    (C) dead writers
    (D) fools
    (E) Saturnists

13. Nashe complains (lines 10–11) that the preachers have no eloquence to hold their audience but only

    (A) repetition
    (B) nonsense
    (C) lies
    (D) irrelevance
    (E) sermons

14. According to the passage, which of the following is NOT a function of poetry?

    (A) to encourage the virtuous
    (B) to purify the language
    (C) to embarrass the villainous
    (D) to illustrate and beautify
    (E) to plagiarize sermons

15. Who first raised the issue of poets' necessity to the state?

    (A) Nashe
    (B) Sidney
    (C) Salustius
    (D) Plato
    (E) Milton

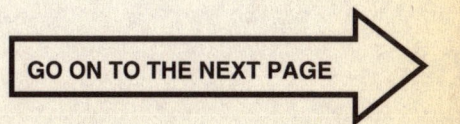

GO ON TO THE NEXT PAGE

Questions 16–29. Choose answers to questions 16–29 based on a careful reading of the following poem by John Donne.

Let me pour forth
My tears before thy face whilst I stay here,
For thy face coins them, and thy stamp they bear,
Line And by this mintage they are something worth,
(5)   For thus they be
        Pregnant of thee;
Fruits of much grief they are, emblems of more—
When a tear falls, that Thou falls which it bore,
So thou and I are nothing then, when on a diverse shore.

(10)   On a round ball
A workman that hath copies by can lay
An Europe, Africa, and an Asia,
And quickly make that, which was nothing, all;
        So doth each tear
(15)   Which thee doth wear,
A globe, yea world, by that impression grow,
Till thy tears mixed with mine do overflow This world;
by waters sent from thee, my heaven disolv'd so.

        O more than moon,
(20) Draw not up seas to drown me in thy sphere;
Weep me not dead in thine arms, but forbear
To teach the sea what it may do too soon.
        Let not the wind
        Example find
(25) To do me more harm than it purposeth;
Since thou and I sigh one another's breath,
Whoe'er sighs most is cruelest, and hastes the other's death.

16. The situation described in this poem is

(A) the end of a romantic relationship
(B) death
(C) the separation of lovers
(D) the end of the world
(E) a pleasure cruise

17. Lines 10–16 are an example of

(A) paradox
(B) dramatic irony
(C) metaphor
(D) metaphysical conceit
(E) dramatic monologue

18. Line 19 is an address to:

(A) the moon
(B) the world
(C) the poet's soul
(D) the workmen
(E) the beloved

19. To what do lines 14 and 15 refer?

I. the speaker's tears which reflect the beloved
II. the beloved's tears
III. the beloved's clothing, which has been torn as a symbol of her grief
IV. the ocean, which is salty like tears
V. the rain on their faces

(A) I
(B) I and II
(C) I, II, and III
(D) I and IV
(E) all of the above

20. Which of the stanzas do NOT include images of roundness?

(A) Stanza 1
(B) Stanza 2
(C) Stanza 3
(D) Stanzas 1 and 3
(E) None: all of the stanzas contain images of roundness

GO ON TO THE NEXT PAGE

21. Which of the following most accurately describes the use of imagery in this poem?

    (A) The sustained images of worthlessness suggest the hopelessness of the lovers' situation.
    (B) The sustained images of the globe suggest the vast distances of the lovers' separation.
    (C) The sustained images of roundness suggest a perfect circle, and therefore the cosmic and permanent union of the lovers, since circles have no end.
    (D) The sustained images of water suggest the shifting faithlessness of the lovers.
    (E) The sustained images of water suggest the sexual bond between the lovers.

22. In line 13, to what does the word "which" refer?

    (A) copies
    (B) the round ball
    (C) the world
    (D) the workman
    (E) the continents

23. Which of the following is NOT an appropriate association for lines 19–20?

    (A) the power of a goddess
    (B) the relationship between the moon and the ocean's tides
    (C) the round shape of the moon
    (D) the folktale of the man in the moon
    (E) the moon as suggestive of unhappy feelings, the opposite of "sunny disposition"

24. What does "diverse shore" (line 9) mean?

    (A) heaven
    (B) hell
    (C) Europe
    (D) a different place
    (E) the ground

25. Which of the following types of imagery is sustained throughout the poem?

    (A) tears
    (B) globes
    (C) coins
    (D) moon
    (E) ocean

26. Which of the following is the best paraphrase for line 4?

    (A) You are not worth the salt of my tears.
    (B) My tears are worth something because they reflect your face.
    (C) My tears are emotionally refreshing.
    (D) My tears are worth something because they are for your sake.
    (E) My grief is a valuable feeling.

27. What does the speaker ascribe to his beloved in lines 20–25?

    (A) the power to break his heart
    (B) the power to kill him
    (C) the power to influence the natural elements
    (D) the power to restrain her grief
    (E) the right to seek other lovers

28. John Donne is a

    (A) Modernist poet
    (B) Postmodern poet
    (C) Romantic poet
    (D) Metaphysical poet
    (E) Cavalier poet

29. In the extended metaphors of this poem, the speaker flatters the beloved through the use of

    (A) hyperbole
    (B) sarcasm
    (C) irony
    (D) parallelism
    (E) eschatology

Questions 30–40. Choose answers to questions 30–40 based on a careful reading of the passage below. The passage, an excerpt from a short story by Mary E. Wilkins Freeman, describes a woman about to be married after a long engagement. She will have to leave her own home to live with her fiance and his mother.

Every morning, rising and going about among her neat maidenly possessions, she felt as one looking her last upon the faces of dear friends. It was true that in a measure she could take them with her, but, robbed of (5) their old environments, they would appear in such new guises that they would almost cease to be themselves. Then there were some peculiar features of her happy solitary life which she would probably be obliged to relinquish altogether. Sterner tasks than (10) these graceful but half-needless ones would probably devolve upon her. There would be a large house to care for; there would be company to entertain; there would be Joe's rigours and feeble old mother to wait upon; and it would be contrary to all thrifty village (15) traditions for her to keep more than one servant. Louisa had a little still, and she used to occupy herself pleasantly in summer weather with distilling the sweet and aromatic essences from roses and peppermint and spearmint. By-and-by her still must (20) be laid away. Her store of essences was already considerable, and there would be no time for her to distil for the mere pleasure of it. Then Joe's mother would think it foolishness; she had already hinted her opinion in the matter. Louisa dearly loved to sew a (25) linen seam, not always for use, but for the simple, mild pleasure which she took in it. She would have been loath to confess how more than once she had ripped a seam for the mere delight of sewing it together again. Sitting at her window during long sweet afternoons, (30) drawing her needle gently through the dainty fabric, she was peace itself. But there was small chance of such foolish comfort in the future. Joe's mother, domineering, shrewd old matron that she was even in her old age, and very likely even Joe himself, with his (35) honest masculine rudeness, would laugh and frown down all these pretty but senseless old maiden ways.

Louisa had almost the enthusiasm of an artist over the mere order and cleanliness of her solitary home. She had throbs of genuine triumph at the sight of the (40) window-panes which she had polished until they shone like jewels. She gloated gently over her orderly bureau-drawers, with their exquisitely folded contents redolent with lavender and sweet clover and very purity. Could she be sure of the endurance of even (45) this? She had visions, so startling that she half repudiated them as indelicate, of course masculine belongings strewn about in endless litter; of dust and disorder arising necessarily from a coarse masculine presence in the midst of all this delicate harmony.

(50) Among her forebodings of disturbance, not the least was with regard to Caesar. Caesar was a veritable hermit of a dog. For the greater part of his life he had dwelt in his secluded hut, shut out from the society of his kind and all innocent canine joys. Never (55) had Caesar since his early youth watched at a woodchuck's hole; never had he known the delights of a stray bone at a neighbor's kitchen door. And it was all on account of a sin committed when hardly out of his puppyhood. No one knew the possible depth of (60) remorse of which this mild-visaged, altogether innocent-looking old dog might be capable; but whether or not he had encountered remorse, he had encountered a full measure of righteous retribution. Old Caesar seldom lifted up his voice in a growl or a (65) bark; he was fat and sleepy; there were yellow rings which looked like spectacles around his dim old eyes; but there was a neighbor who bore on his hand the imprint of several of Caesar's sharp white youthful teeth, and for that he had lived at the end of a chain, (70) all alone in a little hut, for fourteen years. The neighbor, who was choleric and smarting with the pain of his wound, had demanded either Caesar's death or complete ostracism. So Louisa's brother, to whom the dog had belonged, had built him his little (75) kennel and tied him up. It was now fourteen years since, in a flood of youthful spirits, he had inflicted that memorable bite and with the exception of short excursions, always at the end of the chain, under the strict guardianship of his master or Louisa, the old dog (80) had remained a close prisoner. It is doubtful if, with his limited ambition, he took much pride in the fact, but it is certain that he was possessed of considerable cheap fame. He was regarded by all the children in the village and by many adults as a very monster of (85) ferocity. Mothers charged their children with solemn emphasis not to go too near him, and the children listened and believed greedily, with a fascinated appetite for terror, and ran by Louisa's house stealthily, with many sidelong and backward glances (90) at the terrible dog. If perchance he sounded a hoarse bark, there was a panic. Wayfarers chancing into Louisa's yard eyed him with respect, and inquired if the chain were stout. Caesar at large might have seemed a very ordinary dog, and excited no comment

(95) whatever; chained, his reputation overshadowed him, so that he lost his own proper outlines and looked darkly vague and enormous. Joe, however, with his good-humored sense and shrewdness, saw him as he was. He strode valiantly up to him and patted him on
(100) the head, in spite of Louisa's soft clamor of warning, and even attempted to set him loose. Louisa grew so alarmed that he desisted, but kept announcing his opinion in the matter quite forcibly at intervals. "There ain't a better-natured dog in town," he would
(105) say, "and it's downright cruel to keep him tied up there. Some day I'm going to take him out."

Louisa had very little hope that he would not, one of these days, when their interests and possessions should be more completely fused in one. She pictured
(110) to herself Caesar on the rampage through the quiet and unguarded village. She saw innocent children bleeding in his path. She was herself very fond of the old dog, because he had belonged to her dead brother, and he was always very gentle with her; still she had
(115) great faith in his ferocity. She always warned people not to go too near him. She fed him on ascetic fare of corn-mush and cakes, and never fired his dangerous temper with heating and sanguinary diet of flesh and bones. Louisa looked at the old dog munching his
(120) simple fare, and thought of her approaching marriage and trembled.

30. In overall terms, how is Louisa characterized?

(A) as a bitter, domineering woman
(B) as a naive, childish woman
(C) as a frightened, foolish woman
(D) as a sheltered, innocent woman
(E) as a selfish, cruel woman

31. Which of the following statements best describe Louisa's household activities (paragraphs 1 and 2)?

(A) They symbolize the timeless rituals of ancient rural harvest deities.
(B) They demonstrate Louisa's contented absorption in a traditionally feminine cultural sphere.
(C) They demonstrate Louisa's mental illness.
(D) They demonstrate Louisa's repressed artistic genius.
(E) They describe the highest traditional values of Louisa's town.

32. Which of the following statements are TRUE?

The story of Caesar is used in this passage to symbolize

I. the idea that Louisa has grown too accustomed to her circumscribed life to welcome change.
II. he idea that cruelty to animals is an indicator of a cruel society.
III. the idea that marrying is like being conquered by an invading emperor.
IV. the idea that people can be trapped by unchanging and unexamined ideas.
V. the idea that you can't teach an old dog new tricks.

(A) I and IV only
(B) I, II, and III only
(C) V only
(D) all of the above
(E) none of the above

33. Caesar's "ascetic" diet (paragraph 4)

(A) reflects Louisa's poverty
(B) is part of his punishment
(C) reflects a nineteenth-century theory that bodily humours are affected by diet and can change disposition
(D) is part of a religious practice meant to encourage celibacy in hermits
(E) is typical pet food in nineteenth-century homes

34. The word "purity" in line 44 is an example of

(A) irony
(B) metaphor
(C) simile
(D) oxymoron
(E) mock epic

35. The tone of the description of Caesar (paragraphs 3 and 4) is

(A) gently satirical
(B) indignant
(C) pensive
(D) foreboding
(E) menacing

GO ON TO THE NEXT PAGE

36. "Sanguinary" (line 118) means

    (A) expensive
    (B) feminine
    (C) masculine
    (D) vegetarian
    (E) bloody

37. Judging from this passage, which of the following best describes Louisa's beliefs about gender relations?

    (A) Men and women naturally belong together.
    (B) Men and women should remain separate.
    (C) Men bring chaos and possibly danger to women's lives.
    (D) Women help to civilize men's natural wildness.
    (E) Men are more intelligent than women.

38. What does "mild-visaged" (line 60) mean?

    (A) having a calm temper
    (B) having a gentle face
    (C) having an old face
    (D) being confused
    (E) having a kind mask

39. Which of the following are accomplished by the Caesar vignette?

    (A) It shows us Joe's down-to-earth, kindhearted character.
    (B) It symbolically shows us Louisa's fears of the future.
    (C) It serves as a symbol of what happens to those who refuse change.
    (D) It provides a humorous satire of small-town concerns.
    (E) All of the above.

40. In line 46, how is the word "indelicate" used?

    (A) to indicate the differences between Louisa and Joe
    (B) to indicate that Louisa considered her thoughts inappropriately sexual
    (C) to indicate the coarseness of Joe's personality
    (D) to indicate the inferior quality of Joe's belongings
    (E) to foreshadow the vision of Caesar's rampage

GO ON TO THE NEXT PAGE

Questions 41–55. Read the poem below carefully then choose answers to the questions that follow.

Gassing the woodchucks didn't turn out right.
The knockout bomb from the Feed and Grain Exchange
was featured as merciful, quick at the bone
and the case we had against them was airtight,
both exits shoehorned shut with puddingstone,
but they had a sub-sub-basement out of range.

Next morning they turned up again, no worse
for the cyanide than we for our cigarettes
and state-store Scotch, all of us up to scratch.
They brought down the marigolds as a matter of course
and then took over the vegetable patch
nipping the broccoli shoots, beheading the carrots.

The food from our mouths, I said, righteously thrilling
to the feel of the .22, the bullets' neat noses.
I, a lapsed pacifist fallen from grace
puffed with Darwinian pieties for killing,
now drew a bead on the littlest woodchuck's face.
He died down in the everbearing roses.

Ten minutes later I dropped the mother. She
flipflopped in the air and fell, her needle teeth
still hooked in a leaf of early Swiss chard.
Another baby next. O one-two-three
the murderer inside me rose up hard,
the hawkeye killer came on stage forthwith.

There's one chuck left. Old wily fellow, he keeps
me cocked and ready day after day after day.
All night I hunt his humped-up form. I dream
I sight along the barrel in my sleep.
If only they'd all consented to die unseen
gassed underground the quiet Nazi way.

Line (5), (10), (15), (20), (25), (30)

41. What does this poem literally describe?

   (A) World War II
   (B) the elimination of garden pests
   (C) the problems of vegetarians
   (D) a dream
   (E) landscape design

42. Which of the following best describes the theme of the poem?

   (A) The animals are taking over the world.
   (B) We must be ever-vigilant against the battles of everyday life.
   (C) Raising your own food is essential to independence.
   (D) The world is essentially violent.
   (E) Violence and persecution are potentials within everyone.

43. Which of the following is FALSE?

   (A) The poem exploits the Nazi rhetoric of vermin extermination.
   (B) The poem draws parallels between Nazi philosophy and contemporary social Darwinism.
   (C) The poem suggests that political beliefs are as emotional and arational as religious beliefs.
   (D) The poem suggests that all violence is essentially similar.
   (E) The poem suggests that some killing is justifiable.

44. Which of the following best describes the phrase "Darwinian pieties" (line 16).

   (A) antonym
   (B) synonym
   (C) oxymoron
   (D) truism
   (E) metaphor

45. Which of the following statements about line 4 is FALSE?

    (A) The legal rhetoric of this line reminds us of the historical perversions of the legal system.
    (B) "Airtight" puns on its legal meaning and its literal meaning in the context of gassing.
    (C) The pronouns in this line establish an "us against them" mindset.
    (D) The line proves that the speaker's attitudes are correct.
    (E) The aural closure provided by the end rhyme echoes the sealing up of the woodchucks' den and the closed mind portrayed in the poem.

46. Which of the following best describes the tone of the poem?

    (A) righteous outrage
    (B) helpless sorrow
    (C) ironic satire
    (D) indignant protest
    (E) quiet triumph

47. What is the most important thematic point made in the final two lines of the poem?

    (A) If only the woodchucks had all been killed, the garden would be safe.
    (B) Even garden-variety violence is similar to the atrocities of the Nazis.
    (C) If only the woodchucks were all dead, the speaker could sleep better at night.
    (D) If only the gassing had killed the woodchucks, the speaker would never have had to confront the violence in his nature.
    (E) If only the gassing had killed the woodchucks, the speaker would not have had to see their disgusting deaths.

48. Which of the following statements describing the setting of the poem are TRUE?

    I. The stereotypically peaceful garden is an ironic setting for the violence described in the poem.
    II. The garden symbolizes nature and thereby enriches the speaker's allusion to Darwin.
    III. The garden makes this poem a pastoral poem.
    IV. The specific references to the garden provide a realistic setting in which to consider the serious issues raised by the poem.
    V. The garden is an important symbol of threatened civilization that must be protected from encroaching predators.

    (A) I, II, and III
    (B) I, II, and IV
    (C) III and V
    (D) all of the above
    (E) none of the above

49. The word "Nazi" in the final line of the poem is

    (A) a metaphor
    (B) an allusion
    (C) a simile
    (D) a paradox
    (E) a metonym

50. The phrase "beheading the carrots" (line 12) is an example of

    (A) a metonym
    (B) metaphor
    (C) personification
    (D) anthropomorphism
    (E) symbolism

51. "I" in this poem refers to

    (A) the poet
    (B) the father woodchuck
    (C) the poet's persona
    (D) a Nazi
    (E) Darwin

GO ON TO THE NEXT PAGE

52. Which of the following best describes the function of line 24?

    (A) The phrase "came on stage forthwith" emphasizes the artificiality of the cultural attitudes under which the speaker is operating.
    (B) The adjective "hawkeye" emphasizes the natural predatory role of humans.
    (C) The noun "killer" emphasizes the horror of the speaker's actions.
    (D) The alliteration of the line is onomatopoeic.
    (E) The senselessness of the line demonstrates the speaker's confusion.

53. How does the first line of this poem function?

    I. It frames the ensuing narrative.
    II. It raises the question of right and wrong.
    III. It turns on the ambiguity of the word "right" to mean both "effective" and "moral."
    IV. Its understatement ironically foreshadows the conclusion of the poem.
    V. It summarizes the poem.

    (A) II and V
    (B) III and IV
    (C) I and II
    (D) I, II, III, and IV
    (E) all of the above

54. Which of the following best describes the word "airtight" (line 4)?

    (A) metaphor
    (B) oxymoron
    (C) pun
    (D) allusion
    (E) symbol

55. Which of the following best describes the final stanza of the poem?

    (A) The poet's persona endorses fascism.
    (B) The slant rhymes indicate the emotional imbalance the speaker is feeling.
    (C) It contradicts the rest of the poem.
    (D) It makes a strong moral point about environmentalism.
    (E) It abandons the verisimilitude of the poem for a surreal dream vision.

STOP
END OF SECTION I

IF YOU FINISH BEFORE TIME IS CALLED, YOU MAY CHECK YOUR WORK ON THIS SECTION. DO NOT GO ON TO SECTION II UNTIL YOU ARE TOLD TO DO SO.

ENGLISH LITERATURE AND COMPOSTION

SECTION II

Total Time—2 hours

Question 1

(Suggested time—40 minutes. This question counts as one-third of the total essay score.)

The passage that follows is from a memoir written in 1900 by a Native American woman, Zitkala-Sa, describing her departure from her mother's home to a missionary school in the East. Read the passage carefully. Then write a well-organized essay describing the methods the author has used to give her historically particular story a universal appeal. Be sure to consider such literary elements as symbolism and point of view.

The first turning away from the easy, natural flow of my life occurred in an early spring. It was in my eighth year; in the month of March, I afterward
Line learned. At this age I knew but one language, and that
(5) was my mother's native tongue.
 From some of my playmates I heard that two paleface missionaries were in our village. They were from that class of white men who wore big hats and carried large hearts, they said. Running direct to my
(10) mother, I began to question her why these two strangers were among us. She told me, after I had teased much, that they had come to take away Indian boys and girls to the East. My mother did not seem to want me to talk about them. But in a day or two, I
(15) gleaned many wonderful stories from my playfellows concerning the strangers.
 "Mother, my friend Judewin is going home with the missionaries. She is going to a more beautiful country than ours; the palefaces told her so!" I said
(20) wistfully, wishing in my heart that I too might go.
 Mother sat in a chair, and I was hanging on her knee. Within the last two seasons my big brother Dawee had returned from a three years' education in the East, and his coming back influenced my mother to
(25) take a father step from her native way of living. First it was a change from the buffalo skin to the white man's canvas that covered our wigwam. Now she had given up her wigwam of slender poles, to live, a foreigner, in a home of clumsy logs.
(30) "Yes, my child, several others besides Judewin are going away with the palefaces. Your brother said the missionaries had inquired about his little sister," she said, watching my face very closely.
 My heart thumped so hard against my breast, I
(35) wondered if she could hear it.
 "Did he tell them to take me, mother?" I asked, fearing lest Dawee had forbidden the palefaces to see me, and that my hope of going to the Wonderland would be entirely blighted.

(40) With a sad, slow smile, she answered: "There! I knew you were wishing to go, because Judewin has filled your ears with the white men's lies. Don't believe a word they say! Their words are sweet, but, my child, their deeds are bitter. You will cry for me,
(45) but they will not even soothe you. Stay with me, my little one! Your brother Dawee says that going East, away from your mother, is too hard an experience for his baby sister."
 Thus my mother discouraged my curiosity about
(50) the lands beyond our eastern horizons; for it was not yet an ambition for Letters that was stirring me. But on the following day the missionaries did come to our very house. I spied them coming up the footpath leading to our cottage. A third man was with them,
(55) but he was not my brother Dawee. It was another, a young intepreter, a paleface who had a smattering of the Indian language. I was ready to run out to meet them, but I did not dare to displease my mother. With great glee, I jumped up and down on our ground
(60) floor. I begged my mother to open the door, that they would be sure to come to us. Alas! They came, they saw, and they conquered!
 Judewin had told me of the great tree where grew red, red apples; and how we could reach out our
(65) hands and pick all the red apples we could eat. I had never seen apple trees. I had never tasted more than a dozen red apples in my life; and when I heard of the orchards of the East, I was eager to roam among them. The missionaries smiled into my eyes, and patted my
(70) head. I wondered how mother could say such hard words against them.
 "Mother, ask them if little girls may have all the red

GO ON TO THE NEXT PAGE →

apples they want, when they go East," I whispered aloud, in my excitement.

(75) The interpreter heard me, and answered: "Yes, little girl, the nice red apples are for those who pick them; and you will have a ride on the iron horse if you go with these good people."

I had never seen a train, and he knew it.

(80) "Mother, I'm going East! I like big red apples, and I want to ride on the iron horse! Mother, say yes!" I pleaded.

"I am not ready to give you any word," she said to them. "Tomorrow I shall send you answer by my (85) son."

With this they left us. Alone with my mother, I yielded to my tears, and cried aloud, shaking my head so as not to hear what she was saying to me. This was the first time I had ever been so unwilling to give up (90) my own desire that I refused to hearken to my mother's voice.

There was a solemn silence in our home that night. Before I went to bed I begged the Great Spirit to make my mother willing I should go with the missionaries.

(95) The next morning came, and my mother called me to her side. "My daughter, do you still persist in wishing to leave your mother?" she asked.

"Oh mother, it is not that I wish to leave you, but I want to see the wonderful Eastern land," I answered.

(100) My dear old aunt came to our house that morning, and I heard her say, "Let her try it."

I hoped that, as usual, my aunt was pleading on my side. My brother Dawee came for mother's decision. I dropped my play, and crept close to my (105) aunt.

"Yes, Dawee, my daughter, though she does not understand what it all means, is anxious to go. She will need an education when she is grown, for then there will be fewer real Dakotas, and many more (110) palefaces. This tearing her away, so young, from her mother is necessary, if I would have her an educated woman. The palefaces, who owe us a large debt for stolen lands, have begun to pay a tardy justice in offering some education to our children. But I know (115) my daughter must suffer keenly in this experiment. For her sake, I dread to tell you my reply to the missionaries. Go, tell them that they may take my little daughter, and that the Great Spirit shall not fail to reward them according to their hearts."

(120) Wrapped in my heavy blanket, I walked with my mother to the carriage that was soon to take us to the iron horse. I was happy. I met my playmates, who were also wearing their best thick blankets. We showed one another our new beaded moccasins, and (125) the width of the belts that girdled our new dresses. Soon we were being drawn rapidly away by the white man's horses. When I saw the lonely figure of my mother vanish in the distance, a sense of regret settled heavily upon me. I felt suddenly weak, as if I might (130) fall limp to the ground. I was in the hands of strangers whom my mother did not fully trust. I no longer felt free to be myself, or to voice my own feelings. The tears trickled down my cheeks, and I buried my face in the folds of my blanket. Now the first step, parting me (135) from my mother, was taken, and all my belated tears availed nothing.

Having driven thirty miles to the ferryboat, we crossed the Missouri in the evening. Then riding again a few miles eastward, we stopped before a (140) massive brick building. I looked at it in amazement, and with a vague misgiving, for in our village I had never seen so large a house. Trembling with fear and distrust of the palefaces, my teeth chattering from the chilly ride, I crept noiselessly in my soft moccasins (145) along the narrow hall, keeping very close to the bare wall. I was as frightened and bewildered as the captured young of a wild creature.

Question 2

(Suggested time—40 minutes. This question counts as one-third of the total essay score.)

Read the following poem carefully. Considering such literary elements as style, tone, rhyme, and diction, write a well-organized essay that examines the poem's view of patriotism.

"next to of course god america i
love you land of pilgrims' and so forth oh
say can you see by the dawn's early my
country 'tis of centuries come and go
and are no more what of it we should worry
in every language even deafanddumb
thy sons acclaim your glorious name by gorry
by jingo by gee by gosh by gum
why talk of beauty what could be more beautiful than these heroic happy dead
who rushed like lions to the roaring slaughter
they did not stop to think they died instead
then shall the voice of liberty be mute?"

He spoke.   And drank rapidly a glass of water.

–e. e. cummings

Question 3

(Suggested time—40 minutes. This question counts as one-third of the total essay score.)

In some works of literature, mothers or the concept of motherhood play central roles. Choose a novel or play of literary merit and write a well-organized essay in which you discuss a maternal character and the specific ways the character and the concept of maternity relate to the larger themes of the work. Avoid plot summary.

You may select a work from the list below, or you may choose to write about another work of comparable literary merit.

Medea
Sophie's Choice
The Color Purple
As I Lay Dying
A Tree Grows in Brooklyn
Hamlet
The Awakening
The Joy Luck Club
Sons and Lovers
To the Lighthouse
Beloved
Black Rain
Pedro Paramo
The Sound and the Fury
Fifth Business
The Stranger
The Scarlet Letter

STOP
END OF SECTION II
IF YOU FINISH BEFORE TIME IS CALLED, YOU MAY CHECK YOUR WORK ON THIS SECTION.

PART VII

ANSWERS AND EXPLANATIONS— PRACTICE TEST 2

QUESTIONS 1–15

"An Invective Against Enemies of Poetry" is excerpted from *Pierce Penniless, His Supplication to the Devil*, by English satirist Thomas Nashe (1567–1601). A journalist in London, Nashe published *Pierce Penniless* about 1592. Although much of his work would now be considered reactionary bigotry, Nashe is admired for his energetic and relatively modern-sounding prose style. In the passage excerpted here, Nashe is defending poetry as a valuable intellectual contribution to society, especially in contrast to the work of preachers and historians.

1. **The correct answer is (D).** "Eloquence" is the obvious answer here, since it runs contrary to the meaning of the passage. (And you remembered you were looking for the contrary, right? This is one of those "Except" questions.) All the other answers are straightforward accusations in the text, except for (E), which is a little obscure. But when Nashe talks about the preachers' "quarter sermon," he means a sermon given once a quarter, only four times a year. The implication is that the preachers really don't work very hard, unlike poets, as the next paragraph goes on to explain.

2. **The correct answer is (C).** In astrological terms, Saturn was thought to be the planet of depression and gloom, and Saturnists were people ruled by Saturn, hence, depresssed, depressing people. Remember that in the sixteenth century, astrology was considered more scientific than it is today. (A) is meant to lure people who recognize that Saturn is a planet and jump to "astrologer" by association. (B), "nymphomaniac," or sex addict, is there to trick people who confuse "Saturnist" with "satyr." (D), "pagan," picks up on the magical associations of astrology, but is certainly the wrong description of a preacher. (E), "optimistic person," means the opposite of the required definition.

3. **The correct answer is (D).** Unlike the lazy plagiarizing preachers, poets must have new material all the time or the public won't buy their books. (A) is wrong because the various professions presented in these lines are only implied comparisons for a poet's career, not a list of moonlighting poets. (B) is wrong because Nashe's audience does respect good poets; they only reject bad poets who present stale, recycled material. (C) and (E) are completely irrelevant to the passage, but might tempt those who think in terms of marketplace competition.

4. **The correct answer is (A).** Nashe is comparing poets to fishmongers, who must constantly keep their product fresh for the marketplace. He is continuing his thought about poets being superior to plagiarizing preachers. You could make arguments in support of (B), the idea that poetry has slippery meanings, but Nashe is not arguing that; he's defending poetry. (C) and (D) are also interesting ideas, but they are not in this passage, and are in fact contradicted in other portions of the reading, which praise the special cultural meaning and lasting fame of poetry. (E) is just ridiculous and completely contradicts the meaning of the passage.

5. **The correct answer is (C).** Nashe is asserting the purity and beauty of the English language, and argues that London, the seat of literary culture, influences how English is spoken all over the country, like the streams of a fountain spreading out beyond the fountain itself. Therefore, poets who improve English in London have a national influence. Answers (A), (B), and (E) are just incorrect associations with the watery imagery of fountains. (D) is tempting because it includes the idea that London is the source of culture, but does not include the important concept of national influence.

6. **The correct answer is (A).** Lines 39–48 describe how people are motivated by what is said about them, by their longing for fame or their horror of shame, by their reputations. Nashe might agree with (B), but nothing is said about fairness in these lines. (And despite what he may have thought, Nashe was often considered a slanderer during his lifetime, so his contemporaries didn't think he was fair.) (C) is tempting because the passage does mention that soldiers are inspired by poetry, but the concern in this passage is specifically the personal concerns of individuals for their reputations, not the general idea that poetry is uplifting. (D) might trick people who focus on the reference to "those that care neither for God nor the devil," but Nashe is not interested in atheists except as another category of people with reputations to worry about. (E) doesn't really have anything to do with the passage, except for those who overthink and get caught up in why the poets are writing about everyone in the first place. But that's getting far afield from the meaning of the specified lines.

7. **The correct answer is (A).** This question is actually pretty straightforward; the parenthetical phrase directly following the name Salustius tells you he is a French poet, actually more familiarly known today as Guillaume de Saluste du Bartas (1544–1590). (B) might confuse people who know what *nom de plume* means (it means "pen name"). (C) is simply incorrect but suggested by the Latinate name. (D) is right out of left field. (E) is for people whose eyes glazed over reading this passage and just stuck on the Wife of Bath.

8. **The correct answer is (E).** Bath is an ancient town and spa in England. This is a general knowledge question that you are just expected to know; the town shows up not only in Chaucer but also in Jane Austen. Answer (B) might be confusing because there is a famous character in Chaucer called the Wife of Bath, because she's from Bath, and she is mentioned in this passage. If you were getting very frazzled, the notion of wife might sucker you into choosing (C), since wives have husbands. (D) is there to confuse you if you were getting overwhelmed by this list of poets. (A) is just irrelevant.

9. **The correct answer is (A).** Nashe says it is better "to have an elegant lawyer to plead one's cause" than a stuttering townsmen (lines 67–68), and just so, it is better to have a poet write your history than a historian. (B) is wrong because mayors are not even compared to anything here; they are just something chronographers write about. Chronographers are local historians, and poets are said to be better than chronographers, not like them, so (C) is incorrect. (D) is wrong for the same reason: lawyers are better than townsmen just as poets are better than chronographers. (E), angels, is a little tricky, because poetry is said to be "the very phrase of angels" (line 66), which might imply that poets are the angels speaking the phrases. But that sentence is talking about Poetry: The Concept, not poets as members of society. And even conceited poets don't generally compare themselves to angels, certainly not in the middle of such a satirical piece. Even if you were confused by that, you should be able to see that lawyers is a direct comparison, while "angels" requires some overreading and stretching.

10. **The correct answer is (D).** The phrase "the pilferies of your pen to polish" is an example of alliteration, which means using the same initial consonant sound repeatedly in a line. All the other answers are just wrong. A metaphor (A), is when one thing is described in terms of another, but this is not metaphorical. Onomatopeia (B) is when words sound like what they are (e.g. "slither"), but pens and pilferies don't make special sounds. A paradox (C) is something that sounds like a contradiction but turns out to be true in some deeper sense. An apostrophe (E) is when a poem directly addresses someone or something that can't hear the poem ("O Moon! You orb of wonder!"). If you don't know these terms, you should be sure to read over the glossary in this book before the exam.

11. **The correct answer is (E).** "Those" refers back to "the enemies of poetry." This is a straightforward grammar question that requires you to parse the complex opening sentence.

12. **The correct answer is (A).** "Divines" are preachers, here excoriated for giving boring rather than poetic sermons. Nashe is opposing divines to writers, whether great (B) or dead (C). He does say that the divines are fools (D) and Saturnists (E), but those are descriptions rather than definitions. (A) should strike you as the best answer here if you understood the passage.

13. **The correct answer is (A).** This is a pure definition question; you need to know what a tautology is. A tautology is unnecessary repetition, so (A) is obviously the right answer. (B), (C), and (D) all sound like criticisms, and so seem to fit, but do not paraphrase the cited line. (E) merely says that the preachers have sermons, but sermons are not by definition ineloquent, as specified in the sentence cited.

14. **The correct answer is (E).** The selection specifically mentions all other options as functions of poetry: (A) is in line 40; (B) is in lines 34–37; (C) is in lines 40–42; and (D) is a direct quote from line 30. (E) is not a function of poetry, but is mentioned in the selection as a failure of boring preachers.

15. **The correct answer is (D).** This is a hard question asking for general knowledge. You could have reasoned it out if you realized that people have been questioning the necessity of poetry for millenia; this might have led you to choose the correct answer: Plato. (Actually, Plato decides that poets aren't really necessary in his *Republic*.) Nashe (A) is the author of this selection. Sidney (B) and Salustius (C) are other writers mentioned in the text. Milton (E) is the famous British poet who wrote *Paradise Lost*.

QUESTIONS 16–29

John Donne was the finest metaphysical poet of the seventeenth century, and remains one of the greatest English-language poets. His prodigious output of lyrics, satires, sermons, and meditations treat subjects both sacred and profane. He is also, however, notoriously difficult due to his ingeniously figurative language, which is why he tends to show up on English exams frequently.

This poem, "A Valediction: Of Weeping," expresses feelings upon be separated from one's lover. Through kaleidoscopic shifts of perspective, it plays with the paradoxes of presence and absence, distance and proximity.

16. **The correct answer is (C).** It is sometimes difficult to tell precisely what the poem is about, but you can use process of elimination to answer this question. The easiest one to eliminate is (E), since there is far too much crying here for a pleasure cruise. Some of the images sound apocalyptic, so (D) might sound tempting, but you should have realized that this is a love poem and that the end of the world imagery is metaphorical. Likewise, though death is mentioned, it is probably also a metaphorical death, so (B) is wrong. That leaves (A) and (C). It is hard to tell if the relationship is ending or merely being interrupted by distance, but the lovers are definitely being separated. Hence, (C) is the correct answer.

17. **The correct answer is (D).** You should know the definition of "metaphysical conceit," since the AP English exam likes to use metaphysical poets. A metaphysical conceit is an elaborate metaphor or simile that occurs in a metaphysical poem. You should have recognized this as a metaphysical poem, since it is by John Donne. Note that "metaphysical" here has little to do with philosophy, and much to do with depth of meaning. The metaphysical conceit in question is the comparison of tears to globes—each tear becomes an entire world once it

reflects his beloved, just as round balls become globes once someone pastes images of the continents on them. You may have been tempted to answer (C), recognizing that this is very metaphorical, but in this instance the lines are not literally a metaphor but a simile: Note the use of "so doth" (line 14) to indicate the comparison.

18. **The correct answer is (E).** "O more than moon" is an address to the beloved. You should have realized this because the addressed entity has arms (line 21), which narrows your choices to either (E) or (D), the workmen. It is obviously not (A) the moon. The world (B) has no arms. And nothing in this poem mentions the poet's soul (C).

19. **The correct answer is (B).** The tears in lines 14 and 15 are the speaker's tears, which "wear" the image of his beloved, and they are also the beloved's tears "worn" on her face. There is nothing here about clothing. Although seas and rain are mentioned in the poem, they are not specifically referenced in these two lines, and the comparison that is continuing from the previous lines is to globes, not to other waters. Therefore, the first and second choices are correct, as given in (B). (A) only gives the first choice, and is therefore incorrect. (C), (D), and (E) include incorrect choices.

20. **The correct answer is (E).** All of the stanzas contain images of roundness. The first stanza has coins and fruit, and even in a way pregnancy. The second stanza has globes and worlds. The third stanza has the moon and the word "sphere."

21. **The correct answer is (C).** Many, many metaphysical poems contain circle imagery, because the iconography—or pictorial material—of seventeenth-century poetry interprets the circle as the perfect shape. Circles have no end and therefore indicate perfect wholeness and eternity. These qualities made circles especially popular in love poetry, of which this is an example. (A) is wrong because there isn't any imagery of worthlessness, nor is there a sense of hopelessness. (B) is half right, because there are globes and vast distances, but the whole point of the poem is to reduce the vast distances by containing them within the tiny spheres of tears, so choosing (B) is an incomplete reading of the poem. Furthermore, the globe imagery is really only prominent in the second stanza, rather than being sustained throughout the poem. (D) is wrong because there is no suggestion of faithlessness between the lovers. Eliminate (E) because there is little explicit sexuality in this poem.

22. **The correct answer is (B).** This is really a grammar question to see how well you can sort out the sentence structure in this poem. "Which" begins a dependent clause modifying "that." So "which" refers to whatever "that" is. "That" is the object of the verb "make." The subject of "make" is the workman. The workman is making globes out of the round balls that are blank in his workshop. Therefore, both "that" and "which" must refer to the round balls. Although the globes are copied from models, the "copies" are models the workman "hath by" in his shop; he refers to the copies but does not make them into anything, so (A) is wrong. "World" does not even show up in this stanza until several lines later when it is a metaphorized tear, so (C) is wrong. The workman is the subject of this independent clause, but the subject is not being modified by "which," so (D) is wrong. The listed continents are objects of the subject "workman" but are not modified by the dependent clause, so (E) is wrong.

23. **The correct answer is (D).** This is a tricky question because it requires both interpretation of the poem and some familiarity with the conventions of metaphysical poetry, but the process of elimination can help you out here. Remember to read the question carefully; you are looking to identify the **wrong** association here, so you are looking for what **doesn't** fit in the

answers. (B) obviously fits the poem since there is an obvious connection between the moon, the sea, and tides. (C) obviously fits since the round imagery has been sustained throughout the entire poem, and you should remember that you have already been asked about round imagery. Remember to keep your answers consistent across questions. (E) probably fits because the poem certainly does describe unhappy feelings. That leaves us with (A) and (D); you must choose between a goddess and the man in the moon. There is no explicit reference to either a goddess or the man in the moon, but at least the idea of a goddess seems flattering to the beloved and fits the poem better. There is nothing even suggestive of the man in the moon, and in general, metaphysical poems did not draw on folktale material for their imagery, but rather on more classical themes including moon goddesses. Therefore, (D) is the least likely association and the correct answer.

24. **The correct answer is (D).** "Diverse" here just means "different"; the phrase means "a different place." Heaven (A) and hell (B) have no place in the poem at all. Europe (C) is listed as a continent in the poem, but not specified as a destination. The ground (E) is just an answer for the truly desperate.

25. **The correct answer is (A).** Tears are found throughout all three stanzas, though you have to look closely at the final stanza to find the idea in the word "weep" (line 21). Globes (B) are only in the second stanza. Coins (C) are only in the first stanza. The moon (D) is only in the third stanza. The ocean (E) is in the second and third stanzas. Ocean is almost suggested by the mention of shores in the first stanza, but it is not as strong a suggestion as that of "weep" for tears in the third stanza, so tears (A) remains the best answer.

26. **The correct answer is (B).** Line 4 is "And by this mintage they are something worth." "They" refers back to "my tears" in line 2. The tears are said to be coined by the beloved's face (line 3), and the coin metaphor is carried forward into the use of "mintage" here; the process of being coined is the mintage that makes the tears worth something. The tears reflect her face the way that coins show a ruler's face. By showing the beloved's face, the tears become valuable, like coins. Therefore, (B) is the best paraphrase. (A) is contrary to the sense of the poem, since it says the beloved is worthless. (C) does not reflect the meaning of the line, though some readers might be confused if they don't know what "mintage" means. (D) is tempting, because it sounds nice and fits with the meaning of the poem, but it overstates—it goes beyond what the line means. Paraphrases are supposed to restate, not extend. (E) is both vague and sort of New Age, and is not the point.

27. **The correct answer is (C).** The speaker asks the lover to "forbear/To teach the sea what it may do" (lines 21–22) and that she not let the wind "Example find" (line 24) in her behavior. He is saying that the natural elements are watching and learning from her, copying her behavior, an idea that is carried forward from the description of his lover as the moon influencing the tides. One would think, in the face of such great love, that she would have the power to break his heart (A), but that is not mentioned in the specified lines. He does mention dying in these lines (C), but mostly in the context of her power over the elements; he warns her against teaching the oceans and winds how to kill him, not against killing him herself. The lines assume that she has the power to restrain her grief (D), but just tell her to do so; they do not emphasize this power the way they do her power over nature. Nowhere in the poem is there anything mentioned about the right to take other lovers (E).

28. **The correct answer is (D).** John Donne is the most famous Metaphysical poet, which you might have remembered when you read the earlier question mentioning a metaphysical conceit. The only other answer that is close is (E), Cavalier poet, but the Cavalier poets wrote much fluffier poems than the Metaphysical poets, and did not include the elaborate metaphysical conceits so prominent in this selection. All the other types of poets mentioned wrote hundreds of years later than Donne.

29. **The correct answer is (A).** The speaker flatters the beloved by exaggerating her powers over natural elements, by declaring the inestimable value of even the reflections of her image—in other words, through hyperbole.

QUESTIONS 30–40

Mary E. Wilkins Freeman (1852–1930) was a New England writer who was brought up in an impoverished and strictly religious household. As an adult, she wrote fiction that portrayed the psychological effects on women of a traditional and repressive culture. She was well educated, but most profoundly influenced by her discussions with friends of literary classics. She is generally noted as an important early realist and regional writer, but her characters offer a psychological depth unusual in regional writers of her time. Freeman was also one of the few women of her time able to achieve economic independence through her earnings from her writing.

This selection is from the short story, "A New England Nun," published in 1891, about a woman who decides after a very long engagement that she really doesn't want to get married after all.

30. **The correct answer is (D).** This is a tricky question because the portrait of Louisa appeals to many popular steretoypes about women. But this is also a question in which you can use process of elimination. (A) is obviously wrong: Louisa is not bitter or domineering, but that was thrown in there in case you confused Louisa with her fears about her future mother-in-law. (B) is partly right, because Louisa is naive, but she is not shown doing anything childish. You might argue that her preconceptions about men are somewhat childish, but that would be overreading. (C) is also alluring, because "frightened" seems to relate to the end of the passage in which Louisa "trembles," but there are lots of reasons for trembling, and "foolish" doesn't really fit. You might find Louisa's ideas about men foolish, but her contemplation of how her upcoming marriage will change her life is certainly realistic enough in its way. (E) might also appeal because of our sympathy for Caesar, but Louisa also loves the dog, and nothing in her behavior is deliberately cruel. Therefore, the only really acceptable answer is (D). Louisa is certainly sheltered, and knows it; and she is also innocent insofar as she believes what she is told, about Caesar, Joe, and Joe's mother, but more importantly she believes in the conventional wisdom regarding the difficulties of married life.

31. **The correct answer is (B).** Again, you can answer this question through process of elimination and a careful reading of the selection. (A) is almost ridiculous: the only thing that comes close to a reference to farming in this selection is Louisa's distilling of herbs, and that doesn't seem to involve any seasonal harvest ritual. Besides, harvest rituals and their goddesses are usually sexual, which is precisely what Louisa's maidenly activities aren't. (C) is wrong because there is nothing to suggest that Louisa is mentally ill. (D) is wrong because, although Louisa has "almost the enthusiasm of an artist" while cleaning her house, there is nothing to suggest that she is a genius of any kind. (E) is tempting, since Louisa is engaged in many traditional tasks, but since she anticipates that her mother-in-law and husband will make her stop many of her less productive activities, they are probably not the highest values of the town. This leaves (B). Note that (B) uses the phrase "feminine cultural sphere," which is a term widely used in feminist criticism to indicate traditionally feminine activities. The passage suggests this interpretation by its contrast between Louisa's activities and Joe's more masculine aura.

32. **The correct answer is (A).** We can examine each statement separately. (I) expresses the main idea of the passage, and is therefore true. (II) is an interesting idea, but is not relevant to the passage, since even if you disapprove of Caesar's treatment, there is no suggestion that society is cruel in this passage. (III) is there to confuse people who skimmed the passage and thought Caesar was an ancient Roman. (IV) is a theme suggested by the passage and supported by the reactions of the townspeople and by Louisa's reactions to her own life, and is therefore true. (V) is merely a flippant commonplace that sheds no real light on anything: no one is trying to teach anyone any tricks—the statement is false. Therefore, (A) is the only possible answer.

33. **The correct answer is (C).** This is one of the rare AP questions that seeks actual outside knowledge; you wouldn't know this answer unless you had learned it in a literature class somewhere. There was for many centuries a well-regarded theory that said personalities were influenced by "humours" in the body: warm humours in the body caused angry or passionate personalities while cold humours caused unemotional or calm personalities. These humours were affected by diet and by environment. This is where you get the stereotype of the hot Latin lover who lives in a tropical region, eats spicy food, and is given to fits of violent temper. It is also where we get the idea of people being "in a good humour." The bitten neighbor is described as "choleric," which is another reference to the theory of humours. Louisa is deliberately feeding her dog bland food to discourage any further attacks on the neighbors. She is not poor or she would not be able to have such nice things in her house, so (A) is false. The passage does speak metaphorically of Caesar's imprisonment, but Louisa is not deliberately punishing her dog, certainly not for a decade, so (B) is wrong. There are many references to hermits and nuns in this story, but dogs do not practice celibacy as a religious practice, so (D) is wrong. (E) is wrong just from context, since the passage mentions that other kitchens give bones to dogs.

34. **The correct answer is (B).** "Redolent" means "smelling of," and since purity doesn't have a smell, its use here must be metaphorical. Irony (A) is tempting but there is nothing opposed or contradictory here to indicate irony. There is no simile (C) because there is no direct comparison of two things. Since there is no contradiction, there cannot be an oxymoron (D). And while the tone may be gently mocking, there is nothing epic under discussion, so (E) is wrong. If you do not know these terms, study the glossary in this book.

35. **The correct answer is (A).** The story of Caesar is a gentle satire on the minidramas of small-town life, which finds excitement in the vicious reputation of an old dog. Clues to the satirical tone are the many overwritten references to sin and danger, and especially Louisa's vision of Caesar on a rampage through the town. Freeman's treatment of this passage is too humorous to be either indignant (B) or pensive (C). Since it is clear to the reader, and even to Joe, that Caesar isn't really dangerous, there is nothing foreboding (D) or menacing (E) in this passage either. The selection does say that Louisa feels many "forebodings of disturbance," including worries about Caesar, but those are Louisa's feelings rather than the tone of the passage, which indicates the attitude of the author.

36. **The correct answer is (E).** "Sanguinary" means bloody, both in the sense of containing blood and of liking blood. (D), vegetarian, is obviously wrong since it contradicts the meaning of the sentence. The other answers draw on ideas raised in previous questions on this piece; remember to keep your answers consistent. We have already established that financial concerns do not dominate Caesar's diet, so (A) is wrong. (B) and (C) drag in the ideas of masculine and feminine traits that predominate in this selection, but they really have nothing to do with what the dog eats.

37. **The correct answer is (C).** This question tests how well you read Louisa's character, since the entire passage is about her attitude toward gender relations. Her meditations on the disorder her future husband will bring to her house and on the impending danger of Caesar's release are best summed up in (C). Louisa is living in a society that believes men and women belong together (A), but her worries show that she is not entirely convinced of this. On the other hand, she is not explicitly rejecting marriage, so (B) is not the right answer either. (D) introduces the idea of wildness that you might have associated with Caesar, but it is important to note that Louisa does not believe she has tamed Caesar, nor does she think she will have any influence over her husband, so (D) is wrong. Her belief that Joe's decision to release Caesar will prove disastrous shows that she does not think men are more intelligent than women, so (E) is also wrong.

38. **The correct answer is (B).** Caesar has a gentle face; he is mild-visaged. "Visage" means face. (E) might have misled some people because there is the suggestion that Caesar is vicious, and hence could be "masked," but we see Caesar differently than Louisa does. This adjective is just straightforwardly descriptive, not a clue to hidden depths. Don't overread the passage.

39. **The correct answer is (E).** All the statements describe the narrative accomplishments of the Caesar vignette. Joe is shown to be kind and practical (A) when he urges Caesar's release; Louisa's fears (B) are demonstrated in her vision of Caesar on a rampage; Caesar's sad plight is an example of what happens when people refuse change (C); and the inflated terror of the townspeople is a satire of small-town life (D).

40. **The correct answer is (B).** "Indelicate" is a euphemism for "inappropriately sexual." Dirty jokes are indelicate; graphic sexual details are indelicate. The point here is that Louisa's concern about the chaos Joe may bring to her life is connected to her sexual concerns. Although this passage in general ponders the differences between Louisa and Joe, delicacy or lack thereof is not the primary concern of the passage, so (A) is wrong. There is nothing to suggest that Joe is especially coarse, nor that his belongings are shoddy, so (C) and (D) are wrong. (E) is another example of overreading the passage. "Indelicate" does not refer to Caesar in any way, and so cannot foreshadow Louisa's vision of a rampaging dog.

QUESTIONS 41–55

Maxine Kumin is a revered contemporary poet who tends to examine the depths, such as they are, of comfortable suburban life. "Woodchucks" is from her 1972 collection *Up Country*.

41. **The correct answer is (B).** The poem literally describes the speaker's attempts to rid the garden of woodchucks. The final reference to Nazis (A) solidifies the subtext of the poem, and illuminates its underlying theme about violence, but is not the literal subject. There is a dream (D) mentioned in the final lines, but it is a minor detail rather than the main subject of the poem. Landscape design (E) and vegetarianism (C) may come to mind in the description of the garden, but neither are the subjects of the poem.

42. **The correct answer is (E).** The theme of the poem is that violence and persecution are potentials within everyone, even otherwise peaceful suburban gardeners. (D), the idea that the world is essentially violent, is tempting but too general. (A), (B), and (C) are not even close; note that (B), the idea that we must fight the battles of everyday life, might tempt people who misread the poem.

43. **The correct answer is (E).** The poem condemns all killing, even killing often justified as necessary, such as eliminating garden pests. Therefore, (E) is false, and the correct answer. In fact, (E) contradicts the entire sense of the poem. All of the other statements are true. Even if

you did not know about Nazi rhetorics of vermin extermination, you could recognize the presence of this rhetoric in the poem and would hesitate to eliminate (A). Likewise, you should notice the reference to Darwin, even if you are not clear on connections between Nazis and Social Darwinism; therefore, you would hesitate to eliminate (B). The third stanza demonstrates the truth of (C), that political beliefs are quite similar to religious beliefs, although recognizing this requires a sensitivity to tone in the poem. The very comparison of killing woodchucks with Nazi genocide should lead you to see Kumin's point that all violence is essentially similar (D).

44. **The correct answer is (C).** "Darwinian pieties" is an oxymoron because it is a contradiction in terms. Darwin's evolutionary theories are seen by many to be anti-religious since they contradict Fundamentalist beliefs in Creationism. At the same time, "piety" means religious devotion. Kumin is suggesting that people are devoted to Darwin as blindly as they ever were to religion. However, Darwin is used here not so much to suggest evolution as to suggest the political beliefs associated with "Social Darwinism," which sees struggles between groups of people as a violent zero-sum contest for survival in which the winners are proven to be biologically superior. Social Darwinism is often a polite mask for racism and other social biases against groups perceived as inferior.

45. **The correct answer is (D).** The tone of the poem contradicts the speaker's attitudes, so nothing in the poem proves those attitudes correct. All the other statements about line 4 are true.

46. **The correct answer is (C).** The entire poem is an ironic satire against people who refuse to recognize the violence of their lives as part of the violence of the world. (A) and (D) are tempting since both Kumin and presumably the reader feel outrage over the violence in the world and would wish to protest it, but the poem itself remains ironic. There is a sense of triumph (E) in the fourth stanza, but its effectiveness is undercut by the pathetic references to mothers and babies. There is no helpless sorrow (B) anywhere in the poem.

47. **The correct answer is (D).** The entire point of the poem is the speaker's growing awareness of his or her own violent tendencies. The idea that all violence is related (B) is implied in the poem, but is not the main point of the final two lines. The other answers are all variously shallow misreadings of the poem.

48. **The correct answer is (B).** The garden, usually considered a peaceful place, is here the scene of violence, which is ironic, so (I) is true. The garden obviously symbolizes nature, which is the site of Darwinian struggle, so (II) is true. In this poem, the garden is very realistic and specific, suggesting that the issues discussed are specific and realistic as well, so (IV) is true. (III) is false, but tempting because gardens are often featured in pastoral poems. However, pastoral poems focus on the peacefulness of the countryside, which this poem obviously does not. (V) is obviously false, and contradicts the main theme of the poem.

49. **The correct answer is (B).** In the final line of the poem, "Nazi" is an allusion to the atrocities of genocide in World War II. The poem as a whole implies a comparison between the killing of woodchucks and genocide, but this is merely implied and does not become an outright simile (C) or metaphor (A) in the final line. Neither does the final line contain a paradox (D) or metonym (E). If you do not know what these terms mean, you should consult the glossary at the back of this book.

50. **The correct answer is (C).** "Beheading the carrots" is an example of personification because it applies a human quality to an inhuman object: carrots don't have heads to lop off, but describing the woodchucks' actions in this way makes the woodchucks sound more sinister. Anthropomorphism (D) is a more involved form of personification, in which one ascribes human motivations to animals. It does not apply here because you are being asked about carrots, not animals.

51. **The correct answer is (C).** The speaker of a poem is not necessarily the poet, but is known as the poet's "persona." That makes "the poet" (A) the wrong answer. The other answers are pretty ridiculous.

52. **The correct answer is (A).** This question is a little tricky. By switching from a setting of natural gardens to the idea of a staged scene, the poet is emphasizing the artificial cultural script influencing the speaker to act so brutally. There is even a suggestion that such scripts naturalize many brutal actions in human society and so render atrocities acceptable, as in the influence of Nazi ideologies. (B) is tempting because of the influence of ideology; social Darwinism holds that humans are naturally predatory, but the poem as a whole is arguing against exactly this point. (C) is partially true, since "killer" is a harshly clear word, but the effect is not unique to this line; equally harsh words have gone before in previous lines. (D) is wrong because although the line is alliterative, it is not especially onomatopoeic. (E) is just flat out wrong because the line isn't senseless and the speaker isn't confused.

53. **The correct answer is (D).** The way to answer this question is to evaluate each statement as true or false. Statement (I) is true; the first line tells you that you are going to hear a story about gassing the woodchucks. Statement (II) is true; "didn't turn out right" implies that things went "wrong," but what is wrong when you are gassing living creatures? Statement (III) uses a more academic discourse to say almost exactly the same thing as statement (II), and is also true. By the time you get to the end of the poem, you know that "didn't turn out right" is an understatement of what really happened, so (IV) is true. (V) is false, because the first line does not give enough information to be considered a summary of the poem. The first line still seems to be about woodchucks instead of about human nature, and no summary of this poem should focus on woodchucks. (D) is the only choice that correctly lists the true statements.

54. **The correct answer is (C).** "Airtight" is a pun, referring to the legal idea of an "airtight case" to show that the speaker felt justified in executing the woodchucks, but also referring to the physical process of gassing the woodchucks. It is not sustained enough to be a metaphor (A) and it does not symbolize anything (E). It might be read as an allusion (D) to the legal system, but it is not really specific enough to work as an allusion. It does not contradict itself, so it's not an oxymoron (B). If you don't know these terms, be sure to study the glossary in the back of this book. Incidentally, question 45 already told you that "airtight" is a pun.

55. **The correct answer is (B).** This question can be answered through the process of elimination. (A) is wrong because the final lines are certainly ironic. (C) is wrong because there is no contradiction at the end of the poem. (D) is wrong because the poem's strong moral point is about human violence, not about environmentalism. (E) is wrong because the dream mentioned is realistic rather than surreal, and therefore the verisimilitude of the poem is not abandoned. (Verisimilitude means "the quality of seeming real"—it's another good term to know for the exam.) That leaves only (B), which fits perfectly. Slant rhymes are imprecise rhymes, in this case "keeps/sleep" and "dream/unseen."

PART VIII

GLOSSARY

THE GLOSSARY OF LITERARY TERMS FOR THE AP ENGLISH LITERATURE AND COMPOSITION TEST

We've put an asterisk (*) beside the handful of terms that you *absolutely must know*.

Abstract An abstract style (in writing) is typically complex, discusses intangible qualities like good and evil, and seldom uses examples to support its points.

Academic As an adjective describing style, this word means dry and theoretical writing. When a piece of writing seems to be sucking all the life out of its subject with analysis, the writing is *academic*.

Accent In poetry, *accent* refers to the stressed portion of a word. In "To be, or not to be," accents fall on the first "be" and "not." It sounds silly any other way. But accent in poetry is also often a matter of opinion. Consider the rest of the first line of Hamlet's famous soliloquy, "That is the question." The stresses in that portion of the line are open to a variety of interpretations.

Aesthetic, Aesthetics *Aesthetic* can be used as an adjective meaning "appealing to the senses." Aesthetic judgment is a phrase synonymous with artistic judgment. As a noun, an aesthetic is a coherent sense of taste. The kid whose room is painted black, who sleeps in a coffin, and listens only to funeral music has an aesthetic. The kid whose room is filled with pictures of kittens and daisies but who sleeps in a coffin and listens to polka music has a confused aesthetic. The plural noun, *aesthetics*, is the study of beauty. Questions like *what is beauty?* or, *is the beautiful always good?* fall into the category of aesthetics.

Allegory An *allegory* is a story in which each aspect of the story has a symbolic meaning outside the tale itself. Many fables have an allegorical quality. For example, Aesop's "Ant and the Grasshopper" isn't merely the story of a hardworking ant and a carefree grasshopper, but is also a story about different approaches to living—the thrifty and the devil-may-care. It can also be read as a story about the seasons of summer and winter, which represent a time of prosperity and a time of hardship, or even as representing youth and age. True allegories are even more hard and fast. Bunyan's epic poem, *Pilgrim's Progress*, is an allegory of the soul, in which each and every part of the tale represents some feature of the spiritual world and the struggles of an individual to lead a Christian life.

Alliteration The repetition of initial consonant sounds is called *alliteration*. In other words, consonant clusters coming closely cramped and compressed—no coincidence.

Allusion A reference to another work or famous figure is an *allusion*. A classical allusion is a reference to Greek and Roman Mythology such as, *The Iliad*. Allusions can be topical or popular as well. A topical allusion refers to a current event. A popular allusion refers to something from popular culture, such as a reference to a television show or a hit movie.

Anachronism The word *anachronism* is derived from Greek. It means "misplaced in time." If the actor playing Brutus in a production of Julius Caesar forgets to take off his wrist-watch, the effect will be anachronistic (and probably comic).

Analogy An *analogy* is a comparison. Usually analogies involve two or more symbolic parts, and are employed to clarify an action or a relationship. *Just as the mother eagle shelters her young from the storm by spreading her great wing above their heads, so does Acme Insurers of America spread an umbrella of coverage to protect its policy-holders from the storms of life.*

Anecdote An anecdote is a short narrative.

Antecedent The word, phrase, or clause that determines what a pronoun refers to. As *the children* in *The principal asked the children where they were going*.

Anthropomorphism In literature, when inanimate objects are given human characteristics, anthropomorphism is at work. For example, *In the forest, the darkness waited for me, I could hear its patient breathing* . . . Anthropomorphism is often confused with personification. But personification requires that the non-human quality or thing take on human shape.

Anticlimax An anticlimax occurs when an action produces far smaller results than one had been led to expect. Anticlimax is frequently comic. *Sir, your snide manner and despicable arrogance have long been a source of disgust to me, but I've overlooked it until now. However, it has come to my attention that you have fallen so disgracefully deep into that mire of filth which is your mind as to attempt to besmirch my wife's honor and my good name. Sir, I challenge you to a game of badminton!*

Antihero A protagonist (main character) who is markedly unheroic: morally weak, cowardly, dishonest, or any number of other unsavory qualities.

Aphorism A short and usually witty saying, such as: "A classic? That's a book that people praise and don't read."—Mark Twain.

Apostrophe A figure of speech wherein the speaker talks directly to something that is nonhuman.

Archaism The use of deliberately old-fashioned language. Authors sometimes use archaisms to create a feeling of antiquity. Tourist traps use archaisms with a vengeance, as in "Ye Olde Candle Shoppe"—Yeech!

Aside A speech (usually just a short comment) made by an actor to the audience, as though momentarily stepping outside of the action on stage. (See *soliloquy*.)

Aspect A trait or characteristic, as in "an aspect of the dew drop."

Assonance The repeated use of vowel sounds, as in, "Old king Cole was a merry old soul."

Atmosphere The emotional tone or background that surrounds a scene.

Ballad A long, narrative poem, usually in very regular meter and rhyme. A ballad typically has a naive folksy quality, a characteristic that distinguishes it from epic poetry.

Bathos, Pathos When the writing of a scene evokes feelings of dignified pity and sympathy, pathos is at work. When writing strains for grandeur it can't support and tries to jerk tears from every little hiccup, that's bathos.

Black humor This is the use of disturbing themes in comedy. In Samuel Beckett's *Waiting for Godot*, the two tramps, Didi and Gogo, comically debate over which should commit suicide first, and whether the branches of the tree will support their weight. This is black humor.

Bombast This is pretentious, exaggeratedly learned language. When one tries to be eloquent by using the largest, most uncommon words, one falls into bombast.

Burlesque A burlesque is broad parody, one that takes a style or a form, such as tragic drama, and exaggerates it into ridiculousness. A parody usually takes on a specific work, such as *Hamlet*. For the purposes of the AP test, you can think of the terms *parody* and *burlesque* as interchangeable.

Cacophony In poetry, cacophony is using deliberately harsh, awkward sounds.

Cadence The beat or rhythm of poetry in a general sense. For example, *iambic pentameter* is the technical name for a rhythm. One sample of predominantly iambic pentameter verse could have a gentle, pulsing cadence, whereas another might have a conversational cadence, and still another might have a vigorous, marching cadence.

Canto The name for a section division in a long work of poetry. A canto divides a long poem into parts the way chapters divide a novel.

Caricature A portrait (verbal or otherwise) that exaggerates a facet of personality.

Catharsis This is a term drawn from Aristotle's writings on tragedy. *Catharsis* refers to the "cleansing" of emotion an audience member experiences, having lived (vicariously) through the experiences presented on stage.

Chorus In Greek drama, this is the group of citizens who stand outside the main action on stage and comment on it.

Classic What a troublesome word! Don't confuse classic with classical. Classic can mean typical, as in *oh, that was a classic blunder*. It can also mean an accepted masterpiece, for example, *Death of a Salesman*. But, classical refers to the arts of ancient Greece and Rome, and the qualities of those arts.

Coinage (neologism) A coinage is a new word, usually one invented on the spot. People's names often become grist for coinages, as in, *Oh, man, you just pulled a major Wilson*. Of course, you'd have to know Wilson to know what that means, but you can tell it isn't a good thing. The technical term for coinage is *neologism*.

Colloquialism This is a word or phrase used in everyday conversational English that isn't a part of accepted "school-book" English. For example, *I'm toasted. I'm a crispy-critter man, and now I've got this wicked headache*.

Complex / Dense These two terms carry the similar meaning of suggesting that there is more than one possibility in the meaning of words (image, idea, opposition); there are subtleties and variations; there are multiple layers of interpretation; the meaning is both explicit and implicit.

Conceit, controlling image In poetry, *conceit* doesn't mean stuck-up. It refers to a startling or unusual metaphor, or to a metaphor developed and expanded upon over several lines. When the image dominates and shapes the entire work, it's called or a *controlling image*. A metaphysical conceit is reserved for metaphysical poems only.

Connotation, denotation The *denotation* of a word is its literal meaning. The *connotations* are everything else that the word suggests or implies. For example, in the phrase *the dark forest*, *dark* denotes a relative lack of light. The connotation is of danger, or perhaps mystery or quiet; we'd need more information to know for sure, and if we did know with complete certainty that wouldn't be connotation, but denotation. In many cases connotation eventually so overwhelms a word that it takes over the denotation. For example, *livid* is supposed to denote a dark purple-red color like that of a bruise, but it has been used so often in the context of extreme anger that many people have come to use *livid* as a synonym for rage, rather than a connotative description of it.

Consonance The repetition of consonant sounds within words (rather than at their beginnings, which is alliteration). A flo*ck* of si*ck*, bla*ck*-che*ck*ered, du*ck*s.

Couplet A pair of lines that end in rhyme:

> But at my back I always *hear*
> Time's winged chariot hurrying *near*.
>
> —From "To His Coy Mistress" by Andrew Marvell

Decorum In order to observe decorum, a character's speech must be styled according to her social station, and in accordance with the occasion. A bum should speak like a bum about bumly things, while a princess should speak only about higher topics (and in a delicate manner). In Neoclassical and Victorian literature the authors observed decorum meaning they did not write about the indecorous. The bum wouldn't even appear in this genre of literature.

Diction, syntax The author's choice of words. Whether to use *wept* or *cried* is a question of diction. Syntax refers to the ordering and structuring of the words. Whether to say, *The pizza was smothered in cheese and pepperoni. I devoured it greedily*, or *Greedily, I devoured the cheese and pepperoni smothered pizza*, is a question of syntax.

Dirge This is a song for the dead. Its tone is typically slow, heavy, depressed, and melancholy.

Dissonance This refers to the grating of incompatible sounds.

Doggerel Crude, simplistic verse, often in sing-song rhyme. Limericks are a kind of doggerel.

Dramatic Irony When the audience knows somthing that the characters in the drama do not.

Dramatic Monologue When a single speaker in literature says something to a silent audience.

Elegy A type of poem that meditates on death or mortality in a serious, thoughtful manner. Elegies often use the recent death of a noted person or loved one as a starting point. They also memorialize specific dead people.

Elements This word is used constantly and with the assumption that you know exactly what it means— that is, the basic techniques of each genre of literature. For a quick refresher, here's a short and sweet list for each genre:

short story	poetry	drama	non-fiction (rhetorical)
characters	figurative	conflict	argument
irony	language	characters	evidence
theme	symbol	climax	reason
symbol	imagery	conclusion	appeals
plot	rhythm	exposition	fallacies
setting	rhyme	rising action	thesis
		falling action	
		sets, props	

Enjambment The continuation of a syntactic unit from one line or couplet of a poem to the next with no pause.

Epic In a broad sense, an epic is simply a very long narrative poem on a serious theme in a dignified style. Epics typically deal with glorious or profound subject matter: a great war, a heroic journey, the fall of man from Eden, a battle with supernatural forces, a trip into the underworld, etc. The mock-epic is a parody form that deals with mundane events and ironically treats them as worthy of epic poetry.

Epitaph Lines that commemorate the dead at their burial place. An epitaph is usually a line or handful of lines, often serious or religious, but sometimes witty and even irreverent.

Euphemism A word or phrase that takes the place of a harsh, unpleasant, or impolite reality. The use of *passed away* for died, and *let go* for fired are two examples of euphemisms.

Euphony When sounds blend harmoniously, the result is euphony.

Explicit To say or write something directly and clearly (this is a rare happening in literature since the whole game is to be "implicit," that is, to suggest and imply).

Farce Today we use this word to refer to extremely broad humor. Writers of earlier times used *farce* as a more neutral term, meaning simply a funny play; a comedy. (And you should know that for writers of centuries past, *comedy* was the generic term for any play; it did not imply humor.)

Feminine rhyme Lines rhymed by their final two syllables. A pair of lines ending with *running* and *gunning* would be an example of feminine rhyme. Properly, in a feminine rhyme (and not simply a double rhyme) the penultimate syllables are stressed and the final syllables are unstressed.

First person narrator See *point of view*.

Foil A secondary character whose purpose is to highlight the characteristics of a main character, usually by contrast. For example, an author will often give a cynical, quick-witted character a docile, naive, sweet-tempered friend to serve as a foil.

Foot The basic rhythmic unit of a line of poetry. A *foot* is formed by a combination of two or three syllables, either stressed or unstressed.

Foreshadowing An event or statement in a narrative that in miniature suggests a larger event that comes later.

Free verse Poetry written without a regular rhyme scheme or metrical pattern.

Genre A sub-category of literature. Science-fiction and detective stories are *genres* of fiction.

Gothic, Gothic novel Gothic is the sensibility derived from gothic novels. This form first showed up in the middle of the eighteenth century and had a hey-day of popularity for about sixty years. It hasn't really ever gone away. The sensibility? Think mysterious gloomy castles perched high upon sheer cliffs. Paintings with sinister eyeballs that follow you around the room. Weird screams from the attic each night. Diaries with a final entry that trails off the page and reads something like, *No, NO! IT COULDN'T BE!!*

Hubris The excessive pride or ambition that leads to the main character's downfall (another term from Aristotle's discussion of tragedy).

Hyperbole Exaggeration or deliberate overstatement.

Implicit To say or write something that suggests and implies but—gasp—never says it directly or clearly. "Meaning" is definitely present, but it's in the imagery, or "between the lines."

In medias res Latin for "in the midst of things." One of the conventions of epic poetry is that the action begins *in medias res*. For example, when *The Iliad* begins, the Trojan war has already been going on for seven years.

Interior Monologue This is a term for novels and poetry, not dramatic literature. It refers to writing that records the mental talking that goes on inside a character's head. It is related, but not identical to stream of consciousness. Interior monologue tends to be coherent, as though the character were actually talking. Stream of consciousness is looser and much more given to fleeting mental impressions.

Inversion Switching the customary order of elements in a sentence or phrase. When done badly it can give a stilted, artificial, look-at-me-I'm-poetry feel to the verse, but poets do it all the time. This type of messing with syntax is called *poetic license*. *I'll have one large pizza with all the fixin's*—presto chango instant poetry—*A pizza large I'll have, one with the fixin's all.*

*****Irony** This is one term you need to be very comfortable with for the AP test. Irony comes in a variety of forms, and you need to be able to recognize and be sensitive to it. Actually being able to name the specific type of irony involved is not important. ETS doesn't care if you can see an example of tragic irony and call it by name, they just want you to be able to see that it's irony. The reason irony shows up so much on the AP test is that it's a powerful verbal tool, and so good writers use it all the time. ETS also loves irony because ironic writing makes for good questions: strong readers detect irony, weak readers do so less clearly.

One definition of irony is *a statement that means the opposite of what it seems to mean*, and while that isn't a bad definition, it doesn't get at the delicacy with which the authors on the AP test use irony. Simply saying the opposite of what one means is sarcasm. The hallmark of irony is an undertow of meaning, sliding against the literal meaning of the words. Jane Austen is famous for writing descriptions which seem perfectly pleasant, but to the sensitive reader have a deliciously mean snap to them. Irony insinuates. It whispers underneath the explicit statement, *Do you understand what I really mean*? Think of the way Mark Antony says again and again of Brutus, "But he is an honorable man." At first it doesn't seem like much, but with each repetition the undertone of irony becomes ever more insistent.

Lament A poem of sadness or grief over the death of a loved one or over some other intense loss.

Lampoon A satire.

Loose and periodic sentences A *loose sentence* is complete before its end. A *periodic sentence* is not grammatically complete until it has reached its final phrase. (The term *loose* does not in any way imply that the sentences are slack or shoddy.)

> Loose sentence: *Jack loved Barbara despite her irritating snorting laugh, her complaining, and her terrible taste in shoes.*

> Periodic sentence: *Despite Barbara's irritation at Jack's peculiar habit of picking between his toes while watching MTV and his terrible haircut, she loved him.*

Lyric A type of poetry that explores the poet's personal interpretation of and feelings about the world (or the part that his poem is about). When the word *lyric* is used to describe a tone it refers to a sweet, emotional melodiousness.

Masculine rhyme A rhyme ending on the final stressed syllable (a.k.a., regular old rhyme).

Means, Meaning This is the big one, the one task you have to do all the time. You are discovering what makes sense, what's important. There is literal meaning which is concrete and explicit, and there is emotional meaning.

Melodrama A form of cheesy theater in which the hero is very, very good, the villain mean and rotten, and the heroine oh-so-pure. (It sounds dumb, but melodramatic movies make tons of money every year.)

*****Metaphor and simile** A *metaphor* is a comparison, or analogy that states one thing *is* another. *His eyes were burning coals*, or *In the morning, the lake is covered in liquid gold*. It's a simple point, so keep it straight: a simile is just like a metaphor but softens the full-out equation of things, often, but not *always* by using *like* or *as*. *His eyes were like burning coals*, or *In the morning the lake is covered in what seems to be liquid gold.*

Metaphysical conceit See *conceit*

Metonym A word that is used to stand for something else that it has attributes of or is associated with. For example, a herd of 50 cows could be called 50 *head* of cattle.

Nemesis The protagonist's arch enemy or supreme and persistent difficulty.

Neologism See *coinage*.

*****Objectivity and Subjectivity** An *objective* treatment of subject matter is an impersonal or outside view of events. A *subjective* treatment uses the interior or personal view of a single observer and is typically colored with that observer's emotional responses.

*****Omniscient narrator** See *point of view*.

Onomatopoeia Words that sound like what they mean are examples of onomatopoeia. *Boom. Splat. Babble. Gargle.*

Opposition This is one of the most useful concepts in analyzing literature. It means that you have a pair of elements that contrast sharply. It is not necessarily "conflict" but rather a pairing of images (or settings or appeals, etc.) whereby each becomes more striking and informative because it's placed in contrast to the other one. This kind of opposition creates mystery and tension. Oppositions can be obvious. Oppositions can also lead to irony but not necessarily so.

Oxymoron A phrase composed of opposites; a contradiction. *Bright black. A calm frenzy. Jumbo shrimp. Dark light. A truthful lie.*

Parable Like a fable, or an allegory, a parable is a story that instructs.

Paradox A situation or statement that seems to contradict itself, but on closer inspection, does not.

Parallelism Repeated syntactical similarities used for effect.

Paraphrase To restate phrases and sentences in your own words, to re-phrase. Paraphrase is not analysis or interpretation, so don't fall into the thinking that traps so many students. Paraphrasing is just a way of showing that you comprehend what you've just read—that you can now put it in your own words, no more, no less.

Parenthetical phrase A phrase set off by commas that interrupts the flow of a sentence with some commentary or added detail. *Jack's three dogs, <u>including that miserable, little spaniel</u>, were with him that day.*

Parody The work that results when a specific work is exaggerated to ridiculousness.

Pastoral A poem set in tranquil nature or even more specifically, one about shepherds.

Pathos See *bathos*.

Periodic sentence See *loose sentence*.

Persona The narrator in a non first-person novel. In a third person novel, even though the author isn't a character, you get some idea of the author's personality. However, it isn't really the author's personality because the author is manipulating your impressions there as in other parts of the book. This shadow-author is called the author's *persona*.

Personification When an inanimate object takes on human shape. *The darkness of the forest became the figure of a beautiful, pale-skinned woman in night-black clothes.*

Plaint A poem or speech expressing sorrow.

*Point of View The point of view is the perspective from which the action of a novel (or narrative poem) is presented, whether the action is presented by one character or from different vantage points over the course of the novel. Be sensitive to point of view, because ETS likes to ask questions about it, and they also like to you to mention point of view in your essays.

Related to point of view is the narrative form that a novel or story takes. There are a few common narrative positions:

- **The omniscient narrator** This is a third person narrator who sees, like God, into each character's mind and understands all the action going on.

- **The limited omniscient narrator** This is a third person narrator who generally reports only what one character (usually the main character) sees, and who only reports the thoughts of that one privileged character.

- **The objective, or camera eye narrator** This is a third person narrator who only reports on what would be visible to a camera. The objective narrator does not know what the character is thinking unless the character speaks of it.

- **The first person narrator** This a narrator who is a character in the story and tells the tale from his or her point of view. When the first person narrator is crazy, a liar, very young, or for some reason not entirely credible the narrator is *unreliable*.

- **The stream of consciousness technique** This method is like first person narration but instead of the character telling the story, the author places the reader inside the main character's head and makes the reader privy to all of the character's thoughts as they scroll through her consciousness.

Prelude An introductory poem to a longer work of verse.

*Protagonist The main character of a novel or play.

Pun The usually humorous use of a word in such a way to suggest two or more meanings.

Refrain A line or set of lines repeated several times over the course of a poem.

Requiem A song of prayer for the dead.

Rhapsody An intensely passionate verse or section of verse, usually of love or praise.

Rhetorical question A question that suggests an answer. In theory, the effect of a rhetorical question is that it causes the listener to feel she has come up with the answer herself. W*ell, we can fight it out, or we can run—so, are we cowards?*

*Satire This is an important term for the AP test. ETS is fond of satirical writing, again because it lends itself well to multiple-choice questions. *Satire* exposes common character flaws to the cold light of humor. In general, *satire* attempts to improve things by pointing out people's mistakes in the hope that once exposed, such behavior will become less common. The great satirical subjects are hypocrisy, vanity, and greed, especially where those all too common characteristics have become institutionalized in society.

*Simile See *metaphor*.

Soliloquy A speech spoken by a character alone on stage. A soliloquy is meant to convey the impression that the audience is listening to the character's thoughts. Unlike an aside, a soliloquy is not meant to imply that the actor acknowledges the audience's presence.

*Stanza A group of lines roughly analogous in function in verse to the paragraph's function in prose.

Stock characters Standard or cliched character types: the drunk, the miser, the foolish girl, etc.

Stream of consciousness See *point of view*.

*Subjective See *objectivity*.

Subjunctive Mood *If I were you, I'd learn this one!* That's a small joke because the grammatical situation involves the words "if" and "were." What you do is set up a hypothetical situation, a kind of wishful thing: *if I were you, if he were honest, if she were rich.* You can also get away from the person and into the "it": *I wish it were true, would it were so* (that even sounds like Shakespeare and poetry). Go to page 61, question 15 for the perfect example: "Were one not already the Duke..."

Suggest To imply, infer, indicate. This is another one of those basic tools of literature. It goes along with the concept of implicit. As the reader, you have to do all the work to pull out the meaning.

Summary A simple retelling of what you've just read. It's mechanical, superficial, and a step beyond the paraphrase in that it covers much more material and is more general. You can summarize a whole chapter or a whole story, whereas you paraphrase word-by-word and line-by-line. Summary includes all the facts.

Suspension of disbelief The demand made of a theater audience to accept the limitations of staging and supply the details with their imagination. Also, the acceptance on an audience's or reader's part of the incidents of plot in a play or story. If there are too many coincidences or improbable occurrences, the viewer/reader can no longer suspend disbelief and subsequently loses interest.

Symbolism A device in literature where an object represents an idea.

Syntax See *diction*.

Technique The methods, the tools, the "how-she-does-it" ways of the author. The elements are not techniques. In poetry, *onomatopoeia* is a technique within the element of rhythm. In drama, *blocking* is a technique, and *lighting*. Concrete details are not techniques, but tone is. Main idea is not a technique, but opposition is.

Theme The main idea of the overall work; the central idea. It is the topic of discourse or discussion.

Thesis The main position of an argument. The central contention that will be supported.

Tragic flaw In a tragedy, this is the weakness of character in an otherwise good (or even great) individual that ultimately leads to his demise.

Travesty A grotesque parody.

Truism A way-too obvious truth.

Unreliable narrator See *point of view*.

Utopia An idealized place. Imaginary communities in which people are able to live in happiness, prosperity, and peace. Several works of fiction have been written about utopias.

Zeugma The use of a word to modify two or more words, but used for different meanings. *He closed the door and his heart on his lost love.*

The Princeton Review

Completely darken bubbles with a No. 2 pencil. If you make a mistake, be sure to erase mark completely. Erase all stray marks.

1. YOUR NAME: _____
(Print)   Last   First   M.I.

SIGNATURE: _____ **DATE:** ___/___/___

HOME ADDRESS: _____
(Print)   Number and Street

_____
City   State   Zip Code

PHONE NO.: _____
(Print)

IMPORTANT: Please fill in these boxes exactly as shown on the back cover of your test book.

2. TEST FORM

3. TEST CODE

4. REGISTRATION NUMBER

5. YOUR NAME — First 4 letters of last name | FIRST INIT | MID INIT

6. DATE OF BIRTH — Month / Day / Year

JAN, FEB, MAR, APR, MAY, JUN, JUL, AUG, SEP, OCT, NOV, DEC

7. SEX
○ MALE
○ FEMALE

© 1996 Princeton Review L.L.C.
FORM NO. 00001-PR

Section 1

Start with number 1 for each new section.
If a section has fewer questions than answer spaces, leave the extra answer spaces blank.

1. Ⓐ Ⓑ Ⓒ Ⓓ Ⓔ
2. Ⓐ Ⓑ Ⓒ Ⓓ Ⓔ
3. Ⓐ Ⓑ Ⓒ Ⓓ Ⓔ
4. Ⓐ Ⓑ Ⓒ Ⓓ Ⓔ
5. Ⓐ Ⓑ Ⓒ Ⓓ Ⓔ
6. Ⓐ Ⓑ Ⓒ Ⓓ Ⓔ
7. Ⓐ Ⓑ Ⓒ Ⓓ Ⓔ
8. Ⓐ Ⓑ Ⓒ Ⓓ Ⓔ
9. Ⓐ Ⓑ Ⓒ Ⓓ Ⓔ
10. Ⓐ Ⓑ Ⓒ Ⓓ Ⓔ
11. Ⓐ Ⓑ Ⓒ Ⓓ Ⓔ
12. Ⓐ Ⓑ Ⓒ Ⓓ Ⓔ
13. Ⓐ Ⓑ Ⓒ Ⓓ Ⓔ
14. Ⓐ Ⓑ Ⓒ Ⓓ Ⓔ
15. Ⓐ Ⓑ Ⓒ Ⓓ Ⓔ
16. Ⓐ Ⓑ Ⓒ Ⓓ Ⓔ
17. Ⓐ Ⓑ Ⓒ Ⓓ Ⓔ
18. Ⓐ Ⓑ Ⓒ Ⓓ Ⓔ
19. Ⓐ Ⓑ Ⓒ Ⓓ Ⓔ
20. Ⓐ Ⓑ Ⓒ Ⓓ Ⓔ
21. Ⓐ Ⓑ Ⓒ Ⓓ Ⓔ
22. Ⓐ Ⓑ Ⓒ Ⓓ Ⓔ
23. Ⓐ Ⓑ Ⓒ Ⓓ Ⓔ
24. Ⓐ Ⓑ Ⓒ Ⓓ Ⓔ
25. Ⓐ Ⓑ Ⓒ Ⓓ Ⓔ
26. Ⓐ Ⓑ Ⓒ Ⓓ Ⓔ
27. Ⓐ Ⓑ Ⓒ Ⓓ Ⓔ
28. Ⓐ Ⓑ Ⓒ Ⓓ Ⓔ
29. Ⓐ Ⓑ Ⓒ Ⓓ Ⓔ
30. Ⓐ Ⓑ Ⓒ Ⓓ Ⓔ
31. Ⓐ Ⓑ Ⓒ Ⓓ Ⓔ
32. Ⓐ Ⓑ Ⓒ Ⓓ Ⓔ
33. Ⓐ Ⓑ Ⓒ Ⓓ Ⓔ
34. Ⓐ Ⓑ Ⓒ Ⓓ Ⓔ
35. Ⓐ Ⓑ Ⓒ Ⓓ Ⓔ
36. Ⓐ Ⓑ Ⓒ Ⓓ Ⓔ
37. Ⓐ Ⓑ Ⓒ Ⓓ Ⓔ
38. Ⓐ Ⓑ Ⓒ Ⓓ Ⓔ
39. Ⓐ Ⓑ Ⓒ Ⓓ Ⓔ
40. Ⓐ Ⓑ Ⓒ Ⓓ Ⓔ
41. Ⓐ Ⓑ Ⓒ Ⓓ Ⓔ
42. Ⓐ Ⓑ Ⓒ Ⓓ Ⓔ
43. Ⓐ Ⓑ Ⓒ Ⓓ Ⓔ
44. Ⓐ Ⓑ Ⓒ Ⓓ Ⓔ
45. Ⓐ Ⓑ Ⓒ Ⓓ Ⓔ
46. Ⓐ Ⓑ Ⓒ Ⓓ Ⓔ
47. Ⓐ Ⓑ Ⓒ Ⓓ Ⓔ
48. Ⓐ Ⓑ Ⓒ Ⓓ Ⓔ
49. Ⓐ Ⓑ Ⓒ Ⓓ Ⓔ
50. Ⓐ Ⓑ Ⓒ Ⓓ Ⓔ
51. Ⓐ Ⓑ Ⓒ Ⓓ Ⓔ
52. Ⓐ Ⓑ Ⓒ Ⓓ Ⓔ
53. Ⓐ Ⓑ Ⓒ Ⓓ Ⓔ
54. Ⓐ Ⓑ Ⓒ Ⓓ Ⓔ
55. Ⓐ Ⓑ Ⓒ Ⓓ Ⓔ

The Princeton Review

Completely darken bubbles with a No. 2 pencil. If you make a mistake, be sure to erase mark completely. Erase all stray marks.

1. YOUR NAME: (Print) Last / First / M.I.
SIGNATURE: _____ **DATE:** __/__/__
HOME ADDRESS: (Print) Number and Street / City / State / Zip Code
PHONE NO.: (Print)

IMPORTANT: Please fill in these boxes exactly as shown on the back cover of your test book.

2. TEST FORM

3. TEST CODE

4. REGISTRATION NUMBER

5. YOUR NAME — First 4 letters of last name / FIRST INIT / MID INIT

6. DATE OF BIRTH — Month / Day / Year (JAN–DEC)

7. SEX — MALE / FEMALE

© 1996 Princeton Review L.L.C.
FORM NO. 00001-PR

Section 1

Start with number 1 for each new section. If a section has fewer questions than answer spaces, leave the extra answer spaces blank.

Questions 1–55, each with bubbles A B C D E.

Preparing Online Shouldn't Mean Preparing On Your Own

Test Prep Anytime, Anywhere

Experience The Princeton Review difference with tools that adjust to your unique needs, real-time instruction and free extra help.

The Princeton Review

More Confidence. Less Stress.

800-2Review | www.PrincetonReview.com

The Princeton Review

We're All About Better Scores and Better Schools

Get into your first-choice school by combining book test prep with our 1-2-1 Private Tutoring, classroom course, or online course for the most effective test preparation.

Use this coupon to

Save $50

when you enroll with The Princeton Review.

Learn the best techniques and strategies to maximize your score.

The Princeton Review

Expiration Date: September 30, 2002

800-2Review | www.PrincetonReview.com

The Princeton Review

Find the Right School

**BEST 345 COLLEGES
2003 EDITION**
0-375-76255-8 • $20.00

**COMPLETE BOOK OF COLLEGES
2003 EDITION**
0-375-76256-6 • $26.95

**COMPLETE BOOK OF
DISTANCE LEARNING SCHOOLS**
0-375-76204-3 • $21.00

AMERICA'S ELITE COLLEGES
Choosing Wisely, Getting in,
Paying for It
0-375-76206-X • $15.95

Get in

**CRACKING THE SAT
2003 EDITION**
0-375-76245-0 • $19.00

**CRACKING THE SAT
WITH SAMPLE TESTS ON CD-ROM
2003 EDITION**
0-375-76246-9 • $30.95

**MATH WORKOUT FOR THE SAT
2ND EDITION**
0-375-76177-2 • $14.95

**VERBAL WORKOUT FOR THE SAT
2ND EDITION**
0-375-76176-4 • $14.95

**CRACKING THE ACT
2003 EDITION**
0-375-76317-1 • $19.00

**CRACKING THE ACT WITH
SAMPLE TESTS ON CD-ROM
2003 EDITION**
0-375-76318-X • $29.95

CRASH COURSE FOR THE ACT
10 Easy Steps to Higher Score
0-375-75326-5 • $9.95

CRASH COURSE FOR THE SAT
10 Easy Steps to Higher Score
0-375-75324-9 • $9.95

Get Help Paying for it

DOLLARS & SENSE FOR COLLEGE STUDENTS
How Not to Run Out of Money by Midterms
0-375-75206-4 • $10.95

**PAYING FOR COLLEGE WITHOUT GOING BROKE
2003 EDITION**
0-375-76273-6 • $20.00

**THE SCHOLARSHIP ADVISOR
5TH EDITION**
0-375-76210-8 • $26.00

Make the Grade with Study Guides for the AP and SAT II Exams

AP Exams

CRACKING THE AP BIOLOGY 2002-2003 EDITION
0-375-76221-3 • $18.00

CRACKING THE AP CALCULUS AB & BC 2002-2003 EDITION
0-375-76222-1 • $19.00

CRACKING THE AP CHEMISTRY 2002-2003 EDITION
0-375-76223-X • $18.00

CRACKING THE AP ECONOMICS (MACRO & MICRO) 2002-2003 EDITION
0-375-76224-8 • $18.00

CRACKING THE AP ENGLISH LITERATURE 2002-2003 EDITION
0-375-76225-6 • $18.00

CRACKING THE AP EUROPEAN HISTORY 2002-2003 EDITION
0-375-76226-4 • $18.00

CRACKING THE AP PHYSICS 2002-2003 EDITION
0-375-76227-2 • $19.00

CRACKING THE AP PSYCHOLOGY 2002-2003 EDITION
0-375-76228-0 • $18.00

CRACKING THE AP SPANISH 2002-2003 EDITION
0-375-76229-9 • $18.00

CRACKING THE AP U.S. GOVERNMENT AND POLITICS 2002-2003 EDITION
0-375-76230-2 • $18.00

CRACKING THE AP U.S. HISTORY 2002-2003 EDITION
0-375-76231-0 • $18.00

SAT II Exams

CRACKING THE SAT II: BIOLOGY 2003-2004 EDITION
0-375-76294-9 • $18.00

CRACKING THE SAT II: CHEMISTRY 2003-2004 EDITION
0-375-76296-5 • $17.00

CRACKING THE SAT II: FRENCH 2003-2004 EDITION
0-375-76295-7 • $17.00

CRACKING THE SAT II: WRITING & LITERATURE 2003-2004 EDITION
0-375-76301-5 • $17.00

CRACKING THE SAT II: MATH 2003-2004 EDITION
0-375-76298-1 • $18.00

CRACKING THE SAT II: PHYSICS 2003-2004 EDITION
0-375-76299-X • $18.00

CRACKING THE SAT II: SPANISH 2003-2004 EDITION
0-375-76300-7 • $17.00

CRACKING THE SAT II: U.S. & WORLD HISTORY 2003-2004 EDITION
0-375-76297-3 • $18.00

The Princeton Review

Available at Bookstores Everywhere.
www.review.com

When It Is Only About You

Princeton Review 1-2-1 Private Tutoring

Maximize your scores with expert Princeton Review instructors, focus only on areas where you need it, and attend private sessions held at times and locations convenient for you.

The Princeton Review

More Confidence. Less Stress.

800-2Review | www.PrincetonReview.com